Our Game
was
Baseball

Our Game
was
Baseball

Growing Up with
Larry Boyce and
Small-Town Ball Games

to Jeremy —
Best wishes and Enjoy!

John Hodgkins

JOHN E. HODGKINS

Cover photographs:
Baseball: Tage Olsin
Grass: Christoph Michels
Team: The Townies at Hippach Field, c. 1950, author's collection

Design and production by Michael Steere

Printed at Versa Press, East Peoria, Illinois

ISBN 978-1-4507-3580-3

John Hodgkins
73 Sisquisic Trail
Yarmouth, ME 04096

DEDICATION

*Dedicated
to the memory of
Boyce and the Townies;
the only entertainment,
the only inspiration,
the only dream a boy needed.*

CONTENTS

"The only real game—I think—in the world is baseball. . . .
You've gotta start way down (at) the bottom, when you're six or
seven years of age. You can't wait until you're fifteen or sixteen.
You gotta let it grow up with you. And if you're successful, and
you try hard enough, you're bound to come out on top."

—Babe Ruth
Farewell to Baseball Address
April 1947, Yankee Stadium

INTRODUCTION

S ummers in the 1940s in Temple, Maine, I played baseball in the schoolyard or in Art Mitchell's hayfield and dreamed of playing for the Townies, Temple's small-town team of local war veterans, loggers, and family farmers. Then one day in 1949, when I was fourteen years old, manager Lawrence Boyce sent me into a lopsided Townies game in West Sumner in the last inning. For the next eight years I played baseball in a Townies uniform: benchwarmer, pinch hitter, utility infielder, eventually a starter and a Townies' regular. I didn't know then that we were making history.

Small-town baseball in the 1940s and 50s, in Maine and elsewhere, was part of rural life, like gardening and the Grange. It had been since early in the twentieth century, when major-league baseball organized into two leagues, and the season culminated in the World Series, popularizing the sport into every corner and hamlet of America. Even the smallest towns fielded teams. Temple, a town of perhaps two hundred people then, was only one of many. Boyce's 1940s schedule took the Townies to such country cross roads and settlements as East Dixfield, West Peru, and East Wilton; Mercer, New Vineyard, and Lexington. On Sunday afternoons, rural folks crowded the ball fields, cheered for the home team, and wolfed red hot dogs slathered with mustard and piccalilli.

In mid-century the fever waned. Advances in transportation and communication brought rural folks a plethora of Sunday afternoon

11

alternatives. Television and big-league baseball came right into the parlor, and a trip to the coast for lobster only took an hour in a new Mercury Monterey V–8. Folks had too many choices. Small-town baseball teams withered and died. Except for the memories, a way of rural life mostly disappeared.

Several years ago, perhaps during the 1990s, I suggested somewhat offhandedly to Robert Kimber, a Maine author of no little acclaim—*Upcountry, A Canoeist's Sketchbook, Living Wild and Domestic*—that he consider writing the story of the Temple Townies. I suppose he did consider it, or try to, but Kimber had arrived in Temple in the early 1970s, long after the Townies had disappeared from the ball field and he lacked information, memory, and poker-table stories. He had missed the hard-cider days, and I somehow knew when I talked to him that the job of recounting the Townies' history would inevitably be mine. I was the best equipped. I had played for the Townies, and I possessed the scorebooks, photographs, memories, and time. I was committed to preserving a piece of Maine small-town history. Ten or so years after talking to Kimber, I started writing *Our Game was Baseball*.

I discovered during the four-year journey to the final chapter just what the Townies meant to Temple. Prior to the end of World War II, Temple had been destined for mortality, its passing predicted by the Reverend Richard Pierce in his 1945 graduate dissertation, *A History of Temple, Maine: Its Rise and Decline*. But the coming of the Townies after the war thrust new life into Pierce's gasping community, gave the town identity, its residents hope. Invigorated by the returning veterans, the Townies—loggers, farmers, veterans, high school kids, good players and bad—spirited the community. Townsfolk came out their kitchens and barns and worked for the Townies. They built a baseball field, dugouts, backstop, and all that. They worked at fundraisers, beano games, and Saturday-night dances to finance the team. And they applauded the triumphs. The talk around the wood heater at the general store turned from war to baseball. Men went into the woods and the hayfields on Monday mornings smiling. The Townies had won again. Kids played baseball in the schoolyard and dreamed of playing for the Townies. I was a kid then, and I had the dream. Maybe someday, I thought, I'll wear a Townies' uniform.

This is also my story. I dreamed of more than being a Townies baseball player. I dreamed of growing up, becoming a man in the company of men I admired: Lawrence Boyce, my uncle and the Townies manager, the war veterans, and my Pa, who played for the Townies as well. Yes, this is a baseball story. But my growing up took place here under the tutelage of Boyce and the Townies: first job, high school, learning to drive, college.

Baseball is an imperfect game, full of failure. The best hitters fail two-thirds of their turns at bat. The best teams lose forty percent of the time. The World Series champion 1949 New York Yankees won sixty-two percent of their games. During the eleven years of the Townies' existence following World War II, they won fifty-nine percent of theirs. I suspect the writing of our story is imperfect as well. But it is the truth as I know it, lived it, recall it, and learned it. Descriptions of events that I did not see, or dialogue that I did not hear, represent the truth. This is our story: history, memoir, nostalgia. Enjoy.

PROLOGUE

E|very story has a beginning. Almost from the time we can read we want to know how our stories start. We search for genealogical roots. We form historical societies and identify our founders. We read old letters and faded newspapers. We study the backgrounds of worn and cracked photographs and talk to elderly people. We need to find beginnings.

This story begins in October 1947 in Temple, Maine. Ma comes to Temple for a day. She comes from Kennebunk, where she went with my sisters a month previous to enroll them in school there. She comes to divorce Pa, to be present at the proceedings that will seal the separation.

The proceedings are over now. The separation is sealed, and the court has granted her custody of my two sisters. I, the court has also decreed, am to remain in the custody of Pa, who has put me in the care of his sister, my Aunt Marion, and her husband, Uncle Lawrence Boyce. Ma is running here and there in the house, tossing the last remnants of her years here into a paper bag. Her suitcase sits by the kitchen door. She's in a hurry. She puts the bag on the kitchen table, looks out the window, and down the lane. "Where is she?" she fusses. "I have to catch a bus." She paces back and forth on the worn linoleum and looks again.

Fern, who helped Ma through the war years when Pa was away and then moved away from Temple herself, will come and drive her to the bus station. "It's not time, yet, Ma. She'll be here," I say, wondering when I will see her again—or whether I will see her again. She fidgets and paces and lights another cigarette. Then I hear Fern's Plymouth growling up dusty Cowturd Lane and into the driveway. "Here she comes," I say.

Ma hugs me. "Come see me sometime," she murmurs, grabs her suitcase and the bag, and piles into the Plymouth—she, my mother, is gone.

There's a chill in the air, and a faint scent of wood smoke. I stand in the driveway and watch the Plymouth turn and cross the bridge, then disappear on the road to Farmington. I stand there until the dust has settled on the lane, then walk around the house to the backyard. There's no wood to be stacked. The garden has frosted and died. The McIntosh tree is bare. The old-auto graveyard on the stream bank stares back at me through broken and rusted head lamps. Maples along the bank are colorless. The stream is dormant and desperate for rain; leaves float silently in the stagnant millpond. Wherever I walk, I see signs of the end. It's too late, I brood; I can't go back.

I go into the shed where Pa is puttering with something. I need to get away. "I'm going to Auntie May's," I tell him.

It was past noon when Ma left. The bus ride to Kennebunk will take four hours. The Blue Line will carry her from Farmington to Lewiston, where she will board a Greyhound to Kennebunk. For four hours, through tiny East Wilton, Chisholm, and North Turner, she will ride the bus, winding among barren western Maine hills and passing frigid-looking lakes and ice-rimmed streams, through brown country-side, across the Androscoggin River, then through Maine's flatlands, along the coast, and finally to Kennebunk. For four hours she will sit and try to read a book, but mostly she will stare out the window—and wonder if it could have been different.

At the Greyhound depot in Lewiston, Ma fetches her suitcase and paper bag and leaves the Blue Line. She is standing at the ticket counter when she hears her name, "Clarice! Clarice, is that you?" Startled, she turns.

"Anna! My gosh . . ."

They met at Farmington State Normal School in 1929. Ma finished her studies in 1930 and came to Temple to teach in the two-room Village School. Anna Field came the following year to the one-room Red Schoolhouse on the Intervale Road; two young girls starting out alone in remote and friendless Temple at the onset of the Great Depression. Ma lodged at Hathaway's in the village, Anna at Marcus Mitchell's farmhouse a half-mile out the Intervale Road. They were together every chance.

They made the most of their weekends, isolated as they were from each other, living with strangers. On Fridays Anna walked to the village after supper, and they gathered around the Hathaway's pump organ in a musical soiree of such favorites as "Love's Old Sweet Song," the Spanish melody, "Juanita," and Stephen Foster's "My Old Kentucky Home." On Saturdays they walked five miles to Farmington for lunch at Tarbox and Whittier's Soda Shop and a movie at the State Theater. Together they envisioned an ocean-liner voyage to Europe and dreamed of hiking in the Alps. One summer they traveled together to Kennebunk Beach and worked at the Atlantic House resort there.

In time they made friends in Temple: Marion Hodgkins and her younger brother Elliott, Amy Mayo, Roland Ranger, Ardeen Merchant, and others. Eventually Anna bought a car, and they rode to the State for the Saturday movie; sometimes Anna would drive down to Farmington Falls after the movie and they'd park by the river. Other times they'd ride up to Kingfield on Saturday nights in either Anna's coupe or Elliott's roadster and dance at Foster Hill. The two young schoolmarms found delightful times together in the midst of the Depression, falling in and out of love, giggling and dreaming through Cornelia Otis Skinner's "Our Hearts Were Young and Gay," accepting invitations to Friday night dinner at the Hodgkins', or hosting a school social during winter holidays.

In 1934 Anna's high school boyfriend, Norman Harding, came to Temple and asked Anna to marry him. "I can't marry you," she answered. "I'll lose my job. It's the Depression. We could never keep two jobs."

But Norman insisted and Anna weakened. In the summer they traveled to Quebec for the wedding ceremony—so's there'll be no record of it at home an' you can keep your job, Norman said—and moved into the Edes' house, two miles farther out the Intervale Road. Anna kept on teaching at the Red Schoolhouse, and Norman puttered and sought—somewhat half-heartedly, Ma said—work that paid cash.

Ma married in 1934 as well, romantic and adventurous Elliott Hodgkins, and she and Pa bought a house on the edge of the village. Ma and Anna's friendship, of course, waned a bit, but they remained close. There was a baseball field on the intervale then, and Pa and Norman played for the town team. After the Sunday games, we'd go to the Edes' place in the roadster and sit awhile, or Pa would fish for trout in the brook. Anna drove to the village frequently on weekends and sat in Ma's kitchen, and they gossiped and reminisced. And Anna, Ma told me once, went with Ma to the hospital and cradled me in her arms the day I was born.

But neither marriage was what might be called idyllic. By 1943 Anna was tired of Norman's putterings—"I outgrew him," she said later—and they divorced. She left Temple before Pa was drafted and went off to World War II, and she took an upper-grade teaching job in Weld, on the opposite side of Mt. Blue. Ma had not seen her since.

"Clarice, my gosh, how long has it been?"

Ma couldn't remember. Too much had happened since 1943. She exhaled. "I'm leaving him, Anna. I'm going home. I don't want to go home, but I can't stay in Temple any longer." Ma didn't delve into the whole story, except to tell her friend, "It was the war, Anna. The war did it to him. He's a changed man."

"Wha . . ."

"It ended this morning," Ma murmured. "Court was scheduled for nine o'clock. When we arrived the lawyers had already settled it. I'm a single woman, Anna," she sighed.

"Where are the kids?"

"The girls are with Eileen in Kennebunkport right now. They've been going to Park Street School since September. We're staying with Mother until I find a place. Oh, Anna. I must find myself," she moaned.

"Eileen?"

"My sister, the pleasant one."

"And Johnny? Where's Johnny?"

"He's with his Aunt Marion. She always wanted him. Now she's got him. I had no room for a growing boy. He'll be a teenager soon." The two friends were silent, Anna struggling for something to say, Ma trying to collect herself. Finally, Ma said, "It was the drinking, Anna. He just couldn't stop. He's an angry drinker now, sometimes abusive. Oh, Anna, I loved him so!"

"I'm sorry, Clarice. They were such good times, such good times. I'll always remember . . ."

Ma heard the call to board. She hugged Anna—and was gone.

In Temple, I walk to Aunt Marion's. She and Uncle Lawrence live in a rambling Cape Cod cottage across from the village school yard, Cumming's Hill Road they call it. Beyond their house the dusty road leads to the cemetery at the edge of town. Beyond Cumming's Hill is the back way to Farmington,. No children live at Aunt Marion's, but Pa's parents, Grandma Luna and Grandpa C.F., do. Grandpa C.F. is retired from his job as postmaster and occasionally engages in a bit of activity: gardening, making maple syrup, fishing in the stream, or puttering in the barn, where he usually keeps a bottle of something to "strengthen him," he says, as the day wears on. He also, whenever a challenge is sent over from Harold Staples or some other evening lingerer at the general store, plays a game of checkers occasionally. Grandma, who has more of a literary makeup, sits in a parlor and reads—or writes.

Aunt Marion is a professional woman—she sells life insurance, a business that Grandma Luna gave up when the war ended. But she is trained in school as a teacher, graduated from Farmington State Normal School in 1926. During the war, she supervised a cadre of cadet teachers—college students used as schoolmarms around the state to ease a critical teacher shortage—in Piscataquis County. Before that she taught at the Farrington School in Augusta and the one-room Red Schoolhouse in West Farmington.

Aunt Marion is nothing like my mother. She drives a car, a big Chevrolet, the biggest they make, and buys a new one every three years. She is an assertive driver: sits erect; grips the steering wheel with both hands; tips her chin up— to see better I presume—and honks at intersections to scatter pedestrians and warn other motorists of her presence. She is a bold woman, the town's door-knocker during the war: "I'm raising money for the boys in uniform," she announced when the doors opened. Temple never missed its war bond quota.

People buy her insurance policies, too. "You sure $5,000 is enough?" she cajoles them. "You got an awful big family here." More is always better for Aunt Marion. She pays me more than twice as much as other folks—a dollar—to mow her lawn. She knows I like oatmeal cookies and bakes batch after batch until I'm tired of them. I'll never tell her again I like oatmeal cookies. No one in Temple is ever in line ahead of Aunt Marion: she acquired the first snow tires in town, the first electric washing machine, the first oil heater, the first gas stove, the first television, the first—and probably the last—electric ironer and shirt presser. But she is also generous. She distributes vegetables to her neighbors, gives her time to charity fund-raising, and takes a present to every kid in town at Christmastime.

Uncle Lawrence, her husband of some eleven years, is a touch more modest, has a sense of humor, and is not stuck in his ways. He sells bakery products house-to-house in small towns surrounding Augusta in Kennebec County, and is home only on Thursdays—his day off—and Sundays. A short man, lean and agile, with a square jaw, heavy eyebrows, and black hair slicked straight back, he appears the consummate butler in his bakery salesman's uniform standing on the stoop of an Augusta farmstead carrying an armful of cakes and pies. Yet he is a tough and grizzled man who cuts and splits firewood for Aunt Marion's stove, raises a quarter-acre of potatoes every year, and plays nine-inning baseball games on Sunday afternoons. He learned life's lessons on various baseball fields and, though open minded about other folks' affairs, he applies the lessons to a decent and principled personal life—he obeys the rules.

I am in the eighth grade in October 1947 when I move to Aunt Marion's. Uncle Lawrence manages the town's baseball team. He is what some call a baseball aficionado. He has grown up mostly on baseball fields, and folks often refer to him, good-naturedly of course, as a baseball nut. Baseball meant nothing to me when I first met Uncle Lawrence a year or so ago. He showed me how to throw and catch a baseball—"playing catch" he called it—and took me along to the Sunday games that summer. And once he took me to see the Red Sox in Fenway Park: Ted Williams, Bobby Doerr, Johnny Pesky, and all of them. He even encouraged me to learn the game on my own. So when I move into his house, I figure if he is a baseball nut, then perhaps I will be a baseball nut, too.

Chapter One
LAWRENCE BOYCE

T here were no movie theaters in Temple when I was a boy in the 1940s, and no bowling alleys either. Nor was there an ice cream soda shop where kids could hang out and gossip over romances at the Village School, or goings-on in parked cars outside the dance hall on Saturday nights. And we lacked a soccer field, and tennis courts, and a playground where we could throw basketballs up at a hoop. Our game was baseball.

On summer days we played baseball in the school yard, or in a neighbor's pasture, or in a hayfield. We came together early, and when enough kids had showed up for a game—a pitcher, a first baseman, and one fielder were enough for a team—we chose up sides and hit and chased baseballs all day. If more kids came, we added players, and if some had to leave, the teams shrunk back to three again. A kid who stayed all day, one who had no errands to run for his mother and no barn chores to do, might go to bat forty times and rap out more than thirty hits. The score might reach into the hundreds—had we kept score. But winning or losing was not important to us. Baseball was our game. And we played every day—except Sunday.

On Sunday, the Townies, a real baseball team—farmers and loggers and soldiers home from the war—played on a real baseball field at the edge of town, a field with square canvas bags at the corners, a pitching rubber, and a home plate exactly seventeen inches wide. The weekday school-yard players went to the Sunday games and watched, played catch, and chased ground balls during batting practice. And we hung around the dugout and dreamed of wearing a Townies uniform someday. I shagged throws for the team's manager, Uncle Lawrence Boyce, when he hit warm-up fungoes to outfielders, and listened to him explain strategy to his players. And I envisioned him someday asking me in my Townies' uniform to execute some artful diversionary orchestration: *"Try to lay a bunt down toward the third baseman, Johnny,"* I imagined he might whisper, *"and maybe the runner can sneak into third base behind him."*

I idolized the Townies. It seemed they had come home from the war to play baseball. They had fought at Falise Gap and in the Ardennes. They had landed on beaches at Anzio and Cebu Island. They had knocked out German tanks and shot down Japanese bombers. Now it was over. They were home. They went to Lawrence Boyce, a man with a baseball background, a baseball luminary some said, who had played in the old Pine Tree League in South Paris as a teenager and later for Mack's All Stars in Farmington, the originator of the first Temple baseball team in 1930, and they asked him to organize the team again. "We want to play baseball," they told him.

Boyce put on public suppers and beano games in Brackley Hall and bought balls, bats, and bases with the profits. He added a farmer or two to the team's roster and persuaded local businessman Mark Mosher to give up a piece of land a mile or so outside the village center for a field. He marked out foul lines and base paths, and the players brought machinery, scraped the grass off the infield, trucked clay from a riverbank pit, and rolled it smooth. Boyce taught baseball basics at practice sessions and arranged intra-squad games. And in the summer of 1946, he put together a schedule of games against nearby towns.

Most every town around fielded a team then, and Boyce's schedule took the Townies to East Dixfield and Norridgewock, North Jay and Rumford Point, and to Farmington four times, where the Townies faced a different team each time: Fairbanks, Farmington Falls, the Farmington Town Team, and Callahan's Hard Cider Boys. Independent ball, Boyce called it. On Sundays he packed his car with bats and bases and his catcher's mitt and mask, put the score book and a box of baseballs on the seat beside him, and drove to some remote field in an outlying town where the players there, similar to what had happened in Temple, had laid out a new baseball field.

Many times the fields were a greater challenge than the opposing players. The Townies played in hayfields and dusty sandlots. They played in fields where the grass hadn't been cut and a ground ball would stop rolling before it reached the fielder, and in rocky pastures where the grass had been scraped off and a ground ball would carom off a boulder into a player's shin. They could hit the ball far distances in those solitary spaces—slug they called it—and some could catch and throw the ball, as well. And Boyce, undaunted by their freewheeling at-titude toward the game, encouraged them, and mentored them, and tolerated their indiscretions and miscues. And he persuaded them to be proud of their skills.

Boyce was called a baseball mastermind. It was a label awarded him by the lingerers at the general store and sportswriter Cliff Gove at *The Lewiston Daily Sun* for his know-how managing and playing for the Townies, a label he deserved. But before the war Boyce to me was just Uncle Lawrence, Aunt Marion's husband, a man who lived with her in a house across the road from the Village School and worked someplace else. I didn't know he was a baseball man, nor did I know baseball, not until after the war.

He and Aunt Marion gardened and put up a winter's supply of firewood in their spare time. I knew Aunt Marion. She came to visit Ma occasionally, to inspect our garden, exchange gossip, and solicit money for a war bond drive, but Uncle Lawrence remained mostly invisible. He spent his working weeks away. I went to his house on summer mornings and mowed his lawn for a dollar and a handful of warm oatmeal cookies, but my dealings were made with Aunt Marion and I knew little of his whereabouts. Though I didn't know then he was a baseball man, I suspect now that the first time he came to Temple, the first time he saw the general store, the first time he heard the sawmills whining in the village, or smelled the horse manure plopped along the Intervale Road, he was wearing a baseball uniform.

In my earliest memory of Boyce, the baseball man—it was 1946, I was eleven—he is splitting wood outside his shed door on a summer day, stove wood he called it. A pile of stove-length logs lies behind him, produced by handyman Eddie Fontaine's home-fashioned sawing rig, and a pile of split stove wood is growing in front. A short man, his legs bowed from a lifetime of summers squatting behind home plate wearing a catcher's mitt and mask, Uncle Lawrence is dressed in a long-sleeved shirt and baggy trousers, his black hair tousled in the humid Maine air, a bandanna sticking out of a pants pocket. He picks up a log, places it on a chopping block, and swings an axe at it until it will fit Aunt Marion's kitchen stove. Then he reaches for another. All morning he places one stick after another on his block, whacking at each one with the axe. When the chunks surrounding the block interfere with his work, he tosses a few onto a larger pile and then goes back to swinging the axe. He takes no break, no drink of water, no pause to wipe the sweat off his brow with the bandanna. He works. "Winter's coming," he tells me between logs, a slight grin appearing on his squarish, weathered face.

Later, after he has finished chopping for the day, he hands me a baseball glove, "Here, try this on," he says and reaches for his catcher's mitt and a baseball. I have seldom, if ever, worn a baseball glove. I slip it on and pound a pocket into the palm with my right fist, as I have seen my friends in the school yard do. "Does it fit?" Boyce asks and tosses the baseball to me. Then he, the manager of the Temple Townies in his baggy pants and bandanna, and I, an eleven-year-old kid who doesn't know whether his baseball glove fits or not, stand in the driveway some thirty feet apart, and toss the ball back and forth. "Use both hands," he says to me more than once, "and reach for the ball with the palm of the glove open. Let it nestle in there and cover it with the bare hand."

I try it his way.

"That's right," he assures me. "It will seem awkward at first, but you'll get the hang of it," and he spends perhaps an hour, the pile of un-split logs lying on the ground beside us, teaching me the baby steps of baseball.

Boyce was born in Bethel in 1904, grew up there, played base-ball for the high school, and after-ward for the Norway-South Paris Twins in the Pine Tree League. His parents moved to West Farmington in the 1920s, and he went with them. Keen for base-ball, the twenty-something-year-old Boyce contacted Frank "Mac" McLaughlin—manager of an all-star team of Farmington luminar-ies that barnstormed against small-town teams in Franklin, Somerset, and Androscoggin Counties—an asked McLaughlin if he had a spot for him.

Boyce poses on the Intervale Road in Temple, c. 1930.

McLaughlin put him behind the plate, and sometime around 1930 Boyce went to Temple with Mack's All Stars to play a collection of Temple men in Dana Barker's hayfield on the Intervale Road. History has not recorded, nor does anyone alive recall, the details of subsequent visits, but not long after that first visit—again wearing the uniform of Mack's All Stars—Boyce posed in the center of the dusty road near Barker's hayfield while Marion Hodgkins snapped his picture. Soon Boyce was a Temple personality, a player-manager of the baseball team and the suitor of Marion Hodgkins. They married in   the summer of 1935 on a Friday, without interfering with the baseball season.

The Temple team that Boyce adopted and nurtured before World War II put their gloves and spikes away during the war while the players soldiered. Boyce, too old to be called to serve, worked on the Temple home front—as a selectman, clerking in the general store, pitching hay, growing potatoes, splitting stove wood, campaigning for war bonds—and waited. He waited four years.

By the end of the war, Temple had endured fifteen years of troubling times. It was a tired town. For the first thirty years of the twentieth century, Temple enjoyed economic prosperity unknown in its history, a prosperity that came from sawmills located along the stream in the village, where logs, dragged from the woods by two-horse teams and drays, were sawed into lumber, and the lumber sold. But the economic crash of 1929 ruined Temple's independent economy, and the mills went bankrupt. After a fruitless attempt to restart with new money, the mills were abandoned, the equipment auctioned, and jobless townsfolk hunkered down for the duration of the Great Depression.

Rare was a job in Temple during the Depression that paid money, and an out-of-town job was so rare that if one was obtained—Earl Barker went to Eustis to work in a sawmill, say—*The Franklin Journal* reported the news in its next edition. A few sturdy folks, however, continued to cut wood, and an occasional farmer milked a half-dozen dairy cows and shipped the milk to the creamery in West Farmington, but most families eked out a living on small farms: a cow or two, a hog, a few chickens, a huge garden, and a deer rifle. They swapped labor and services with neighbors, and bartered with townsfolk for goods they could not produce themselves. The population of Temple fell to 240 in the 1940 census—a historic low. The public school nurse reported a higher frequency of underweight school children and the published list of delinquent taxpayers grew longer. And the lifestyle thrust upon the town in the Depression lingered into the 1940s and the onset of the war.

More stress was placed on the town during the war: bond drives depleted meager savings accounts and the draft board called the town's young and strong men away from their work in the barns, fields, and forests. Women and kids, in addition to their work in the kitchens and schoolhouses, harvested hay, tended to barn chores, and gardened. Older men filled gaps in logging crews, and every family member worked to keep the home place warm in winter. The end of the war was a welcome sight, particularly of course to those who had served in it, but also to those who stayed behind, and they greeted homecoming soldiers with exhausted joy. "Life will be easier now," they exclaimed. "We'll have jobs and money, and folks will come back to the town and kids to the schoolhouses."

But Richard Donald Pierce, pastor of the First Congregational Church in Temple, and candidate for the degree of Doctor of Philosophy from the Boston University Graduate School, thought otherwise. Pierce had researched Temple's past, and in his 1946 dissertation, *A History of Temple, Maine: Its Rise and Decline,* he stated that Temple's disintegration was well underway, that it was likely too late to make the adjustments necessary for economic and cultural survival. He cited economic failure, increased immorality and illegitimacy, the steady impairment of cultural and social life, a sense of despair over public responsibility. Institutional life—the Grange, the churches, schools, and other civic organizations—"is so decimated," he wrote, "it depresses those who do attend." Its demise undoubtedly certain, he foretold the end of Temple's history and predicted the town would soon revert to a plantation with an ever-decreasing population.

Admittedly, Temple was weary in 1945 and in need of an infusion of energy and a revival of spirit. But the townsfolk were not inclined toward hopelessness. They remained unaffected by Pierce's prediction—most of them likely had no knowledge of it—and set about reviving their town. The energy came in the form of returning soldiers, who tried to put their wartime experiences out of mind. They went back to work in logging crews, construction crews, sawmills, and nearby businesses and shops. They married, built homes, and started families. Their energy, in Temple and elsewhere, loosened up the economy, and money began to flow again. People found jobs and accumulated a little cash to spend after the taxes were paid.

And Boyce and his ball team, the Townies, brought a new spirit to the town. They entertained folks, took them out of their kitchens and barns, brought them together, and caused them to laugh and cheer. They brought hope to the town. Folks had a place to discard their troubles, and kids a place to dream—the baseball field. Townsmen went there to mow grass, rake the infield, and build dugouts and bleachers. They went to watch Boyce prepare the team for the coming summer— and to socialize with their neighbors. They applauded their inexperienced and unpolished baseball players with unbridled support. And evening checker-game chatter at the general store turned from war to baseball: "Casey, you git any hits last week?" Pierce's depressing prediction was lost in the clamor of the game; the race for third base between a runner and a baseball; the exuberant, shouting fans; the nuances of a box score. The Townies breathed spirit into Pierce's disintegrative town.

Except for Boyce, however, the Townies lacked baseball savvy. They had pitched hay, pushed and pulled a crosscut saw, tended animals, dug potatoes, and learned to fire an M-1 rifle and a .30-caliber machine gun, but seldom since their time in the village school yard, had they swung a baseball bat. Some had gone to the high school in Farmington, but only one—Al Bergeron—had played baseball there.

Some left school to work, and more than one had chores at home that kept him away from high school sports. And only one or two had perhaps played ball with Boyce and the pre-war Townies. So as they prepared for the 1946 season, they appeared to Boyce to be more enthusiastic than skilled.

But Boyce was a player's manager. He had grown up in a hard America and had no stomach left for pessimism, intimidation, or hard-nosed management. He didn't act more baseball-wise than his players, nor did he demand excellence. He was supple in his dealings with the Townies. He tolerated—even embraced—the few hard-drinking playboy veterans who might show up on time, or arrive late, or not show at all, and he made last-minute adjustments in his lineup without rancor. All his players were contributors to the team, he felt, and none gave less than he was capable of. Aware of their limitations, Boyce was willing to accept only what they had to give. They were *his* teammates, too.

Though he knew a great deal about baseball and how to play to win, he taught the Townies only the fundamentals and then let them play. No trickery, no nuance, no complicated tactics. His treatment of that first post-war team is the best example. He made it simple for them. "See the ball and hit it," he told his batters. To the base runners, he said, "Pressure the defense, make them throw the ball." And to the defenders, "Catch the ball, don't hold onto it, throw it ahead of the runner." It was elementary learning, tactics they could execute without stopping to think. Boyce knew that a relaxed and confident player, one not measuring himself against the manager's expectations, was a more skillful player.

He bolstered them. He knew their inexperience would cause anxiety and countered it by continually telling each player how good he was. They believed him, and he rewarded their successes with publicity, putting their names in *The Franklin Journal*. And he included the town's youth in the team's doings, too. He knew we were the team's future, and he gave us side-line duties as ball boys, batboys, gofers. He helped us and taught us and prepared us for the coming of our dream—playing for the Townies—and when we were ready, he gave us a uniform and put a bat in our hands. "He was like a father to me," more than one of us remarked later of Boyce.

Boyce thought his strategies would win ball games. "But if we don't win," he said more than once, "it won't matter. We're here to play, to do our best and maybe have some fun." Boyce really had no alternative. He knew his players wouldn't accept any guff from him—or anyone else. They'd had enough of someone else's orders. So he treated them as teammates. He *showed* them what he wanted. "We'll see what happens," he told Aunt Marion.

Chapter Two

THE TOWNIES GO TO
THE ANDOVER FAIR

F or many, the start of a new baseball season symbolizes re-
newal. The slate is wiped clean. It's a new beginning, a time
of hope. Managers and coaches—not only in the major leagues, but
everywhere—all predict they'll finish the new season higher than last
year. And the previous year's last-place finishers all fill their ballparks
with expectant fans on opening day.

So it was in Temple in 1946. Hope had come back. Talk around the
wood heater at the general store turned to the Townies—"*Waal*, this *is*
next year. You pickin' the Townies to win?" The townsfolk watched the
snow melt in the fields, committed their summer Sundays to rooting
for the Townies, and ignored Dr. Pierce's disastrous foretelling of the
future. The players, too—war veterans, farmers, and loggers who had
lived through the Great Depression—felt the new awakening. They
went to the baseball field and celebrated their victory over oppression,
and laughed, and began again.

The upstart Townies—no uniforms, perhaps a sweatshirt or two
left over from the 1930s team—play their first game in June. They

score eight runs in the first inning at Farmington Falls and go on to win 16–4. Jules Vernesoni, just out of a German prisoner of war camp, pitches for the Townies, allows nine hits, and strikes out eight Falls batters. Boyce, a veteran catcher, and the most destructive hitter on his team, puts himself fourth in the batting order and scores three times during the afternoon. The game will become a precursor to their first season.

Boyce takes me with him to the ball fields in 1946, and I watch it happen. The Townies open a new era in Temple. They start with a rush. Following the conquest of Farmington Falls, they go to Fairbanks and score twenty-nine runs—and Boyce isn't satisfied. "We're not ready yet," he tells Aunt Marion. He needs to juggle the defense, he says, balance the players' skills with what the positions call for. He moves Elmer Wirta, an anti-aircraft gunner in Belgium the previous two years, to third base where his quickness will protect the hot corner. He puts Dick Blodgett, a former army flyer, at second base, where his weak arm will not be as evident. He moves Bruce Mosher from second base to right field, where most of the ground balls hit toward him the week before skittered to anyway, and shuffles Howard Mitchell from right field to left to make room for Mosher. He keeps rangy Vilio Hellgren, who had served with Wirta in Belgium, in center field and puts newcomer Al Bergeron, home only a few days from tending navy aircraft on Pelilieu Island in the South Pacific, at shortstop.

Still, Boyce has not settled on his pitching. He knows he will need a reliable pitcher, and more than one if possible. Vernesoni pitched well enough to win the first two games, but Boyce knows, too, that the Townies won't consistently score twenty-nine runs, not against the competition he has in mind. "I need to experiment with the pitching a little more," he tells the baseball buffs one evening at the general store.

On Independence Day the Townies inaugurate the new baseball field in Temple: a screened backstop, dugouts to the left and right, a clay infield, pitcher's mound heaped up in the center, clipped grass in the outfield. The woods in left are reachable to a long hitter and will stop a flying baseball, but right field tips slightly downhill, and a ball that skids by the right fielder can roll maybe a quarter-mile before he can retrieve it. During the pre-game warm-ups, infielders backhand ground balls on the rolled clay, and outfielders chase fly balls without fear of tripping over a boulder. "Be hard to make an error on a field like this," Dick Blodgett says later in the dugout.

"You'll find a way," someone answers.

The Independence Day game brings out a crowd. Home folks—wives, girlfriends, and mothers; school-yard players; and curious folks from outback farms—turn out in numbers for the celebratory game and sit on just-built bleachers behind the screened backstop. Someone brings a gas stove and steams red hot dogs, someone else has a cooler and a supply of soda. They will sell everything—dogs for twenty-five cents, drinks for a dime—and turn the profits over to the team for new baseballs.

The East Dixfielders arrive in time for a brief warm-up. Boyce recruits Adrie Mosher as scorekeeper. "Sure," she answers, "How do you do it?" John Hardy, who played first base for the Townies in the Farmington Falls game, volunteers to call the balls and strikes from behind the plate, and East Dixfield's Jake Coolidge, who likely owns some relationship to four players in the East Dixfield batting order with the same surname, agrees to umpire the plays at the bases. At two o'clock they are ready to play. Amid a smattering of a firecrackers here and there, Tarmo Sade (he preferred it pronounced Say'-dee), Boyce's choice as pitcher-for-the-day, walks to the mound and throws the first pitch of the game.

Sade has no baseball experience. He was born in a logger's camp at the base of Mt. Blue in the Temple outback in 1920, went to the Village School and then the high school in Farmington, and then back to chopping wood. He and center fielder Hellgren traveled to New Hampshire and Massachusetts with bucksaws and crosscuts during their youth, worked in the woods where the pay was better, and came back to Temple in time for World War II. The 1946 Townies are Sade's first opportunity to play ball. Boyce, who has noted Sade's strong arm at shortstop in the previous two games, picks him to pitch in the home opener in front of the home folks.

The Townies fans are well rewarded for their curiosity. And Sade, handed command of the pitcher's mound, does not disappoint. He faces thirty-two batters in nine innings, gives up just five hits, fans ten, and holds East Dixfield scoreless. And the Townies knock out thirty-two hits and score twelve runs in a demonstration of their batting power. It is their third straight win, but this game, more than any other, defines the future Townies. In just three games, Boyce has sorted out the players, many of them men he hadn't seen play, learned their strengths and weak-

Tarmo Sade stuffs bats into a World-War-II duffel bag after a game at Hippach Field. Al Mitchell is in the background, c. 1949.

nesses, and put them into the lineup at positions they will occupy for years. He has framed a team that seems after three games indestructible: eight war veterans, a farmer, a logger, and Boyce. Boyce has hit .706, Bruce Mosher .684, Dick Blodgett .667, and Sade has claimed the role of signature player.

The winning streak lasts five games. On the strength of some hefty swinging by Vilio Hellgren and Elmer Wirta, and Sade's fourteen strikeouts, the Townies outscore Norridgewock the next week 9–5. They look doomed, however, the following week when potent North

Jay comes to the Temple ball field and jumps into to a 4–2 lead after three innings. But Sade comes alive in the fourth inning and whiffs ten batters over the rest of the game—perhaps someone fed him black coffee between innings—and they escape defeat when the Townies' hitters rally for five runs in the fifth inning and four in the eighth. Boyce, who preaches modesty, doesn't boast over the five-game winning streak, nor do his players swagger. "This game will humble you eventually," he reminds them. "If you don't believe it, wait and see."

As Boyce predicted, the streak bedevils them, becomes an unexpected burden. The Farmington Town Team is scheduled to come to Temple on a Tuesday evening, two days after a Sunday Townies game with the Norridgewock Chiefs. Boyce, curious over how his Townies would measure up, scheduled the Farmington game for an evening. "It's just a workout," he claims, "an exhibition for the local fans." But the Townies suddenly feel the weight of entertaining the shiretowners undefeated. "Farmington!" someone exclaims. "Good gawd, the folks will expect us to beat them, too."

Boyce puts Bergeron on the mound at Norridgewock and rests Sade for the Farmington game. The Townies fail to produce a single run for Bergeron. They lose 6–0, a three-hitter by the Chief's strong right-hander Lyons, and the winning streak is over. They lose, as well, to Farmington on Tuesday evening in front of the biggest crowd of the season. A rested Sade whiffs five but yields six hits in the five-inning affair, losing 6–2, and the loyal fans go home quietly. They lose on Sunday to the Farmington Falls Yankees when the Yankees score seven runs in the closing innings. And they lose the return game with the Farmington Town Team at Hippach Field the following Tuesday, when, except for a bit of unfortunate laxity in the second inning—when Sade walks three batters, and the infielders make three errors while six shiretowners scamper across the plate—they might have won. But the losing streak has reached four games.

Their fortunes turn the following Sunday at Rumford Point. Sade

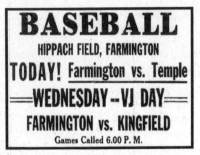

Announcement in the Franklin
Journal, *August 1946.*

strikes out the last batter with the tying runner on second base for a 5–4 win. They follow with five more victories to end the season, the last one at Hippach Field against a Farmington team that calls itself the Aces. The Aces comprise a mixture of remnants of the renowned Mack's All Stars, aging veterans, and emerging high school and college phenoms, all led by shadowy sports promoter Jack Callahan. They'll soon be known as Callahan's Hard Cider Boys and wreak havoc on full cider barrels and beer kegs Sunday afternoons for years to come all over Franklin County and even into Canada. Sade fans fourteen Aces in their debut, but Aces pitcher Vint Davis gives the Townies fits—eight strikeouts and three hits in five innings—with his own version of a menacing fastball and threatens to steal the game with a towering home run over the left field fence in near darkness.

Sade, the tall, muscular Finn, emerged as the Townies' marquee player that season. He intimidated batters and baffled even the best of them. He won seven of the nine games he pitched, losing only to the Farmington Town Team when the Townies couldn't produce runs. He inspired his teammates to believe they could win, and they responded with standout performances of their own—Blodgett batted .491, Boyce .439, and burly Elmer Wirta, another Finn who could stalk a baseball like a cat, committed just two errors all season at third base. The Townies were the talk of the town, their fans exuberant. Uncle Austin, owner of the general store, called every player who came through the front door "Casey."

As for me, I watched and listened to Boyce teach his collection of veterans and farmers the rudiments of the game. And as the season progressed, I ran errands for him, retrieved foul balls from roadside bushes, chased grounders during batting practice—and dreamed. Near the end of the season he rewarded me, "How'd you like to be our bat-boy?" he asked.

At season's end the Townies are invited to make an appearance—"a celebrity appearance," one of them calls it—at Andover Fair. "They want us to come over and play an exhibition game," Boyce tells them. "Said they'd pay us a thirty-five-dollar appearance prize if we'd come over and play Rumford Point again."

"Rumford Point?" someone cries out. "Hell, ain't we beat them enough already?"

Boyce smiles. "We need the money," he says, "and they probably still think they can beat us."

So the Townies travel to Andover Fair on a sunny Thursday in September. Schoolmarm Marjorie Josselyn closes the Village School for the day, and Uncle Austin locks the doors to the general store. Mothers pack picnic baskets, and families carpool to Andover in time to catch a ride on the Ferris wheel or watch the oxen pull before the game. Aunt Marion packs a picnic of ham sandwiches, blueberry pie, and oven-baked oatmeal cookies, and fills a one-gallon cooler with lemonade—"made in the shade by the old maid," she proclaims—and she tucks a blanket and two folding chairs into the trunk of her Chevy. Uncle Lawrence pulls on an old Temple baseball sweatshirt, gathers up his score book and a box of fresh baseballs, and at nine o'clock we leave a deserted Temple for the Andover Fair.

The Townies arrive early, in time for a warm-up session. I decline an invitation from Aunt Marion to ride the merry-go-round so I can carry out my batboy duties—stack bats, chase errant balls, fill water jugs—and maybe snag a few ground balls during batting practice. I choose to wait and listen to my schoolhouse friends' tales of Ferris

The Townies at the Andover Fair, 1946.

wheel rides and visits to the pulling ring. I keep close to the action at the baseball field.

As noon approaches, folks return to the field from the exhibition hall or beano tent and spread blankets on the sidelines, where they open picnic baskets and shout support for the Townies between bites. Scorekeeper Adrie Mosher lists the starting lineups in the score book for each team, and Boyce provides a seat for her at the end of the bench. He picks Sade to pitch, a choice not hard to make since he won seven of the nine games he pitched during the regular season, including two victories over Rumford Point. The Rumford Point manager names right-hander Bob Elliott—whose fastball is familiar to the Townies—to pitch, and he also includes three unfamiliar names in the batting order that haven't appeared in the previous two games. "Probably some ringers, Boyce speculates. "Come up from Lewiston," he grins when Adrie points out the strange names.

Sade's fastball and curve are hard to hit that day. He gives up one run in the second inning when Bruce Mosher, who usually spends his weekdays twitching logs on the back of Wilder Hill, stumbles chasing a fly ball in right field. The ball caroms off his shoulder and falls to the ground, and before he can retrieve it, a Rumford Point runner crosses home plate with the first run of the game. But Sade keeps command. At the end of eight innings, he has yielded just three hits and no more runs.

Meanwhile, the Townies score two in the third inning on Wirta's single to take the lead, and three more in the fourth on a key hit by Vilio Hellgren. Sade weakens in the ninth inning, however, and Rumford Point scores three times to pull within a run. With two outs and the tying run on second base, Boyce trots out to the mound to talk to Sade. I suspect he tells Sade that the Townies are being paid thirty-five dollars to come to Andover and play this game and he, Boyce, does not want to take any tainted or unearned money home. "Don't worry, boss," Sade likely answers. "I'll take care of that right now." And he strikes out Rumford Point's long-ball-hitting Elliott on three pitches, the third one a sharp-breaking drop that Boyce can't catch, but he smothers it with his chest and arms, grabs the ball in his bare hand, and throws the runner out at first base. Game over: Townies 5, Rumford Point 4.

After the game, folks traipse back to the beano game or the gambling rings on the midway for another chance to win a stuffed teddy bear or a table lamp while their kids beg for one more ride on the Ferris wheel. But for Boyce, the win and the thirty-five dollars are enough. He congratulates his players, packs away the balls and bats, retrieves the score book from Adrie Mosher, and stuffs the thirty-five dollars into his billfold. "Looks like we got ourselves a team here," he says to no one in particular.

The Townies played sixteen games that summer and won twelve.

Their record validated Boyce's managing. He worked them hard in fundamentals at weeknight practices, but Sunday afternoon baseball, I observed, was a social affair. The Townies was simply a collection of grown men having fun. They relaxed, and Boyce let them play. They boasted and tossed up rowdy challenges to their opponents, who were often their friends and would provide a case of Krueger Ale after the game.

The Townies played reckless baseball. They took chances on the base paths. They swung at pitches they could see regardless of the strike zone. They challenged opposing runners to try for the extra base. They challenged and teased each other. They laughed. They found humor in their embarrassment. One Sunday in front of the home folks, Boyce rounded third base and sprinted for home plate trying to beat the throw. He attempted to reach the plate with a stretched-out toe, sliding feet-first on his backside, but the ball arrived first, and he was ruled out. Boyce stood up to discuss the call for a minute with the umpire, smoke pouring from his pants pocket. Larry Barker yelled at him from the dugout, "Hey, Larry, your arse is on fire."

"You're damned right it is," Boyce yelled back. "I was safe by a mile."

"No. Really!" Barker shouted, and shouting broke out all along the bench.

"Huh? Where?"

"Your backside, your pocket. Chrissakes, smoke's rollin' outa there like you jes' farted a smoke shell."

"Damn!" and Boyce swiped at the smoke and smothered the fire while the Townies roared.

"Why'd you have them matches in your pocket?" someone chided. "You figger on stoppin' at third for a smoke?"

"No, I jes' wanted to light a fire under some of you hitters, try to get a few runs here, that's all."

"Goes to show he's not a hard-arsed manager a-tall," someone said, and chuckled, "just a *hot-arse*. Ha, ha, ha." They laughed—at them-selves and at each other. They were loyal to Boyce and the team, and they preferred to win, but when all was said and done, it was a game. And they acquired a reputation during the 1946 season that followed them for the next ten years: they were winners—and they made it look easy.

Chapter Three

HARD CIDER BALL GAMES

B oyce prepared the Townies for the 1947 season on much surer footing than the previous year. He had endured his indoctrination. The team was established and he knew well the skills of the position players. Bergeron was the sparkplug at shortstop, no doubt there. Boyce had settled on him midway through the '46 season, and he had played errorless shortstop in six of seven games. The team's top hitters—Blodgett, Hellgren, Boyce, Mosher, and Mitchell—all hit over .400, clustered in the middle of the batting order. Sade had developed a sharp-breaking drop to go with his fastball and curve, and he dominated the mound. Boyce's team, by all accounts, was expected to roll through another winning season.

They arrive opening day at the Temple ball field in new uniforms. No longer will they dress in pieces of baseball suits from the past or hand-me-down lettered sweatshirts from the 1930s town team. Boyce has parlayed the thirty-five dollars from Andover Fair along with beano profits and a few donations into gray flannels trimmed in blue, a cursive Temple stitched on the shirtfronts. "You'll look like baseball players now," Boyce tells them.

Opening day at the Temple ball field.

"Heck, boss, we always looked like baseball players," Blodgett retorts.

Before the game the Townies pose for a team picture on the infield clay. In bright sunshine, caps pushed to the back of their heads, arms folded or an elbow resting on a knee, they appear detached, perhaps a tinge defiant. Some smirk, some look determined, and some appear grim, perhaps in reaction to the presence of the Farmington Town Team waiting behind the camera for the game to start. Bergeron wears a hint of a smile, and John Hardy squints into the photographer's lens. Boyce alone bears a faint look of confidence.

It's the opening game of the season for both teams. Farmington, the pre-season favorite to capture the flag in the North Franklin League, has come to Temple presumably for a Sunday afternoon work-out. Most folks in Temple think the Townies have no business playing Farmington. Its population is twenty-five times that of Temple, and its ball players are veterans of the high school and college teams there. But Boyce, predisposed to testing his team whenever the opportunity comes, is drawn to such contests. "Farmington is the best around," he repeats several times the week before the game. "Now we'll find out just how good we are." He reasons, too, that if the Townies play the best around long enough, they could be struck by a miracle.

Farmington brings its first team: Larry Davis on the mound; center fielder Stoogie Whittier batting cleanup; third baseman Refino "the Iceman" Collette, formerly of Mack's All Stars; lanky Bob Stevens at first base; and lusty hitters Stan Robash and Clayton Berry, the same team that edged the Townies—and Sade—twice last year. The anticipated pitching duel between Sade and Larry Davis, however, does not occur. Farmington scores three times before the first out. "Where was the drop?" Boyce asks Sade when he comes into the dugout.

"It's been too long between games," Sade mutters.

The Townies come back a short way with three runs in the fourth off Davis, but at the end of five innings, they trail 8–3. In the sixth, Boyce moves Sade to shortstop and puts Bergeron on the mound, another experiment, I presume, and for the remainder of the game, the shiretowners run around the bases while the Townies admire themselves in their new uniforms. Final score: Farmington 28, Townies 8.

Determined to redeem himself, Sade comes back strong the following Sunday at Rumford Point. The Rumford Pointers are not our favorite opponent. Most games are fun, win or lose, but the games at Rumford Point, set apart by what the Townies allege is unscrupulous umpiring, are akin to a family feud, the rancor so harsh that we usually go there knowing the game will sink into an expletive-laden shouting match, or worse. This game is no different. The Townies grab an early lead, 2–0, but in the fifth inning, an error by Blodgett leads to a Rumford Point run—then more. Sade is disgruntled at the error, and gives up the tying run when the Pointer's light-hitting shortstop, who has struck out twice in the game, singles. Sade then plunks the next batter in the ribs with a fastball—perhaps trying to get even with someone. After the shouting, the Pointers react with their bats and rally for the lead. It is the Townies' only loss to Rumford Point in four games, and it comes after several futile chances to regain the lead. Even Pa, making his Townies debut, comes to bat twice with runners on base and botches both chances to pull the Townies out of the funk. They lose again, a dismal start to a promising season. They need a break to recoup. Instead, they get more suffering.

Though most small-town ball teams can come up with at least nine players for a Sunday afternoon game, Mercer shows up the following week with only eight. Boyce does what any small-town manager would do in this situation. To avoid disappointing the crowd, that's come out to see if the Townies can start a winning streak, he offers the visitors a ninth player. When Mercer takes the field, the Townies' Bill Mosher, who soldiered the past two years in the Pacific war, and spent the 1946 baseball season in Japan helping secure the country, is at third base and batting seventh in the Mercer batting order.

The Townies score three in the first inning, more than enough to win. Sade is virtually untouchable. He strikes out nine batters in the seven innings and gives up only one hit, a single by the spunky Bill Mosher in the second inning. The Townies win easily—but not before the suffering comes.

In the fourth inning the Townies lead 8–1. Boyce is first at bat. He pops a pitch straight up over his head, and the Mercer catcher snags it for the out. Howard Mitchell comes up hitting .600 and slaps a ground ball toward shortstop. When the throw skids by the first baseman and settles in the roadside bushes, Mitchell coasts into second. Then Wirta bounces a hit to second baseman Buddy Harlow, who bobbles it momentarily. Mitchell sees the miscue, rounds third base, and dashes for home. Harlow retrieves the ball and throws toward the plate. Mitchell attempts to avoid the tag with a wide slide but catches a spike of his new baseball shoes in the turf. We hear his left leg snap in the dugout.

"Good gawd!" someone yells. "Howard's broke his leg. Get a car down here and get him to the hospital."

Howard Mitchell was the head of a baseball family. The Mitchells lived in a small farmhouse in a large hayfield, perhaps five acres, a mile out of the village on the Intervale Road. They farmed the five acres—a large vegetable garden, a couple acres of commercial string beans, and enough hay to feed a cow or two—and Mitchell chopped and pressed apples into cider at a mill he'd built on the back edge of his hayfield. On Saturdays and Sundays in the fall, townsmen brought apples to Mitchell's mill and he filled fifty-gallon wooden barrels with a year's supply of sweet cider suitable for fermentation, and had enough left over to fill his own barrel. Inside the farmhouse, Howard and Wilena brought up three sons and a daughter—and Howard made sure there was enough room on the five acres for his sons to play baseball.

Mitchell possessed exemplary baseball credentials. He played outfield for the pre-war team and, following the hiatus for World War II, appeared in the first Townies' lineup in 1946 as left fielder. Mitchell's three sons were old enough then to go to the games, and Sunday afternoons at the ball field, Mitchell, a muscular, stocky man proportioned somewhat like Babe Ruth, demonstrated to his sons the skills he was teaching them in the hayfield. Mitchell had a graceful swing that consistently made solid contact with the pitch. He hit .469 for the 1946 Townies, second only to Dick Blodgett's .491, and was seldom guilty of a miscue in the outfield.

After his leg mended, Mitchell tried to pinch-hit in a practice game at the Temple ball field, but his graceful swing was gone and, unable to run, he required a pinch runner standing behind him to make the dash to first base; he couldn't make it work. His career with the Townies was over. But he had infused his sons—Albert, Arthur, and Ronald—with a love for the game, and two of them would follow his lead and eventually wear a Townies uniform.

*　　*　　*

Following the Mercer match, the Townies continue their reckless version of America's game. The formidable Phillips Legionnaires come to Temple, an open date for the defending North Franklin League champions. Manager Fillmore Harnden starts a rookie right-hander on the mound, and the Townies build up such an early lead that not even pitching ace Bill Burnham, who comes on to pitch the second half of the game, can rescue the Legionnaires from defeat. The Townies score an unforeseen win. Then Sade throws another one-hitter at Mercer, a single by Mercer's first batter the only hit, and the Townies win their fourth in a row, 3–0.

It's now mid-July and the Townies are out of the doldrums. Their cheering fans follow them from town to town on Sunday afternoons. Talk at the general store is that the Townies will be unbeatable the rest of the way. Then word comes to Boyce that Howard Mitchell's hay has dried and is ready to put in his barn. Boyce rouses the Townies early Sunday morning, and they meet in Mitchell's hayfield—Blodgett, Sade, Wirta, Hellgren, Pa, and the rest. Mitchell's cast prevents him from climbing onto a hay rake or treading on a load, but while the Townies rake, and load, and pitch the hay into the barn, Mitchell limps back and forth to his cider barrel in the cellar for the thirst-quencher. The last bit of hay is pitched into the mow about noon, and the Townies' stagger home for dinner before the game. Andover is coming for a two o'clock contest. "I think they're comin' to check us out for the fair," someone hiccups.

The Townies rout the Andover team. Boyce, who has shied away from the morning refreshments, puts his first team—the tipplers—in the lineup. The Townies score seven runs in the first inning and keep up the barrage. Sade whiffs fifteen. His teammates play errorless defense behind him, and tipplers Blodgett, Hellgren, and Pa each knock out three hits against a proclaimed superior team. They score seventeen

The Townies and friends in Howard Mitchell's hayfield, July 1947. (Temple Historical Society)

runs, the highest run total since the game in Fairbanks more than a year ago. Blodgett, after the game, endorses the use of Howard's hard cider as a thirst-quencher. "Hell," he says, "put it right in the water jug; pass it around in the dugout before the game."

The streak has reached five, and Callahan's Hard Cider Boys are next. The Townies score five times in the first inning at Hippach Field and run away with it. Jay comes to Temple and loses, the seventh straight Townies victory. Next, outfielder Larry Barker pitches a five-inning two-hitter against East Wilton on a Thursday evening at Temple, winning 14–1. The following Sunday it is Jay again. Boyce names Bergeron to pitch, and when Barker comes on in the sixth to finish up, the Townies have a 12–4 lead. The streak reaches nine. Boyce is ready for the rematch with his formidable and usually victorious rival, Farmington.

Boyce prepares for the Farmington rematch in advance. He keeps

Sade off the pitchers mound. The last time out, Sade whiffed eighteen Jaymen, and Boyce, fearing overwork and fatigue, wants a rested pitcher for the big game at Hippach Field. Also, at the weeknight batting practices, he works the team on bunting. Boyce doesn't usually call for the bunt in a game. He knows the value of bunting but avoids asking the veterans—men who come to the ball field to wield a heavy bat and pound out as many runs as they can—to sacrifice an at-bat to advance a runner a single base. Bunting isn't fun for them. Bunting is for winning and getting out of slumps, and half the time it doesn't work. The veterans, the good hitters, can drive a double into left center as often as they can bunt successfully anyway. But before the Farmington game, Boyce asks them all to lay down a few during batting practice. And he also rehearses a new set of signals he'll flash from the third-base coaching box. He explains the delayed double steal, a situation where two runners work together to pilfer a run, and he wants hitters to take a pitch on certain counts. He warns us that he will have us running whenever he thinks he can pull a surprise on the shiretowners. "And the new signals should confuse their thieves," he says.

Finally, Boyce is mindful of his own weak throwing arm. He can no longer muster a throw to second base that threatens the safety of a runner stealing the bag. Farmington ran freely against him in June, tallying nineteen stolen bases, and he knows their young speedsters will take copious advantage of him again. He goes to Strong and asks Connie Ladd, who caught for Strong during the North Franklin League season, to catch Sade in the Sunday showdown. "Sure, I'll catch," Ladd tells him. "I need to stay in shape for the all-star game coming up anyways."

The Townies score first. With two outs in the second inning, Al Bergeron singles off Farmington starter Bill Lane. Pa drives a Lane pitch into right field, and Bergeron scoots to third base. With runners on first and third, Boyce then signals the delayed double steal, a new piece of trickery for the baseball fundamentalist, and they execute it perfectly. Bergeron scores on the play before the Farmington infield can run down Pa for the third out. Townies lead, 1–0. In the fourth, the shiretowner's Lou Collette, whose speed will later earn him a center field job in the St. Louis Cardinals minor-league system, singles, promptly steals second base, and scores on a Bob Stevens drive that falls in front of Bruce Mosher in right. It's a seat-squirmer with the score tied 1–1; three hits by each team; no errors; Sade and Lane both in command; two innings left. I'm hopeful—and careful not to cross any bats.

Pa strokes a single to lead off the sixth, but is stranded when the heart of the Townies batting order—Ladd, Hellgren, and Blodgett—all fly out. Sade goes to the mound and strikes out Apple Oliver and Clayton Berry to start the Farmington sixth. His strike-three pitch to Berry, the drop, gets away from Ladd. Ladd is unaccustomed to Sade's drop. He doesn't realize he has to smother it to contain it, and he looks surprised when the ball squirts away. Fortunately he retrieves it in time to throw out Berry at first base.

With two outs, Sade teases speedster Lou Collette with fastballs off the corners of the plate. But Collette is patient, and Sade eventually throws ball four. With Collette on first, Bob Stevens comes up. Sade grimaces and strikes him out with the sharp-breaking drop, but the ball breaks away from Ladd again, this time all the way to the grandstand and beyond. Before Ladd can reclaim it, Collette is on third and Stevens on second. The next batter, Jimmy Conway, singles them both home. In the top of the seventh, the Townies go down in order. Game over: Farmington 3, Townies 1.

Boyce and the Townies could deservedly pine a few minutes over what might have been, but instead they rejoice. They have played well—their best. They kept the outcome in doubt until the final inning. They came up short, but they have no regrets. "A helluva game, wa'n't it? Who we play next?"

They go back to Hippach Field the next week and face the Hard

Cider Boys. Undertaker Vint Davis, whose line-drive hitting is a threat to a third baseman's health, pitches for the Cider Boys and holds the Townies scoreless into the fifth inning. Meanwhile the Hard Cider Boys romp around the bases for eleven runs before Sade can get his arm loose and work up a sweat. Boyce sticks with Sade, however, and in the fifth, the Townies begin to stir. They tighten the gap in the sixth, and in the seventh they pull within a run, 13–12. Then the game is abruptly called off by the home plate umpire. Boyce converses briefly with the umpire and the Cider Boys' wheeler-dealer Jack Callahan about the matter, throwing his arms into the air and slinging his ball cap on the ground to emphasize his frustration, while the Hard Cider Boys all snicker in the dugout, but Callahan holds fast. "The game is over," he declares.

"I can't figure out what the hell they're up to," Boyce reports back in the Townies' dugout. "Far's I can see, they figger they'll quit while they're still ahead. I call it no contest."

"We'll play 'em again, boss. We'll beat their arse," someone says.

"Damn right."

But first the Townies entertain undefeated Farmington Falls. The Yankees have won eight straight, and the Townies are their last barrier to an undefeated season. Unfortunately for the visitors, however, the Townies feast on Falls' pitching, push over fourteen runs on sixteen hits, and stop the Falls' streak head-on. Falls' center fielder Gee Dumeny manages three hits off Sade while his teammates whiff sixteen times. "He'll be talking about those hits at Croswell's Store all winter," Sade says with a chuckle. Tuesday's *Franklin Journal* simply reports the Falls' streak a victim of the mighty Temple nine.

The win over undefeated Farmington Falls puts the Townies in an agreeable spirit, and they settle the unfinished matter with the Hard Cider Boys peaceably. The game brings out a large crowd, perhaps a record, to watch the Townies try to even the score, reminiscent of the opening day game against Farmington. They have come all season, come to greet their townsfolk and see the Townies win. A crowd has turned out at every game, and they have not been disappointed—the Townies have won ten of thirteen. They will win this one. Callahan's bandits, as Boyce has good naturedly tagged the Hard Cider Boys, run often on Boyce's arm—six stolen bases by those few who manage to get on base—but Sade fans fourteen in a lopsided victory. Anticipating the outcome, the Cider Boys have brought a jug to share. "Good stuff, ain't it," someone says.

For years, Uncle Austin, proprietor of the general store in Temple, has conceded the end of summer to the Skowhegan State Fair, which comes in the middle of August. He returns from the last day of harness racing at Skowhegan in 1947 and moans as usual to the townsfolk loitering on the store's platform, "Well, the fair's over. Winter's next, I s'-pose."

The townsmen nod in polite agreement. But regardless of Uncle Austin's dreary outlook, the loiterers know that summer hasn't ended, not until the Townies have played their last game. "Where do they finish this year?" one asks.

"I dunno. Mebbe at another one of them celebrity appearances," another answers.

The Townies play deep into September. The return game at Farmington Falls turns out virtually the same as the first—Townies 7, Yankees 3, Sade fifteen strikeouts—except that center fielder Dumeny is absent. "Probably somewhere talking about the three hits he got off me the last time," Sade laughs.

The return game in Phillips is not the same. The heavy-hitting Legionnaires have rolled to the North Franklin League championship in a showdown game with Farmington in front of a reported one thousand fans at Hippach Field, their third victory over the shiretowners this season. Legionaries manager Harnden doesn't risk another rookie on the mound, and the Townies are impotent against luminary Bill

Burnham. They drop their fourth game, but Boyce sees the loss as a workout for the last game of the season—at Andover Fair.

The invitation came in August, about the time Uncle Austin waxed his snow shovel. The Andover folks, impressed by the Townies' headlong brand of baseball—and perhaps the new gray flannels—offered the Townies another thirty-five dollars to come to the fair and play Andover. "They want us to come to the fair?" Blodgett queried. "Must be the hard cider."

Boyce doesn't hesitate when the call comes. "We'll be there," he answers.

"Gosh," Aunt Marion remarks, "You and your team are getting to be quite the celebrities."

The Townies go to Andover on a clear and chilly September 24. It seems as though it hasn't rained since June. "I don't think it'll rain today," Boyce remarks, readying to leave Temple. "Snow maybe, but not rain." Townsfolk are excited again at being picked to entertain the fairgoers, and most travel to Andover for the game. But Mrs. Josselyn keeps the Village School in session, prompting Pa, who Boyce says will start at first base this year, to say he'll take me to the game anyway. But Aunt Marion, an unyielding advocate of school attendance, objects to Pa's laissez-faire disposition—"My gosh! He's going to school, and that's all there is to it. Who would think?" she retorts—and Pa is persuaded by the possibility of a confrontation with Aunt Marion to send me to school. Boyce is forced to make other arrangements for the bats.

The Townies manage well enough without me. Although Andover keeps the outcome against the superior Townies in doubt until the final inning, pitching ace Sade doesn't weaken. He whiffs nineteen batters on a day so cold that Boyce, shivering behind home plate, has trouble hanging on to Sade's drop and on four occasions is forced to chase the third strike and throw the batter out at first base. The Townies push the winning run across the plate when Bergeron drives a liner into the outfield in the tenth inning, scoring Bruce Mosher. The victory runs their season record to thirteen wins and four losses. Boyce collects thirty-five dollars for their appearance at what one player calls Andover's winter carnival and drives home to Aunt Marion's warm kitchen.

Chapter Four

AUNT MARION (I)

D uring her years in Temple, Ma had trouble making life work. Once during the war, when Pa was battling the Germans in Europe and she was tangled up in some family squabble, she told me, "Johnny, I don't know why it is. I've always been either in the wrong place or doing the wrong thing. I just can't get it right." I thought Ma unduly harsh on herself, but not knowing exactly how to answer her, I blurted out, "Not *always*, Ma."

Before coming to Temple, Ma had lived a puritanical existence in Kennebunk. Her parents, keepers of the strict British lifestyle—church, duty, no movies or dancing, and all that—brought her to Maine from England in 1913 when she was four years old. She tolerated life at home but after high school she left for Farmington, where she graduated from the State Normal School in 1930. Temple, then a town of three hundred or so woodchoppers and sustenance farmers five miles west at the end of the road, lacked a teacher. Ma accepted the job, boarded at Hathaway's in the village, and walked to the schoolhouse and back each day. But Temple was the wrong place for Ma. She met Pa there, and in 1934, they married—a marriage that turned out wrong. I was born in the midst of the Great Depression, and for years after we suffered from depression-based shortages—money, warmth, food, transportation—and too much of Pa's poker playing. When World War II broke out, Ma tended three youngsters and a sparse kitchen on the edge of the village and taught school only on days when the regular schoolmarm couldn't get there. When Pa left for the war in 1943, he asked her to wait in Temple. She acquiesced and tried to manage the place herself. But Temple was still the wrong place, and after two years and with Pa still in Germany, she abandoned it for the security of Kennebunk and her parents.

But Ma was a gamer. When Pa came home, she returned to Temple and tried to rebuild life with him there on the half-acre farm— the wrong place again. The war had changed Pa, and after two years of domestic tumult, Ma and Pa divorced, and she returned to her parents—the wrong place, again. "I just don't know why I can't get it right," she wailed.

It is October 1947. I am twelve years old. My house is empty. My parents have left, Pa to his brother's in Farmington, Ma to her parents in Kennebunk. Except for Aunt Marion and Uncle Lawrence, I am alone, orphaned. Now I walk the quarter-mile to Aunt Marion's, wondering whether *I'm* doing the right thing, or if *I'm* in the right place. But there is no way I can know, no decision I can make, no problem I can solve, that will tell me. Aunt Marion has always been good to me, and I know she will continue to be. But will I be able to grow up here? The thought is constant: *What is next for me?*

Aunt Marion is a formidable woman: big, strong, and loud, given to outbursts of the truth. "I have to speak what's on my mind," she says. "That's the way I am." She is afraid of no one, hesitant about nothing, determined to have her way. "If people don't like it, that's too bad," she says, though she doesn't mean to hurt anyone. She has to be herself. She runs through life with her chin jutting out. She gardens. She cooks. She keeps house. She runs Grandma's errands. She grocery shops with a ten-gallon cardboard box and picks wild strawberries into an eight-quart pail. She takes Grandma to alumni gatherings at the Farmington Normal School and me to boy scout troop meetings. She doesn't miss a meeting of several women's groups in Farmington, or church in Temple on Sunday. And she doesn't interrupt her life for the movies on Saturday night, or the comics on Sunday. "Foolishness," she calls them. She distances herself from many of life's little pleasures—caffeine, sugar, tobacco, alcohol—afraid, I suppose, of conceding to the devil's excesses, or perhaps violating her mother's preachings. Living at Aunt Marion's will not be the same for me.

"C'mon Johnny," Aunt Marion beckons. "I've some scrapbooking to do. I'll show you how it's done. Have you ever done scrapbooking?"

"No," I answer. "We didn't do things like that." I suspect she feels a need to show me how industrious folks entertain themselves when faced with idle time, or perhaps after a month of me in her house, she has an urge to try some parenting.

"There's a stack of last month's news clippings on the kitchen table," she says, pointing. "They're about the fires. Trim them up for me, and I'll glue them in."

The fires. I know about the fires.

Forest fires devastated Maine in October 1947. Following a run of dry weather that stretched back into June, they broke out all over, first in Topsham and Bowdoin and then spreading west. Ten days later, fifty forest fires were reported burning in the state. A huge blaze burned thousands of acres in Newfield and Shapleigh and Waterboro and spread toward Kennebunk and Kennebunkport. Ma wrote me that downtown Kennebunk, where she lived with Grandma and Grandpa Watson, was in the fire's path and she had fled with Nancy and Patty to the ocean at Kennebunk Beach. They would stay there until the fires were stopped. The newspaper reported that fires burned hundreds of acres and nearly as many houses and millionaires' estates on Mount

Desert Island alone, and the National Guard made plans to evacuate the trapped population of Bar Harbor by sea. Two weeks passed before the firefighters brought the blazes under control. From time to time during those two weeks, I could smell smoke in Temple. Folks spread rumors: "Fire up to Varnum," or "Mt. Blue's ablaze." Aunt Marion clipped stories from the newspapers every day for more than two weeks and stacked the clippings in a safe place. Yes, I know about the fires.

We sit at the kitchen table and trim and arrange and glue until twilight. *This is fun,* I think—and I then hear a commotion outside.

It must be Eddie Fontaine. He is tinkering on his sawing rig in the barn, where he's stored it for the winter. The barn is connected to the house by a shed, and hay for mulching the garden is kept in the loft. The shed holds wood for the stove, gardening tools, household discards, and other paraphernalia. Fontaine winters his sawing rig on the barn's lower floor. *It must be him,* I think.

Then I hear Fontaine shouting, "Marion! Marion!" he roars, pounding—thump, thump, thump—up the walkway in the twilight. "Marion, the spark, she catch!" He bursts into the kitchen, ashen faced. "Marion, the spark, she catch, and she burn now—get help!"

"Oh, my Lord! Oh, my Lord!" Aunt Marion dashes to the hand-crank phone on the wall and rings the general store. "Hurry! Hurry!" she shouts into the mouthpiece. "The house is afire!"

Bill Mosher, Townies third baseman, is one of the first to arrive. When he confronts the barn in the coming darkness, he sees a tongue of flame leaping into the near-empty hayloft and spreading toward the shed. More men come, and pandemonium breaks out. There is no water to spray on the leaping fire. The overwrought men carry water in pails from the kitchen faucet and throw it into the barn. They shovel snow into the barn door opening and pitch snowballs into the loft. Someone brings small, fragile-glass globes filled with water, and the men heave the water bombs into the flames now in the loft and spreading toward the shed. They shovel more snow. Then a voice, "Iffen we could blow that shed off, we could save the house. Anyone got any dynamite?"

"Harry Blodgett's got enough dynamite in his barn to blow that gawdamm shed to smithereens," another voice yells."

Jules Vernesoni races off in his car a mile up the Intervale Road to retrieve the dynamite and doesn't come back. The frantic Mosher and the others keep lugging water, throwing snow, and toting goods from inside the house—tables, chairs, beds, rugs, kitchen appliances, cupboard contents, everything—out the front door and across the road to the school yard. They call the Farmington Fire Department twice from the hand crank in the kitchen, but no one appears. They grab hangings off walls and pass armfuls of home-canned fruits and vegetables, enough to last the winter and more, up the cellar stairs and outside.

When the frustrated men are done carrying, they can only watch. The barn falls, then the shed. The house, stripped clean now by townsmen who yanked the bathroom lavatory off the wall, lifted the kitchen sink out of its cradle, and pulled the shiny flush toilet clean from the floor, is now ablaze.

"Where the hell is the fire department?" someone asks.

"An' what the hell happened to Jules?"

Jules is stuck in a snowdrift on the Intervale Road, and the dynamite lays untouched in Harry Blodgett's barn. They wait in vain for the fire department. Then the house falls in, and it's all over.

During the pandemonium, someone wraps a coat around Grandma Luna and escorts her and Aunt Marion up the snowy road to Uncle Austin's. Aunt Marion calls Uncle Lawrence in Augusta. "All is lost," she sobs into the mouthpiece.

He is home in an hour, but there is nothing for him to do. The house is gone—a chimney, a fireplace, and a pile of coal in the cellar that will smolder for a week are all that remain.

"The snowdrift on the Intervale Road," Bill Mosher will say later, "made the difference. If we'd a-had the dynamite, we coulda stopped it

before it got to the house. Gawd, we had plenty of time. We jes'
watched it burn."

And now I am homeless, too. *What will be next*, I wonder?

Easter is not a conspicuous holiday in Temple. In 1948, most folks
keep close to home and attend to their usual weekend duties: barn
chores, gathering maple sap from a few pails hung in the backyard,
cleaning up the shed where the winter's wood has been stacked, and, in
sunny spots, channeling meltwater away from the driveway and into a
ditch. Uncle Austin keeps the general store closed, as he does every
Sunday—except when someone from the outback needs to make a critical purchase: a flashlight battery, a pack of cigarettes, a can of beef
stew, or a similar item of necessity, in which case he'll rise from the sofa
and tend to their needs. But most folks, except those whose nature dis-
poses them toward church services, spend a quiet day at home.

Easter morning Aunt Marion dresses up in a flowery hat and a
netted veil and takes me, outfitted in my new tweed eighth-grade-
graduation suit, to Temple's First Congregational Church to hear the
Reverend Richard Pierce—now professor of history at the prestigious
Emerson College in Boston and lecturer in church history at Andover
Theological Seminary in Newton, Massachusetts—conduct the Easter
service. From our pew near the front, Pierce is a handsome man, a bit
portly perhaps, but pleasantly urbane, confident that his message will
be heard. In Temple just for this Easter service, he will soon leave here
altogether and will later maneuver up through the church hierarchy,
eventually becoming Dean of the College at Emerson. I wonder, as he
stands to deliver the service, what brought him here in the beginning?
Why Temple?

A smattering of local parishioners, predominately wives and mothers, and perhaps Marcus Mitchell or Old Carr, come to the church as
well, and we hearken to Dr. Pierce's version of the Easter story: death
before eternal life. I endure the hour-long service without discomfort

and react with no particular emotion to actually being in church, except for a slight self-consciousness at being so conspicuous among many of the town's older women. Reverend Pierce's sermon does, however, cause me to wonder where I stand on the life-after-death continuum. Have I already suffered and begun to grow—and will later flourish and experience what Pierce refers to without details as eternal life? It's too profound for me, I conclude, as Aunt Marion hustles me out the door. "Come. Aunt Viola's waiting a ham dinner for us," she says, leaving me no opportunity to question Dr. Pierce.

On the drive back to the village, she queries me about the summer. "Are you going to work with Uncle Lawrence on the bakery truck?" she asks.

"I don't know," I answer.

"Well, make up your mind," she says. "He's waiting."

"I don't know whether I want a job. I'd be giving up my summer days."

"Well, you know we're not going to be here. We're moving to Farmington as soon as I find a place."

In Aunt Viola's kitchen, I gaze out a window across Temple Stream to the general store. There I envision my friends and me weaving bicycles among parked cars while loiterers chat on the platform and Uncle Austin leans against the door opening in the summer sunlight. I replay Aunt Marion's words: I won't be in Temple? What will I do in Farmington? Who will my friends be? Where will I roam? Or explore? I have no answers. Except that life will not be the same as I've known it. I'm a teenager now; perhaps a job is on Dr. Pierce's continuum; perhaps I should go to work for pay. A dite frightened by my thoughts, I go to Uncle Lawrence, "I'll do it," I tell him.

It is May. Lilacs are budded. Fishermen are on the stream banks. Baseball practice has started. Mrs. Josselyn at the Village School is holding graduation rehearsals. Aunt Marion, not one to put a project aside for later, comes back from a shopping trip in Farmington and bursts breathless into Aunt Viola's kitchen. "Well! We're moving," she announces.

"Oh?" Aunt Viola answers.

"We're going to Christine's."

Aunt Viola puts a puzzled look on her face, "I didn't think you were going to Christine's?"

Marion and Christine, sisters, each view themselves as the head of the family: Aunt Marion, a successful professional woman, takes responsibility for the parents and is the family's advocate and decision maker, the family go-to person, so to speak; Christine, a persnickety Farmington housewife and social gadfly, is two years older. Their behavior in the presence of Grandpa C.F. and Grandma Luna is entertaining to the family, but some think hurtful to themselves and their parents. But the rivalry flourishes. Marion, a presumptuous political manipulator, and Christine, a self-proclaimed highborn, maintain a minimum level of civility toward each other. But they are not close. The news that Marion will be tenant and Christine—who with her husband Roy owns two apartments in their oversized Farmington home—the landlord is a surprise.

"Why, yes, of course we are," Aunt Marion answers, "Christine has a vacancy, and I've decided. We're going there as soon as school is over. I need a cup of tea. Is there a teabag here someplace?" She pours boiling water into a flowery teacup and dips a teabag into the steamy water.

"What does Roy think?" Viola continues.

Aunt Marion sips her tea. "Roy wasn't there. And I asked Christine to lower the rent."

Aunt Viola looks up, "Christine lowered the rent? Without Roy knowing it? That's a new one, isn't it?"

"I told her," Aunt Marion adds, "that Mother will be with us, and I didn't expect to pay the full price. And as long as Mother lives there, I don't want the rent to go up."

"What did she say then?"

"Well, how could she say no, for goodness sakes? She's *her* mother, too."

Aunt Marion knows, and so does Aunt Viola, that Christine's husband, Roy Stinchfield, a miserly businessman who suffers from a nervous tic when finances are mentioned in his presence, will have nothing to do with lowering the rent—for any reason. Roy's eyes will dart at Christine, and his voice will squeak, and his face will twitch when he hears her news. And sparks will fly at the landlords' supper table before he acquiesces.

Moving to Farmington was hard for Aunt Marion. Born in Temple and raised on the family homestead on the edge of the village, she had known no other place, nor had she ever wanted to. She moved away after college—schoolteacher—but she called Temple home. It had always been her home and she believed it always would be her home.

The Temple Aunt Marion grew up in was prosperous. Dams in two places on Temple Stream, where it dropped through a rocky gorge in the village, powered a succession of sawmills that employed hundreds. From the kitchen of her childhood, she watched a parade of two-horse drays haul logs over Mill Hill into the village and listened to the saws whine on the stream. From the platform of her father's general store, she watched the lumbermen grapple the logs and stack the timbers, and she greeted them when they passed and repassed to the cash register inside. She married in Temple and weathered it during the hard years of the Great Depression and World War II.

Aunt Marion loved Temple. Yet I think she loved not the real Temple but the fantasy that she called Temple. She dwelled on its charm, its history, and its locally famous names: Gordon, Dryden, Parker, Mitchell. She attended the one-room schoolhouse, and Dr. Pierce's church, and bought a house there when she married. She served the town as treasurer and solicited Temple's quota of money for war bonds during the war. And during the hard years, she promoted the business of the general store and post office by buying everything she could there, and wheedled others to do the same, lest the businesses be abandoned and closed. Aunt Marion repelled any knowledge of Temple's seamy side. She denied the alcoholism and poverty, knew nothing of the existence of locally-born Dorcas Doyen—aka Helen Jewett, an upscale New York City prostitute—and thought the Reverend Richard Pierce, who predicted the early demise of immoral Temple in his 1945 dissertation, a local celebrity. She boasted the town at every chance. Temple was her town. Temple blood ran in her veins.

We move to Farmington in May before school ends. Aunt Marion doesn't wait for graduation at the Village School, nor does she fritter away her time waiting for Christine's husband, Roy, to object to the lowered rent. We move to Farmington not because her house burned, but because I will graduate from the Village School and start high school in the fall. Though in the 1920s she commuted to the high school in a horse-drawn wagon—or sleigh—with her brothers and sisters, she doesn't expect me to do the same. Nor does she want me to miss the school's extracurricular activities because I have to catch an afternoon ride to Temple. She gives up Temple and we move to her sister Christine's on Lake Avenue, within walking distance of the high school, before Roy has time to find a tenant agreeable to paying the full price.

Lake Avenue in Farmington is Queen Anne style: huge houses showing off a wide array of irregular architecture, painted in a potpourri of gentle colors. Leaky roofs and cracked windows and dilapidated, unpainted sheds don't exist on Lake Avenue. Aunt Christine's Queen Anne style house, three stories high, comprises a main house, two ground-level apartments, a screened front porch, a barn, and outbuildings: a playhouse, a tool shed, and a place for the dog, had we a dog. A clipped lawn sidles up to the sidewalk, and a postman ambles by each day to put letters and newspapers into a mail drop. Perhaps

Aunt Marion thinks Aunt Christine's place will seem more like home than something on the other side of town, but I think it will take some getting used to.

"Hello, my name is Dave Smith," the voice behind me says. I am greeted by a robust man with a sparkle in his eyes. "Welcome to Lake Avenue." He introduces Verlie and their lanky, redheaded son, Allan, who looks to be a few years older than me.

Allan produces a ball, and we toss it back and forth on the grass and test each other's knowledge of the goings-on in major league baseball. "Williams is best," I say.

"Musial's my man," Allan counters, and we parry with each other over the skills of players we read of in the daily box scores: Enos Slaughter, Whitey Kurowski, and Red Shoendienst, he tosses my way; Bobby Doerr and Birdie Tebbetts, I throw back at him. We keep tossing the ball, and tossing names. Finally, he shouts Eddie Kazak. *Eddie Kazak?* I wonder. Allan is the first person I've known not to be a Red Sox fan. He is for the Cardinals. "Billy Hitchcock!" I shout. In these few minutes our differences, batting averages, home runs, ball parks, and home towns, bring us together, the beginning of what will become a lifelong friendship.

I'm anxious to know what the high school is like. "Do you play for the high school?" I ask.

"Center field," he says. He tells me, too, that he's a senior now and then asks, "Do you have a summer job?"

"I'm going to be a bakery salesman," I say, pointing to the van in the driveway. "And the boss says he wants me to taste-test the jelly doughnuts every day." He laughs. I try the high school again. "How far away is the school?"

"About a ten-minute walk," he answers. "You'll meet new people there, too, and play sports and join groups. Do you like music?"

"Do they have a freshman baseball team?"

"There's a jayvee basketball team," he says. "And there's a hoop in the barn here—where you can practice." I wonder whether I can find my way into the high school, use the right door, find the right room. Perhaps he'll walk to school with me the first day.

I get no idling time after eighth-grade graduation to prepare for the summer job. No time to unwind, to go fishing, or watch a ball game at Hippach Field. "You don't need any," Aunt Marion says.

Uncle Lawrence wakes me at 4:30 a.m. He takes me to Augusta, for breakfast at George's Diner on State Street: coffee, poached eggs, and toast. He drives to the Hallowell pick-up spot, an old garage off Water Street, where a few minutes earlier a trucker from Portland dropped off our goods. We pack the van with still-warm bread and fruit pies and jelly doughnuts, and then drive to the outskirts of Augusta, where we make our first call at seven o'clock.

Uncle Lawrence impressed me. He could pull all his duties together and keep them running. The sum of the demands of his family, off-field preparations for the baseball team—find money, buy supplies, schedule games, manage practices—and his distant job all put him on the edge. But he didn't slip. He organized and concentrated and avoided mistakes. He was not careless or sloppy. He was thorough. He worked from a plan, not a plan on paper, but a plan in his head. And no place was the plan more evident than on his bakery route.

He has created a routine, organized a team so to speak, to transfer bakery goods from his van to bread boxes all over Kennebec County. It starts at the diner. George knows what Boyce eats for breakfast and starts preparing it when we come through the door. Boyce's second cup of coffee gives the trucker from Portland a few minutes of leeway in case he's running late. And at seven o'clock, the first customer unlocks her kitchen door and looks out the window to see if Boyce is coming up the walk.

We call on nearly one hundred customers. Boyce has arranged his route to visit the outlying farm families, the early risers, first. We call on bleary-eyed urbanites later in the day, when they have finished the newspaper and their second cup of coffee. At noon, our calls usually take us to an in-town lunch spot: a riverside parking area where we eat a sandwich prepared at home; or a lunch counter at a local diner, where Boyce chats with the chef; or perhaps a school parking lot where we watch a school-yard baseball game for thirty minutes while we eat the sandwich. After lunch, Boyce smokes a cigarette, and I read *The Kennebec Journal* while our afternoon customers finish their lunch.

We keep up the regimen, house after house. At many stops, he knows the menu and senses how much the customer has eaten since his last call. In most cases, I go to the door with the expected purchase— and perhaps a special or a slow-selling item he is pushing—and close the deal while Boyce records whether the last customer paid and pre- pares an armful of goods for the next stop. Nearing suppertime, we scurry to finish before our customers are at the table, hoping the lady of the house will find it convenient to buy a pie for dessert. Then it's back to George's Diner for supper and the Lawrence House, a Grove Street rooming house, for the night. At the Lawrence House, Boyce sets his alarm clock for 5:00 a.m., turns on his portable radio to Jim Britt and the Red Sox, and falls asleep.

Selling bakery products was not fascinating work. Nor was it bor- ing or unpleasant. But given other choices I'd have opted not to be a bread and cake salesman. It was busy work. The days were intense. I missed hanging out with my friends. I missed the idleness I knew at the general store in Temple. I missed being lazy. But Boyce demonstrated an impressive work ethic that first summer, a work ethic I was not ac- customed to or even familiar with. I was determined not to be seen as a slacker, though, and I honored my commitment. I worked as hard as I could every day for two dollars and jelly doughnuts. I chose not to complain. I worked willingly. I needed Boyce. He was my ticket to the baseball team.

Later in the summer, Boyce completes arrangements with the Cushman Company to open a route in the Farmington area. "They told me to give it a try, see if I could make a go of it," he tells Aunt Marion. "I figure with Farmington, Strong, and Phillips, I can come up with a hundred customers. That's all I'll need."

"Where do we pick up the goods?" I ask.

"Dryden," he answers. "Down beyond the woolen mill, a little garage. They say the goods will show up there before five o'clock."

We move our weekly routine fifty miles northwest, eat lunch at Lake Avenue three times a week and a sandwich on the riverbank in Phillips twice, and sleep at home every night. The van's daily newspaper changes to *The Lewiston Daily Sun*, and I learn the eating habits of a different set of farm families.

"We'll hold practice twice a week now," Boyce tells me. "The extra workout might turn this season around."

Chapter Five

THE CURSE

T o me the most serious deficiency at Lake Avenue is its location—five miles from the Temple ball field. Boyce and I live farther from the playing field than even the most remote outback farm in Temple. But Boyce manages the Townies from here without a hitch. In May, after the snow is gone, he assembles us at the ball field on Thursday evenings for batting and fielding workouts.

In 1948, for the first time, Boyce puts youngsters into the Thursday practice sessions. Many of us who played in the school-yard games—Cal Tyler, Keith Porter, Al Mitchell, Art Mitchell, Vern Hodgkins—are teenagers now, and we've watched the routine. "Be here on time," Boyce tells us. "I'll find time for you in the batter's box."

At practice the players swing at Larry Barker's batting-practice pitches. When Barker is absent, Bergeron throws, or perhaps Sade. The batsmen follow the batting order, and each one hits five fair balls. When the regulars finish, the reserves hit. We, the youngsters, are last. Boyce eyes us in the box. When we struggle at contacting the ball, he shows us how to position the bat, shift our weight, or turn our belly button into the pitch. "See the ball all the way to the bat," he lectures. And he tells us to go out for the high school team. "You can't get too much baseball," he says. We listen—he has hit over .400 for the Townies for years.

Boyce has many reasons to be optimistic at the opening of the 1948 season. The infield, except for Wirta, is a repeat of the previous year. The stocky Wirta, a fixture at third base for two years who showed wide range and a strong arm, moved out of Temple after last season and retired from playing baseball. But Bill Mosher, who played a few innings of third base last year and hit .286, is looking for a place in the everyday lineup. Boyce puts him at third. The outfield is set. Boyce has a plethora of outfielders to chose from: regulars Hellgren and Bruce Mosher; Larry Barker, who went to left field after Mitchell's injury and, though he didn't hit as well as Mitchell, played a solid defense; John Hardy, a sometimes outfielder who hit .385 last year in six games; and youngster Al Mitchell, who played his second season for the high school. Sade is the pitcher, and Boyce will catch again. Prospects for another successful season look bright.

On opening day a large crowd follows the Townies to New Vineyard. Sade's arm is slow to loosen up and the Townies trail 4–0 before some of their fans can find the ball field, located a quarter-mile walk into a hayfield off highway twenty-seven. Crafty New Vineyard right-hander Elwyn McAllister whiffs eight Townies in the first four innings. Eventually Sade's arm comes around, and he strikes out eleven, but the Townies cannot overcome the early New Vineyard lead. Boyce is right. Baseball will humble the best, and most often it will happen when they least expect it.

At Hippach Field in Farmington the following Saturday, the Townies show a bit more promise and come away with a narrow victory over a team billed as Callahan's Hard Cider Boys, but whose lineup—Don Green, Lou Collette, Cecil Kendall, Dick Green—is changed considerably from a year ago. They look remarkably similar to the 1948 Farmington Flyers, who will compete in the North Franklin

League. But Boyce is undaunted by the similarity, and Pa and Bill Mosher spark a late-inning rally against relief pitcher Red Morrill to claim the victory 8–6. Then comes a disgraceful loss—to the same Hard Cider Boys.

It happens on Sunday, a week later in Temple. The so-called Cider Boys reveal their true identity. They score five runs before the Townies come to bat, pummel Sade with nineteen hits in the game, and prevent the Townies from making any realistic challenge to the final outcome. Callahan uses sixteen players trying to keep the game interesting for the Townies' fans, but he fails. His Cider Boys run around the bases until they have eighteen runs and could have kept on had the umpires let them play more than nine innings. The following week the Townies square up the New Vineyard series at Temple, 14–5, behind the robust hitting of Dick Blodgett and John Hardy. Sade fans fifteen, and the record improves to two wins and two embarrassing losses. Then comes the long trip to South China.

Dowe's Diner in South China was the lunch counter of choice for Boyce in 1947. His bakery route took him by Dowe's about noontime twice a week, where he sat on a swivel stool at the counter and exchanged views on the weather and politics with the locals over a sandwich and a cup of coffee. Most days the conversation eventually turned to baseball, the Red Sox and all that, and Harris Plaisted, who played for the hometown China Clippers, would often join the conversation. Boyce couldn't resist telling the folks about his Townies and the success they were having up in Franklin County. Someone mentioned that perhaps the two teams should play a game somewhere, and Boyce struck an agreement with Plaisted over a second piece of custard pie. The Townies and Clippers would play a home-and-home set of games during the 1948 season. Boyce wanted, the story goes, to test the Townies, to see what they could do. Someone even went so far as to say that Boyce wanted to show the suburban Clippers some good, old-fashioned country baseball.

Now, in June 1948, Boyce prepares his players for the first game. He lectures to them, builds on the drama of the Townies' venture into unknown territory, tells them they are reaching way out this time, putting themselves at risk of embarrassment or, worse, humiliation. He doesn't know just how good the Clippers are, he says, and cites the seriousness of baseball in Kennebec County and the shaky position he is in at Dowe's. "They're waitin' for us," he says, urging them not to win, but to do their best. "I'm relyin' on Sade's arm to keep the score close. And our hittin' is improvin'. Gosh," he remarks, "pitchers can't get Blodgett out. Eight hits in the last two games. And John Hardy will be there, too. I believe with a few hits we can do it."

"Who do they play?" someone asks.

"They play independent ball. Pittston, I guess, maybe Vassalboro. Their best hitter is Harris Plaisted—he hits a long ball. I don't know what they have for pitching—but they win."

The game is played at the Erskine Academy field in South China, a two-hour drive from Temple, in front of a scant crowd. When the Townies arrive, Boyce puts the fielders through a short drill to erase any anxiety and then pencils first-team starters into the score book: Pa at first base leading off; Bill Mosher, who's hitting .454 since he started playing regularly, at third base; John Hardy, who has recently put some new punch into the lineup, in left field. Sade, who has arrived in time to loosen his arm thoroughly, is on the pitchers mound. There is not a weak spot in the lineup.

The Townies score first. In the second inning an error and four singles off the big Clipper right-hander John Boynton bring in three runs. The Clippers answer in the third with one run. The Townies add one more run in the fifth on a ground ball by .077-hitting Bruce Mosher that squirts through the infield and scores Dick Blodgett from second base. Sade pitches a spectacular game. He allows one hit and whiffs thirteen batters in eight innings. But in the ninth with the Townies leading 4–1, the Clippers, whose three pitchers have kept the Townies'

The Townies pose after a loss to the Farmington Flyers, Strong, 1948. (Temple Historical Society)

bats quiet since the second inning, strike back. An error, a single, and a walk load the bases. Boyce goes out to calm Sade. But it's too late. A dropped fly ball and a blast by Plaisted bring home four runs. The Townies are beaten in a shocking finish.

Boyce is undaunted. He knows the South China Clippers are a superior team, and he puts the game behind him. He and the Townies go back to the practice field. Behind Sade, they win the next three, the first a come-from-behind win at Jay. Sade then strikes out twelve of the potent Chisholm-Livermore Townies, perhaps the primary triumph of his pitching career, and the Townies score nine runs in the fifth inning off pitching ace Drig Fournier to win easily at Temple. Next, they hold off a Jay uprising in the ninth at Temple to win again, running their record to six wins and four losses.

Then the Townies are cursed again. They lose to South China at Temple, Harris Plaisted's first inning blast over Boyce's head in right field with the bases full settling the outcome early. And they lose to the Madison Eagles in extra innings when they fail to produce a timely hit and leave runners stranded. Ahead in the Madison game 3–2 in the seventh inning, Sade goes to the mound to face the bottom of the Eagles' batting order. The first Madison batter swings at a fastball and bounces it straight back to Sade who tosses to Pa at first for the first out. Sade strikes out the next batter but then loses concentration and walks the shortstop Gary Spencer. On Sade's next pitch, Spencer goes for second base, and Boyce throws him out for the third out. *Unusual,* I think. Runners have been running on Boyce's weak arm all summer. Spencer is the first base stealer he has caught at second all season.

Boyce walks off the field holding onto his elbow and sits in the dugout. "I've had it up to here with runners who think my arm is no good," he says, holding his hand at nose level, "but by gawd, I got that one."

"What happened to your elbow, Larry? Why you hanging onto it so?"

"Gawd, didn't you hear it snap? I dunno what it was. Hurt for a minute," Boyce answers.

He sits quietly in the dugout while the Townies bat. With two outs, Pa drills a single into right-center but is stranded when John Hardy swings over a fastball for strike three, the third out. Boyce stays in the dugout and watches the players move toward the field. "Hey, Bill, Bill Mosher," he yells. "You ever catch?"

Mosher, who has started out to third base, turns and answers him. "I caught one inning in Mercer last year,"

"Can't lift my arm," Boyce says. "It's dead. You catch."

"Me? Why me?"

"Well, you catch more than any of the others."

The Townies score a run in the eighth inning to lead by two, but the Eagles score two in the ninth to tie it and two more in the tenth to win, 6–4. Boyce's catching career is finished. After some rest, his arm will strengthen a bit, and he'll continue to play from time to time. But he will not catch again.

The Hard Cider Boys—the honest version: Refino Collette, Winston Clements, Ken Brooks, Jack Callahan, et al—come to Temple. Boyce is at second base, Blodgett moves to third, Bill Mosher is catching. Al Bergeron is absent. Boyce puts Al Mitchell at shortstop, the first of the young school-yard players to appear in a starting lineup. The Townies score seventeen runs. Mitchell has three hits and scores twice.

But the Townies finish their season with two shameful losses to New Sharon: the first when New Sharon scores nine in the ninth inning, the second when they score four in the last inning as well. The Townies' season record stands at six wins and eight losses, and they are not invited to the Andover Fair this year. A frustrated Uncle Austin paces back and forth in the general store moaning that winter will come if the Townies don't find any September games to play.

An invitation comes to play in Strong at the Labor Day festival there, though the invitation avoids mentioning thirty-five dollars. Boyce pays no mind to the absence of cash. He knows he will be facing the Farmington Flyers, Cash Clark's collection of youthful ballplayers who finished second to the powerful Phillips Legionnaires in the North Franklin League and swept the Farmington Town Team in a post-season, intratown series. "Of course we'll go. Maybe it'll be warmer than last year at the fair," he remarks to

LABOR DAY CELEBRATION
MON., SEPT. 6 - STRONG
—— LEGION FIELD ——
3 BALL GAMES
FARMINGTON FLYERS vs. TEMPLE 10.30
STRONG vs. RANGELEY 1.30
WINNERS AT 3.30

PARADE AT 8.30 A. M.
DOLL CARRIAGE and BICYCLE--Prizes
HORRIBLES and FLOATS

BEANO and other games of chance-- BOWLING

DINNER - SUPPER on grounds
Served by the Auxiliary

SPONSORED BY
JOHNSON-COX POST AND AUXILIARY NO. 78, STRONG

Announcement in the Franklin Journal, *September 1948.*

Aunt Marion. Boyce has not shied away from playing a Farmington team—ever. Twice this season the Townies faced the Farmington Flyers—masquerading as Callahan's Hard Cider Boys—and came out even. Boyce is more than eager—he's excited and honored—to play again. He knows about the law of averages, and he's aware, too, of the possibility of miracles.

But Boyce does not wait for divine intervention. Mindful that the Townies face a potential shellacking at the hands of the upstart Flyers, and wary of Sade's inclination toward end-of-season fatigue—a tired Sade lost the last two scheduled games to New Sharon—he recruits brothers Stan and Harold Horne, stalwarts for the hard-hitting Dixfield Dixies in the Timber League, and puts them into the Townies lineup. The Dixies make annual trips to Pettingill Park in Auburn, where they threaten to take the state amateur championship away from the best teams in Maine, and the Horne brothers are largely the reason they are so successful there. Unfortunately for the Townies, however, the outcome in Strong would have been the same had Boyce recruited Cy Young to pitch. The Flyers' young and brash hitters drive home six runs in the second inning. The Townies' twelve hits are useless. They fail to score at all against Flyers' left-hander Ken Gray.

The loss to the Flyers marks the end of the Townies' first losing season. "Winning is easy," Boyce tells me when it's over. "Losing is hard work." He knows. He knows he can't go back.

"We've got work to do," he says.

Chapter Six

AUNT MARION (II)

A t Lake Avenue, Aunt Marion is boss. She has wheedled the apartment from her sister at a discount, and she takes ownership of our living there. Brusque, no sense of humor, she is a strong woman, alert and centered, and capable of carrying the burdens of her disjointed family. She manages the details, is the hub of our doings. She tracks our comings and goings—and will have it no other way.

She spends days at home and works evenings. She poaches eggs for Uncle Lawrence's before-daylight breakfast, and on his up-country days wraps a lunch for him to eat beside the road. And she has his favorite hot supper ready when he arrives home at night: cube steak, fried tripe, or macaroni and cheese. She cares for Grandma and drives her to appointments, literary meetings, and visits with friends. She sees to essential clothing for me, a mackinaw, raincoat, and rubber galoshes. She treats me with hot lemonade and cod liver oil when I am sick. She entertains me with card parties and birthday cakes on special days. She doles out spending money. She bosses and scolds and keeps account of our whereabouts.

In Aunt Marion's world everyone works. She sets the example. After her bustling days at Lake Avenue, she calls on life insurance prospects in the evenings and seldom returns home without a contract for a new policy. Proud of her achievements, she seems inexhaustible. She has no time for trivial matters. She doesn't sit and read a book. If she discovers her friends discussing a popular title, she skims a library copy. Her definition of relaxing or recreating is a card game, usually Sixty-Three, at home with a half-dozen relatives and refreshments.

She seldom watches the Townies play baseball. They are not to entertain her, nor are their games a place for her to socialize with neighbors. She backs the team by working: tending tables at beano games, steaming hot dogs at Saturday-night dances, and running errands for her husband when he is desperate for help. To just sit in the bleachers and watch a Townies' game for more than fifteen minutes is more than she can handle. She prizes usefulness.

Aunt Marion is a frugal woman, too. She insists on growing enough vegetables to last until the following year's harvest, and her cellar shelves are stocked with preserves made from wild strawberries, raspberries, and blueberries she picked herself at locations known only to her. She limits the use of hot water—maximum of two inches in the tub on Saturday nights—and writes letters rather than make long-distance phone calls. She mends worn clothing, tosses kitchen waste on the garden, and burns what little trash she accumulates. She lives without credit, puts off buying until she can pay cash, and deposits extra cash in a savings account. And she frequently calls to my attention her own childhood learning, "A stitch in time saves nine," she says. Or "See a penny, pick it up, and all the day, you'll have good luck."

Uncle Lawrence, on the other hand, seems the opposite. At home he is nearly invisible. He is a reticent man, keeps to himself, manages his own affairs, and though quick to help anyone who needs it, he doesn't interfere. He knows Aunt Marion is boss. But he is seldom idle at home, either. On his day off, he takes a week's accumulation of nickels, dimes, and quarters to the bank and then tends to a list of chores: the needs of his bakery truck, the baseball team, and Aunt Marion's garden. He doesn't need to split wood at Lake Avenue, but he does occasionally shovel snow from the front walk. He is unalterably reliable and fair. Though he smokes regularly, he doesn't drink any palpable amount of booze. He doesn't gamble or carouse with seedy pals, or put demands on others to serve him. To Aunt Marion he is predictable and attentive. To me he is the example of strength and unspoken faith.

During my first days at Lake Avenue, I suffered from an infection. When I failed to make any progress toward recovery, Dr. Weymouth, who knew me from my first minute on earth, admitted me to the hospital and suggested I be tended for a few days by professionals. I was anxious about going. I had not been in a hospital since I was two days old. I thought hospitals were where people went to die. But Aunt Marion would have no whimpering. "Oh, pshaw," she retorted to my nervous curiosity, "there's nothing to it. You'll be fine." But it was a new experience for me, and not sure how much trust I should invest when the outcome was in the hands of unknowns, I looked for reassurance. Uncle Lawrence saw my concern and on the ride to the hospital spoke with quiet conviction, "The doctor will know what to do."

Grandma Luna is more of a mystery. Retired from selling life insurance, she spends her days in an overstuffed chair in the parlor, surrounded by books, magazines, and other literary rubble, searching for the possible existence of important relatives. Her ancestry, whatever it is, has led her to think she is kin to United States Senator Margaret Chase Smith and writer Mary Ellen Chase, and she searches through the bits and pieces for validation of her righteousness. "Maybe we are descendants of royalty," she says to me. Perhaps so, I muse, but I avoid telling her that my first twelve years in Temple persuaded me that royal blood does not likely exist anywhere in our family.

Grandpa C.F. lives in two places. He alternates between Lake Avenue and his son Philip's place on Main Street, headquarters for Uncle Phil's Triangle Bus Company and within walking distance of Hippach Field. Grandpa goes to Uncle Phil's whenever the weight of satisfying the "wimmen," on Lake Avenue becomes too heavy to carry. But he usually comes back after the Flyer's have closed out the baseball season, when the loneliness at Uncle Phil's tips the scales toward the hubbub at Lake Avenue.

Grandma didn't know until after their wedding, the family story goes, that Grandpa C.F. is disposed to drinking an alcoholic beverage now and then, and when she learned that he tippled, she felt betrayed. To protect herself from such disturbing behavior, she eventually retreated from a meaningful relationship with him to her insurance business, a litany of literary clubs, and finally to the parlor chair in search of genealogical respectability. But Grandpa C.F. doesn't seem downtrodden over his artificial marriage. At Uncle Phil's, he walks to Hippach Field evenings and watches the semipro Flyers. At Lake Avenue, he putters in a garden spot or tosses a basketball at the hoop in the barn or plays checkers with me, all the while occasionally tossing an empty whiskey bottle out his upstairs bedroom window into the snow pack on the ground below. He is a loveable man and adds a whit of color to the collection of characters sharing the apartment.

But Grandma's treatment of Grandpa C.F. is unyielding. Except when he interferes with her view of the world, she ignores him. On occasion when he seems insufferable to her, she simply drives him away with a succinct lecture. One Sunday he totters down the stairs about midday and reaches for his coat and hat in the hallway. "Where are you going?" she grouses from the parlor chair.

He looks at her, leans forward somewhat unsteadily, one hand touching the rim of his fedora, the other resting on the doorknob, and says, "I'm going to pay my last respects to Temple's Moses Mitchell. He died Friday."

"But look at you," she retorts, "you're in no condition to go anywhere. You'll just make the fool."

He grins. "I'm in better condition than he is, my dear." And he disappears out the door.

84

These characters are a new family for me. I have come to Lake Avenue full of anxiety that I will not fit, that no room will exist in the house or in their hearts for me. But Aunt Marion is good to me. She beams at her own goodness, and I'm enriched by new clothes, warm wash water, a few social lessons, and the character benefits of hardship stories: the daily five-mile commute to high school in a one-horse sleigh, mentoring her older (and somewhat slower) brother Philip in schoolwork, and the inevitable and lengthy list of after-school family chores.

Aunt Marion uncharacteristically posts no strict rules for me, but I know she has rigorous expectations: be on time, be involved, be truthful, be pleasant, be sociable. It's all in the Boy Scout law. She assigns me suburban chores—no cows at Lake Avenue—mow the lawn, rake leaves when they fall, and clear the snow from the steps and the walk. And she sends me off to my freshman year of high school with another bit of uncomplicated philosophy. "A person is known by his friends, John. Find good friends that stay out of trouble and you'll stay out of trouble, too."

It's September now, still dark. I hear footsteps, a knock on my door, and Aunt Marion's voice. "You awake?" I stir, and the footsteps recede down the stairs. The kitchen is filled with the aroma of perked coffee and fried pieces of bacon from a dead hog somewhere in Temple. She's making me breakfast, a big one: eggs poached in deep water in the skillet until the yolks gel, toast, bacon, and a bowl of sliced peaches. "Eat it up," she says. "You'll need your strength today." It's the first day of high school. I walk to school full of fear. Allan tries to bolster me, but I'm too deep in thought to grasp what he says or to notice the sparse traffic on High Street, the slight tinge of red in street-side maples, or a co-ed's smile when we pass the college. The thought of high school gnaws at me. My class will comprise fifty students, not two or three. The teacher likely won't realize I'm there until the year is half over. Nor will my classmates, who have been together for eight years, know my name—or even want to. I'm weighted down with worry. We climb the steps. Allan points out where my class assembles. I step through the door and find a calm spot in the crowded room.

Aunt Marion told me I'm here to be educated, but the high school baseball team is the only subject that interests me. I'm not afraid of biology or algebra or even Latin. But all the rest—how to dress, what to say in the hallway, one-act plays and junior proms, classroom romancing—is unfamiliar territory, a minefield of potential blunders that terrifies me. Fortunately, my classmates don't notice me when I enter. I find an empty seat, and the classroom, a beige-painted compartment of student desks, slate blackboards, and fluorescent lights, goes quiet. Miss Scales, who is also new to Farmington High School but has the appearance and demeanor of a veteran schoolmarm, reads the class roster. At the sound of my name, heads turn and look. I raise my hand. Four years from now I will graduate somewhere in the upper quarter of these fifty students prepared, Aunt Marion will tell me, for advanced learning at a university. Today I am so shaky I can't raise my hand above my head.

I make an effort to observe Aunt Marion's advice to make friends, socialize, and stay out of trouble, but it is a difficult mission. My classmates are friendly and engaging, but I am too self-conscious, fearful of saying the wrong thing, or I'm wearing the same shirt I wore yesterday. Considerable time will pass before I feel comfortable with these stylish teens.

I make friends here, however, friends with similar backgrounds: boys from the Boy Scout troop, boys from New Vineyard and Industry, boys from the Village School, more friends actually than I had in Temple. And I learn from them. I learn what Aunt Marion intended to be socializing. I learn a higher level of profanity, words that not even Pa uses in my presence, words unknown to the playground at the Village School. I learn to smoke cigarettes, not in the boiler room, but behind the jay-vee basketball bus while the varsity plays inside the gym. I don't resist. I have spent my life with smokers. Smoking, I observed in my boyhood, is necessary to a full social life.

I learn to drink booze, to open a beer bottle with a "church key." It happens in the rear seat of an old Chevy filled with schoolmates who have also found friendships in boys like themselves. I'm not proud of what I'm doing, but I don't think it terribly wrong either. Ma and Pa drank beer and whiskey without restraint. I consider the opportunity a rite of passage, part of growing up. I learn early in high school, as Pa likely did before me, that such behavior yields friends, or what I refer to as friends, people who are searching for what I am searching for: acceptance. I ignore the more difficult challenge handed me by Aunt Marion and melt into somewhat marginal behavior.

"Idle hands are the devil's workshop," Aunt Marion, a twenty-year veteran of school teaching, proclaims. I suppose her words are another of her childhood credos. And she doesn't choose to deliberate whether I will practice good study habits. She provides a table, a book shelf, a typewriter, and space in the parlor. "You'll need to submit tidy homework," she comments when I ask why the arrangements. "You'll spend your evenings here." Thus, evenings in the parlor—a place similar to what I envision Grand Central Station to be; a place suited to reading, entertaining guests, and holding smoky discussions on the affairs of Farmington politics; a place where we say our hellos and goodbyes, yak on a dial telephone, engage in conversations with neighbors; a place where Aunt Marion expects me to do my homework—I hunch over a table and read, or study a textbook, and peck on the Smith-Corona while she hums over the dishpan in the kitchen. Saturdays I'm up and out on the bakery van at five o'clock and back after six at night, shivery cold and exhausted.

Coach Carlson calls the first high-school baseball practice in March. The outside temperature is in the thirties, and snow has barely begun to melt as I glove my first grounders on the gymnasium's hardwood basketball floor and swing a baseball bat at a teed-up rubber ball in a batting cage. I feel capable, powerful, in this confined space. Every bounce is true. Every throw is accurate. Every swing makes contact. In a few weeks Coach moves us out to Hippach Field and continues workouts. At the end of spring practice, five freshmen make the varsity team. I am one of them.

Opening game is at home against Strong High School. It's a non-league affair that Coach has arranged to give us real-game experience. The veteran first-sacker is injured, unable to play, so I start at first base. Later at Jay, in the league opener, I sit on the bench and watch the Tigers rout us. I watch from the bench for the remainder of the season. I don't like it. But I know that's where freshmen sit. We keep on playing and keep on losing—by lopsided scores. Not even such experienced players as Townies Al Mitchell and Cal Tyler can stem the rush of defeats that come over us, a hapless bunch. The season grows long, and I grow restless.

One Friday night I walk uptown, "to see a movie at the State," I tell Aunt Marion. I stop in front of the soda shop, lean against a parking meter, and eye the traffic, that vast complexity of vehicles that idle up and down Farmington's streets on weekends. I need these moments, I think. They are of the world. And then an old Chevy full of teenagers pulls up and stops. I get in the back seat. "Where to?" someone asks.

"Bean's Corner," someone else answers.

"Anyone have money for gas?"

"Yeah, somebody does." It's a conversation by boys who want to be men, short questions and direct answers. At Bean's Corner, a lonesome crossroads on the back road to Jay, we find a barn dance and play the role of men there for a time.

I arrive at Lake Avenue late, not in violation of a curfew—Aunt Marion doesn't impose curfews or deadlines—just late. Quite late. Aunt Marion does, however, expect forthright answers.

"I heard you come in last night," she says at breakfast.

"Oh?"

"It was late, must have been after midnight. How long did the movie last, for gracious sake?"

"I dunno. We went somewhere afterward."

"Is that all? You went someplace?" She is angry. "You can come right home every day after school for a while, now," she sputters.

"For how long?"

"Until I say so."

I have no interest in aggravating an angry adult, but baseball is dear to me. Hesitant, afraid that I will reveal too much, I appeal. "I have baseball afternoons," I groan.

Her jaw juts out. "No baseball either," she exclaims.

I surrender. I leave my baseball glove home. After school Monday I wander a circuitous route toward Lake Avenue. Aunt Marion pulls up beside me in her Chevrolet and stops. I open the door. My first-baseman's mitt lies on the seat.

"I changed my mind about baseball," she says. "I don't mean to keep you away from baseball." *It must be Boyce who changed her mind*, I think.

Chapter Seven

TEENAGERS

I t is 1949. Boyce is unhappy. He expected more from the 1948 Townies. But they were dull at the end, no fire, no passion, no fun. They scored nine runs in the last three games, and Sade was the losing pitcher in all three. "We can do better," Boyce tells me. "The fans expect better. I gotta figure out how to revive 'em." The nucleus of the team is still in place: Sade, Bergeron, Blodgett, and Hellgren up the middle. Bill Mosher adapted to the catching job and by season's end was solid behind the plate. "It's the same team," I say. "They can win again."

"No spark," Boyce answers. "Some of 'em have lost their spark. And I need another pitcher. I need to rest Sade once in a while. I need to keep the fans with us, too."

Boyce puts four high schoolers on the team: pitcher Cal Tyler, who has thrown off the high school mound for three years; outfielder Al Mitchell, a Boyce protégé with some late-inning experience at third base; Al's younger brother Art Mitchell; and me. We work out at spring practices, take batting-practice swings, and chase fungoes during defensive drills. "You'll get playing time," Boyce tells us. "Put a little spark in the lineup."

He knows he's taking a chance. He knows, too, that the townsfolk want to see their youth on the team. "You'll be startin' the season in right field," he says to Al Mitchell. "I need an arm out there. I'm tired of runners taking an extra base on our outfielders' arms." Mitchell is the best of the new young players. His experience on the high school team shows that he is ready. As a junior, Mitchell started in the outfield, and Coach put him in the middle of the lineup, where his potent bat would drive home the most runs. He won his letter.

Tyler, a senior, won his letter, too, and Boyce names him the team's relief pitcher, the first one ever for the Townies. "That'll be your job," Boyce tells him. "Sade's backup. I'll use you. You'll be ready to start when the time comes."

He keeps high school senior Granville Knowles, who played three years for the high school team and has been Pa's backup at first base for the Townies, on the bench. Knowles, a fearsome hitter but a whit slow afoot, hit .375 in his backup appearances in 1948.

Boyce moves Bruce Mosher, whose main strength is hitting, to left field, and names Larry Barker a starting pitcher. "I need to give Sade a day off once in a while," he tells Barker. He puts Art Mitchell and me on the bench with backup pitchers Tyler and Barker, and pinch hitter Knowles, for company. We wait for an opportunity.

The Townies open the season with five straight victories. Sade dominates the first four. His arm is rested, and the long winter has rekindled his enthusiasm. He strikes out eleven West Sumners in the opener before giving way in the sixth to Tyler. He fans nine East Wiltons in a six-inning twilight game at Temple. He throws a complete game against North Jay, strikes out eleven, and puts down an uprising in the ninth to preserve the victory. And in his strongest game of the streak, he blanks West Sumner on no hits, striking out thirteen. He looks his best since the 1947 streak. Following the West Sumner game, Boyce gives him a day off, and Larry Barker pitches a decisive win over Callahan's Hard Cider Boys. The Townies have recovered from their mediocre 1948 season. So much so, in fact, that they draw attention from sportswriters.

A feature piece in *The Lewiston Daily Sun* cites Boyce's management of his "snappy combination" of veterans and high-school-age newcomers as the reason for the Townies success. Boyce, the paper states, has worked wonders with a roster of young candidates and aging veterans, and shaped them into a team that has fans shouting. The Sun cites youngsters Granville Knowles, Al Mitchell, Cal Tyler, and me, a veteran's son and member of the town's most prominent family, the paper reports, as beneficiaries of Boyce's coaching. Art Mitchell is a mite piqued, the Mitchells being among the earliest settlers and the oldest family name still living in Temple. "What's this about Temple's most prominent family?" he snickers.

"Well," I kid him, "Grandma says we have royalty in our family someplace." He blurts out something unintelligible. "But that's not so," I quickly add. "And anyway, everyone knows the most prominent family in town is the Moshers."

Boyce has found the spark he was looking for before the season— the teenagers. But the fast start cannot be sustained, and the streak ends in Temple in mid-June, when the middle of Jay's batting order breaks up a 1–1 pitchers' duel with consecutive doubles in the eighth inning and the Tigers best the Townies, 2–1. By then, however, the Townies are a coffee-break and barbershop topic all over the county, and the close loss to Jay does not dampen our spirit.

We win three of the next four. Cal Tyler relieves Sade in the first Lexington game to earn his first win and, following the perennial Sade loss to South China, Tyler pitches a complete-game victory at Lexington a week later. We are on a run. Our fans, the townsfolk, are exuberant. But inexplicably, after we rout the state tar crew, a team of tar-stained workers from the highway department's West Farmington camp, 12–0, we go into a funk and lose five of the next six. At Erskine Academy, Sade, behind 2–1, gives up five runs in the seventh inning to the South China Clippers and, though we out-hit the Clippers, we lose, 7–2. Al Mitchell shows Clippers' fans his arm in the first inning when, with a runner on second base, Clippers' hitter Tracey lines a pitch into the gap in right. Mitchell cuts off the drive and hurls to Bill Mosher in time to nip the runner at the plate. And Mosher's relay to Blodgett catches Tracey diving into second base for the double play. "Routine play for us," Blodgett will say later. Routine loss for us, too.

But the slump is not routine. We have not slumped since the middle of the first season, when we lost four in a row. Now we lose five of six. We lose to North Jay by a run when Sade gives up four in the eighth and one in the ninth. East Wilton scores six times in the first two innings. Strong scores three in the first off Sade and three more in the fourth, and we lose 6–5. Sade is being pummeled: four consecutive losses. Boyce is fed up. He starts Tyler at Andover. Tyler, leading 6–4, starts pitching wild in the sixth, and Boyce beckons Sade, who retires ten consecutive batters to save the game—and his job. Buoyed by Sade's performance at Andover, Boyce starts him the following week at North Jay, the last scheduled game of the season. He allows five runs in the third inning, and the North Jays edge us again by a run, 6–5. It is our fifth loss in six games and drops our season's record to nine wins and seven losses—after winning eight of ten at the start.

The slump was an oddity in an otherwise exemplary season. During the slump we outhit our opponent game after game. Had we been able to come up with a hit or two at a critical time, perhaps we could have won them all. Perhaps Boyce should have pitched Tyler more often and limited Sade to a few innings late in the game. Perhaps fatigue crept into our game; perhaps we lost concentration; perhaps we got smug; perhaps Sade's arm was sore. Townsmen around the checkerboard at the general store tried to zero in on exactly what went wrong, but failed to come up with an answer. Boyce explained it this way: "Slumps are part of baseball."

Boyce tried everything to get us out of it: he juggled the batting order; he inserted teenagers into the lineup; he started Cal Tyler on the mound. Though his changes worked well enough, we didn't turn the slump around. The rookies Tyler and Al Mitchell were bright spots in the lineup. Mitchell started in right field, hit .292, and convinced opposing runners to hang close to the bag and not go for an extra base. Tyler pitched and won three games in his first season on the mound. Boyce used potent Granville Knowles in six games, and he hit .350. Art Mitchell hit .250 in three games. I appeared in six games, started three, and managed to hit .133. And not even I could stem the Townies' downslide.

Boyce didn't look for a reason, he didn't point his finger at or blame anyone. But I think Sade was the difference. He was the workhorse. He pitched against all the tough teams, and though Boyce rested him more, he faltered. He lost intensity. He threw well, but hitters were no longer afraid of him. They knew he would have a weak moment and lose his concentration, they waited, and then they pummeled him. He could no longer intimidate a team.

It is nearing the end of summer. I am riding north on State Highway 4. Boyce is driving. We are working down the list of one hundred bakery customers. We're a team: he drives the van and manages the in-van accounts; I knock on doors and greet customers. By the summer of 1949, I am an old hand at the door-knocking routine, and I know what goods to carry up the walk without ever having seen the breadbox inside. Housewives know me now and linger on the step to chat with me. But I am focused. My mind is on snagging caroms off the granite steps at Lake Avenue before supper or baseball practice at the Townies' ball field. Boyce has made me into a baseball nut for sure. Then one day, without warning, he pulls the van over to the side of the highway and looks at me. "It's time you learned to drive," he says.

It takes a minute to grasp his words. I'm fourteen years old. I don't need to know how to drive. Someone drives me to every place I must go. "What do I do?" I ask, holding the steering wheel and listening to the logging trucks whining by my window on the road beside me. He briefs me on the driving components: steering wheel, clutch, brake, shifter. "Try it," he says.

For perhaps twenty minutes, I show him the dreadful mistake he has made. I likely frighten him as well: I start with a jerk and then another jerk, threatening whiplash; I stall his precious cargo in the center of State Highway 4; I let his van drift to the left over the centerline and to the right onto the gravel; I stomp on the brake and a loaf of homestyle bread soars into the front seat. But he is tolerant. For twenty minutes, I test his patience—and self-control. He doesn't judge. When I am done, he says simply, "You'll learn. Just keep trying. It will come." I relax and confess that it might take awhile.

The bakery route is the perfect place to practice driving. It involves so much more than just the highway. I learn to cope with driveways, traverse barnyards, and navigate country lanes. "Make believe there's a half-glass of water sitting on the dashboard," Boyce tells me. He asks me to drive again. And then again. Soon I manage my anxiety, and I catch on to using feet, hands, and eyes simultaneously—without spilling any water from the imaginary glass. Boyce has taken a chance on me, I muse, and despite my transgressions, he doesn't lose patience or raise his voice. He remains calm. "It's all relative motion," he says, a term I will come to understand much later after I have learned what it means.

Though at fourteen I am not licensed to drive, Uncle Austin says okay to driving the Jeep. The Jeep is owned by a man he calls Charlie, an out-of-stater who comes to Temple every year for hunting season and parks his Jeep in Uncle Austin's side yard to use again the following year. "Take Charlie's Jeep," he says when I mention going up to Mitchell's for a ballgame. "Just stay off the paved roads." Local law enforcement, I deduce, doesn't stretch to our unpaved road network. And when the solo turns out harmless, Uncle Austin asks me to take

Charlie's Jeep and deliver a box of groceries to an outback customer who has no way to get in to the village. Now my driving has value.

Pa, too, has confidence in my driving. When we fish Temple Stream on Sundays, he often asks me to walk back upstream and retrieve the coupe. Only once does he ever question my driving ability—when I am fifteen and an experienced driver. We fish the stream above the village, start at the upper end of Jenkins Road by Dr. Little's farmhouse, and work our way downstream. I carry a rod, but the stream is too small for both of us, so I walk along the bank with Pa, and he points out trilliums and jack-in-the-pulpits and often snags a small trout. Frequently he asks me to retrieve the coupe and each time he cautions me not to break the bottles in the rumble seat. When I catch up, he stops fishing to paw through the bottles back there. "Any stubbies left in here?" he asks. Not until mid-afternoon, with all the stubby stops, do we reach the Burt Mitchell place, two miles downstream. Here, Pa collapses his fishing rod and puts it away—and takes the last stubby out of the rumble seat. "Time to go home, isn't it?" he says.

It is eight miles to Farmington. I look at him, wobbling unsteadily on his feet, a stubby of beer in his hand. "I'll drive," I say.

"Sure, go ahead," he mutters.

At the village, the gravel road turns to pavement, and I am conscious of how conspicuous I am to whatever agency enforces the driving laws. Pa relaxes and lights a cigarette. Less than a mile later, near the Charles Cony place, he drops the cigarette on the floorboard near his feet. He gropes for it but fails to come up with it. "I'll get it," I say and reach across the seat and down. Before I can straighten up, the coupe careens off the roadway into a swampy ditch and comes to rest in an alder patch.

It's eerie quiet here, I notice. We get out and stand on the road, Pa puffing on the cigarette. "I don't think it'll come out without some help," I remark, trying to shield any guilt.

"Someone'll come along. We'll jes' wait a minute," he answers.

An empty logging truck pulls up and stops. The driver comes around the back of the truck, smiles, and nods at Pa. After a brief greeting—I suspect they know each other—he reaches up and retrieves a chain from the truck body. In another minute or two, while I watch and Pa puffs on the cigarette, he hooks the chain to both vehicles and yanks the coupe out of the alder bushes and up onto the roadway. He unhooks the chain, throws it up onto the truck body, and dusts off his hands. "There," he says, "that oughta get you going again." Then he grins, looks at Pa, and then at me. "Johnny," he says, "I think you better drive the rest of the way," and he climbs into his truck and leaves.

"The hell you are," Pa exclaims, reaching for the driver's door. "Get in the other side before you run over somebody."

Chapter Eight

LEGION FIELD AND
THE RANGELEY LAKERS

T he disappointing loss to North Jay at the end of the 1949 season dropped our record to a mediocre 9–7 and left us in a gloomy mood. For three years prior to 1949 the Townies had been invited to play in September exhibitions. We gave the credit to Boyce. He not only knew the importance of certain baseball skills—strong pitching and good defense in the middle of the playing field—he knew that a positive attitude also makes a difference. And he never stopped believing in us.

Boyce looks for places to show off his team. We're fun to watch, he says, a freewheeling, spirited group delighting in baseball. We have personality. Crowds follow the unpredictable Sade, who owns arguably the best breaking pitch in the county, the workhorse veterans Hellgren and Bill Mosher, the popular youngsters Tyler and Al Mitchell—and Boyce, the high-spirited manager. "Forget the seven losses," Boyce says. "We belong in a gala." He wheedles an invitation to Strong to play in the Labor Day festival tournament there. "I believe we'll do okay up there in spite of our record," he says.

The powerful Phillips Legionnaires, a perennial North Franklin League contender, will be at the festival, too, with fastballer Bill Burnham, and all-star hitters Milt Stinchfield and Rink Avery. Rangeley will bring high school pitching phenom Johnny McPherson, and long-ball hitter Skeet Davenport. Strong, who threatened to grab the North Franklin League title away from the Legionnaires, will be there with their heavy-hitting second-base combination Vern Sample and Lewis Mason. Not ones to boast over good fortune, the unassuming Townies take it in stride. "It's not surprising to me we're going," center-fielder Hellgren says. "We're a damned good ball club."

The townsfolk are jubilant, particularly Uncle Austin, who sees the invitation delaying the coming of winter. When Labor Day comes, folks drive over Porter Hill in full cars and then up the hard-surfaced State Highway 4 to the ballpark on South Main Street. They go to spur the Townies, to be part of the outcome.

Built before the war, Legion Field is one of the county's classiest ball fields: chalk stripes outline the batters box and delineate the foul lines; the infield grass is cut smooth; the spacious outfield is on the level with home plate and stretches five hundred feet to a snow fence in center field bordering the Sandy River. Wooden bleacher seats flank the infield; a screened backstop protects spectators behind home plate; dugouts on either side of the baselines provide refuge for players.

When the Townies arrive the stands are filled. Folks had arrived early, marched down Main Street with the 8:30 parade and crammed the sideline bleacher seats before the morning contest between Strong and neighboring Phillips. Now folks from Rangeley and Temple arrive and look for places where they can see the ball field, too. They squeeze into bleacher seats, lounge in lawn chairs behind the backstop, and socialize in parked cars along the left field foul line, where they can sip from bottles in brown paper bags.

Other folks roll the dice at games of chance and eye the gaudy parade floats and dainty doll carriages on display behind the back-stop—but they keep a wary eye on the scoreboard. More play beano in the gaming hall next to the river, and they receive reports of the games from an observer posted in the doorway. Still more stand behind the screened backstop and talk, here on this end-of-summer holiday only to be sociable with other folks—and to appraise the umpire's calls.

The Townies play at one o'clock. Boyce names Tyler to pitch what he calls the first game, as though we have come here sure to play two. "Sade will pitch the second," he says. "Probably face Phillips, maybe Bill Burnham. What a helluva matchup that'll be." It turns out Boyce is right about Phillips. They eliminate Strong 3–1 without using the indomitable Burnham on the mound. But the Townies need to win to face Burnham. Rangeley and lefty Johnny McPherson come first.

Pa hasn't arrived by game time. No one knows why. "Don't worry; he'll be along about the fifth inning," Hellgren says, laughing. "Probably thinks it's a two o'clock game." Boyce puts Sade at first base. Sade hits better than I do, for sure, but he's not any better with the glove. I could play out there—if I wasn't so damned nervous in the batters box. I can play first base as well as any of 'em, and, but for that damned left-hander McPherson, I might be out there. Boyce knows I can't hit a lick off McPherson, and that's why I'm not playing. Sade, who bats righty against the left-hander McPherson, might come up with a hit.

Tyler's into the sixth inning now. Rangeley scored twice in the second when McPherson singled in Lakers' second baseman Quimby, who had hit safely and advanced on a walk, and shortstop Barrett drove McPherson home with a well-placed liner into the gap in left center, but that's been all. Tyler's focused, and tough to hit with men on base. The Townies have parlayed McPherson's wildness and a couple of singles into four runs and a 4–2 lead. Sade, I notice, doesn't have a hit off McPherson. Actually, McPherson hit Sade in the fourth inning, plunked him in the ribs with a curve ball that drifted too far inside. Sade slowed on his way to first base and chatted a moment at McPherson out of the corner of his mouth, but McPherson didn't want to talk. Earlier in the game, McPherson had drilled Hellgren too, with a curve ball. But nothing came of it.

It's the top of the sixth now. The Townies' rookie stands on the pitcher's mound and fingers the baseball, turning it over and over in his right hand, feeling the stitching, searching for an edge, waiting for Bill Mosher to fasten a chest protector. When Mosher nods, Tyler tosses warm-up pitches to him, slower at first then faster, until his arm is ready. He pauses, then hitches up his pants, takes off his hat, and wipes his forehead with his sleeve.

I watch from the Townies' dugout. I like Tyler. He's the antithesis of a macho athlete: a four-year art student at the high school, he's polite and studious with long locks of wavy dark hair. He scans the field. He checks the scoreboard in left and sees the 4–2 lead posted there. He looks toward the Townies' dugout where Boyce sits, the game scorebook open on his lap. Tyler fidgets and paces and tugs on his cap, waiting for a batter.

Tyler is an experienced pitcher. He played his first baseball game in the school yard at the Village School and, when he wasn't working at home, played in pasture games on summer days. He pitched for the high school for three years, sometimes hitchhiking the five miles home to Temple after practice. He was not always the team's best pitcher but one who had done his work and was ready when Coach wanted him. He throws overhand, sidearm, and underhand in a variety of speeds. He flings the ball at the plate, launches it, lets it fly. Hitters wait there unsettled for a glimpse of where the ball will first appear, reluctant to take a solid stance in the box. He's undefeated in three games this year, and Boyce is confident he can move the Townies into the day's final game against Phillips. "Throw strikes, Cal," Boyce remarks from the dugout in a voice too low for Tyler to hear.

Tyler is not nervous, fussy perhaps, but not nervous. He's not calm, either. A passion shows in his eyes. The dogged rookie has earned this chance to win the Townies' biggest game of the year. When he's ready he takes a deep breath, toes the pitching rubber, and looks for a sign from Bill Mosher.

Rangeley second baseman Quimby steps up. He looks for a pitch like the one he hit in the second inning, when he singled and scored Rangeley's first run. But since then Tyler has held the Rangeley batters to just one hit, a harmless double by Davenport. Quimby bounces a roller toward the left side, an easy chance for Bergeron, but the reliable shortstop misplays the hop, and Quimby gets to first. Lakers' hitter Ross tries to bunt Quimby over to second, but he fouls two pitches and then swings under a fastball for strike three. Right-fielder Philbrick, batting eighth in the order, steps into the box, looks at Manager Prince Edwards in the Rangeley dugout, and pushes Tyler's first pitch toward Freddy Dunn at third. Dunn throws him out at first, but Quimby advances to second, scoring position.

Beside me on the bench, Art Mitchell murmurs, "Maybe he'll get out of this without a run—if he's careful with McPherson." Johnny McPherson is not only an outstanding pitcher, but a line-drive hitter as well. He has singled and walked in his two times up. Tyler slings fast-balls at him. With two strikes, McPherson drives a fastball into right center out of Hellgren's reach. Quimby trots home with Rangeley's third run, and McPherson jogs to second.

Tyler looks anxious. He paces, rubs the baseball, and smooths the dirt in front of the pitching rubber with his spikes. The Rangeley shortstop Barrett comes up. Tyler throws the first pitch wide. He flings a second one wide as well. He's eager now to throw the next pitch, anx-ious to end the inning. He strides toward the plate, snags Mosher's toss, strides back to the mound, and hurls again. He repeats. A fretful Art Mitchell on the bench groans, "If he don't stop that walking, he'll walk two miles before this inning is over."

But Tyler is unsettled and walks Barrett. Boyce trots to the mound and talks to Tyler, a ploy to give him time to calm down a dite. He talks until the umpire motions for play. Then Rangeley third baseman Novak, hitless in the game, steps in. Tyler throws a fastball, and Novak slices it toward Bergeron. For the second time in the inning, Bergeron misplays the ball. It slithers into the gap in left center, where Hellgren and Bruce Mosher converge on it. McPherson scores easily from second, and Barrett, running at the sound of the bat on the ball, races around the bases, while the fans rise and scream and propel him forward. Barrett beats the throw to the plate and the Lakers go ahead by a run. Tyler, in danger of giving up the game, takes a deep breath, spends a few moments staring at the ground under his feet, then throws three curve-ball strikes by the next batter for the third out. He walks quietly toward the bench. The Townies toss their gloves aside and run off the field. Bergeron slumps on the bench and hangs his head, "Damn," he mutters.

Behind now 5–4, Boyce turns to Sade, "I'm puttin' you on the mound in the seventh," he says.

"You sure you want to do that, boss?"

"Tyler's pitched well," Boyce answers, "but they got to him that inning. I'm goin' with you now."

"I'm pitching the second game, you know," Sade announces.

"There won't be a second game if we don't get this one," Boyce answers. "Get your arm loose."

Boyce walks to the end of the bench. "Johnny," he says to me. "Tyler's up first this inning. I want you to hit for him an' then play first base. Sade's gonna pitch. Grab a bat an' start it off."

Boyce liked to use pinch hitters. Though his bench was inexperienced and lacked all-around strength, he often used his benchwarmers to pinch hit. And he occasionally pinch hit himself, perhaps to demonstrate what he expected of us, often driving the ball into an outfield gap. Though we honed our swings at practice to earn just such a chance as this, Boyce didn't use pinch hitters just to keep the benchwarmers practicing. He knew the baseball percentages, too. At times a player sitting on the bench was a better hitter, as in the case of Granville Knowles, or a more effective hitter against a certain pitcher or was more likely to put the ball in play in a situation that required contact, such as a runner on third base. Boyce would know. In this situation he wants a runner on base and thinks my strengths outweigh Tyler's. My on-base average is higher than Tyler's this year—though it's not one I boast about—and Boyce needs base runners. I'm smaller than Tyler, too, and Boyce thinks perhaps I can work a walk out of McPherson.

Boyce has used me as a pinch hitter twice this year, and I have delivered one hit. In West Sumner in June, the Townies led the West Sumners, 17–0. Sade was pitching a no-hitter. With one out in the top of the ninth inning, Freddy Dunn, the Townies' new third baseman, lofted a short fly ball to right field that the West Sumner outfielder Matson dropped for an error. Dunn stood on first base, and Boyce looked down the length of the bench. "Johnny," he called. "Go up and hit for Knowles." Boyce didn't need runs in that situation, but he wanted Sade to have the best defense he could put on the field. And he wanted to put a youngster into the trailing edge of a game.

I swung a couple of bats to loosen my muscles, tossed one aside, and stepped into the batter's box. I was nervous. It was my first time at bat for the Townies, and I knew I didn't hit well in game situations. In the school yard and at the high school, I wasn't what folks called a good hitter. I stared at the pitcher, waggled the bat, and set myself for the pitch. The second or third pitch came in over the outside part of the plate. I swung and sliced a short fly ball into left field. The ball curved toward the foul line too deep for the shortstop. The left fielder came on and tried to make the catch, but he couldn't reach it. The ball fell in fair territory just inside the line and bounced away from him. *Double,* I thought, *take another base,* and I raced toward first. *I can get to second. I know I can,* but as I turned at first, I saw Dunn pull up and retreat to second. The left fielder's throw came in to third, and Dunn was forced to stop. I settled for a single.

In the bottom of the ninth, I went to first base for Knowles. I was aware of the picture: fourteen years old, playing in a Townies' uniform in front of a crowd, Sade on the verge of a no-hitter, the war veterans in the field with me trying to protect Sade's pitching. In eight innings Sade had whiffed ten and denied the West Sumners even a single hit. In the ninth, he faced three batters. The first, Rowe, grounded a ball to me at first base—I handled it smoothly and stepped on the bag. Sade confounded the next batter with his sharp-breaking drop for his eleventh strikeout and then forced Henry Stevens, who batted third in the West Sumner batting order, to hit a ground ball to the right side. I moved to my right, backhanded the ball, and raced Stevens to the bag for the out. Sade—and I—had preserved the no-hitter. Boyce's pinch-hitting experiment had worked well.

In July, I pinch hit again for Knowles. With Sade on first base and no outs, I looked for the bunt sign from Boyce, but he didn't show it. Then I slapped a pitch toward second. The second baseman snagged it, tagged Sade going by, and threw to first ahead of me for the double play. A strikeout would have done less damage.

I played in six games that summer, mostly as a late-inning substitute at first base, or in right field when the Townies were far enough ahead. Once, when the South China Clippers came to Temple and Pa showed up late, Boyce started me at first base. "We need you today," he said to me. I played defense well in the six appearances that season, but I managed only two hits in fifteen at-bats, a puny .133 batting average. Weak hitting would hinder my all-round playing ability for years. But for the most part, Boyce didn't need hits when I played.

The state tar crew came to the Temple ball field this past July for an after-work, seven-inning contest. They had sprayed hot tar and broomed heavy sand over several miles of State Highway 4 during the day, and the sultry evening air diminished their intensity for baseball playing. The Townies romped to an early 8–0 lead. With no likelihood that the tar-crew batters, who featured well known long-ball hitters Bob Parlin and Blaine Linton, would recover and solve Sade's assortment of fastballs and drops, Boyce put me in the game. "Go in at first base next inning," he said.

Sade overheard Boyce's instructions, grinned from ear to ear, and looked over at Pa. "Too tired to play anymore, Monty?"

Pa is the only Townies player with a nickname. All the others—Larry, Dick, Al, Elmer, Bruce, Vilio, Tarmo, and so on—are known by their first names. We had no Lefty, Ike, Dusty, Dutch, Scooter, Jocko, or Bobo on our team. We had one nickname: Monty. I never knew the source of it. I first heard it after the war. It may have come from Pa's introduction of Three-Card Monte—or Monte Bank—a card game likely learned in the barracks at Fort Bragg, to his table of poker-playing friends at the West Farmington Fire Company; or the name might have come from his being the only soldier in Temple to have served under British Field Marshall Bernard Montgomery. Whatever the source, his friends used it, and Sade joshed him. "Siddown, Monty. Get some rest—and watch the kid. Maybe you can pick up a pointer or two."

"Boyce jes' wants to see what he can do," Pa said.

"Yeah?" Hellgren, who seldom misses a chance to tease a teammate, laughed. "We all know what he can do. Gobbles up those ground balls and low throws like he had a smelt net out there. You oughta get him to give you a lesson."

"Lesson! Hell, I don't need no *lesson*. He's jes' takin' after his ole man. Chip off the old block."

"Chrissakes, Monty, you got bruises all over your body where you been getting hit with them things," Hellgren chided.

"Yeah," Sade joined in. "Do you good to sit here and watch how it's done. That's what the boss wants—for you to see how it's done."

"See how it's done? Hell, no. That's not what Boyce wants. He's trying to teach the kid how to *play*. He's jes' learning."

"Sure," Sade smiled. "Sure. He's just learning."

I was proud to be on the team with Pa, but for some reason he avoided teaching me how to patrol the first base area: how to hold a runner close to the base, how to apply the tag on a pickoff attempt, how to stretch for a wide throw and tag the base at the same time. He hit well enough for Boyce to put him second in the batting order, but he didn't offer me any batting tips either, a vital piece of my missing know-how. Nor did he suggest any piece of baseball lore that might give me an advantage when I faced a crucial moment in a game, such as now, going up against lefty Johnny McPherson in the Townies' most important game of the year. I could use some of his batting advice right now, I think, but he hasn't offered any.

In the on-deck circle, I pick out a bat, swing it a few times, and plot a strategy. Boyce isn't sending me up to pinch hit against left-hander McPherson because he needs a double or a homer, for sure. Hitting lefties for me is like falling on a sword. "Get on base somehow," Boyce tells me. "We need a runner." I take a position in the batter's box, and waggle the bat. It's my first time against McPherson; I don't know much about him. Today I have watched him spin his nerve-racking curveball at the Townies and hold them to three hits all day. But he's allowed five walks as well. Clearly the walk is my only chance.

It happens quickly. McPherson bewilders me with three deceptive curveballs, and I am out on strikes. Then Bergeron, at the top of the batting order, looking for redemption for his miseries at shortstop, drills a single to center field. A moment later, he advances to second when McPherson slings a fastball by Sade and up against the backstop. Sade then lofts a hit to left-center where left-fielder Ross makes a running catch for the second out. Freddy Dunn comes to the plate with a runner on second and two outs.

Dunn, since June when he played his first game for the Townies, has been potent at bat. He has hit .320 and homered once, a seventh inning blast against North Jay right-hander Jay Donald a week ago in a futile attempt to snatch the victory. Last week's homer is likely on his mind—Boyce's, too—as he sets himself in the batter's box. He hits the first pitch hard, a low liner to center field that drops safely, and Bergeron comes home to tie the score. Second baseman Blodgett, the Townies' surest hitter, advances Dunn to second with a single, and Sade stirs in the dugout. "Guess I better loosen the arm," he says to Hellgren. "Boyce says I gotta throw zeros the rest of the way."

With two runners on the bases, Al Mitchell, who singled in a run off McPherson in the first inning, steps in. McPherson delivers a curve. Mitchell is late and bounces it to the left side. Shortstop Barrett can't decide where to throw the ball, leaving the bases loaded for the Townies' next hitter, catcher Bill Mosher.

Mosher first played for the Townies in 1947. He appeared in three games that summer and batted .250. The following year he played regularly at third base and was hitting .395 in August when Boyce injured his throwing arm. Though he had never caught, the plucky Mosher put on shin guards, chest protector, and mask the next inning and has caught every game since.

The army drafted Mosher in 1944 and trained him in infantry. On completion of training they assigned him to the 182nd Infantry Regiment, then fighting with the Americal Division on Leyte Island in the Philippines, as a replacement infantryman. In March 1945, he participated in the assault against Cebu Island, and later, at the conclusion of the war, he was ordered to Japan for duty with the U.S. Army of Occupation. He arrived at Tokyo Bay on September 2, 1945—surrender ceremonies were taking place there aboard the USS *Missouri*—and spent the following eighteen months in Japan on security duty. He arrived home after the start of the '47 baseball season and went to work in the family logging business—in those days a profession nearly as dangerous as the infantry. On Sunday afternoons he put on the gray-flannel uniform of the Temple Townies.

Mosher had not played a baseball game until then. Not in high school. Not in the army. After learning the technique of playing third base, Boyce summoned him to the catcher's box, and he started learning again—with Sade on the mound. Pitch by pitch he wrestled with Sade's round-the-house curveball and tabletop drop. He, like Boyce before him, was vulnerable to Sade's wandering missiles. Catching the drop, Mosher said once, was a tough, gutsy job. He'd call for the pitch and not know whether it would actually drop. Many times it broke wide or into the ground, deceiving over-anxious batters into swinging. With runners on base or with two strikes on a batter, Mosher blocked such errant pitches with his chest, thighs, knees, whatever part of his body he could throw in front of the skittering ball, and kept it in play. As many as sixteen times this past season, the Townies' scrappy catcher has retrieved a pitch that caromed off his body and hurled the ball, sometimes from his knees, to second or third—to hold a runner in place—or, in the case of a two-strike pitch, to first base for the out.

Mosher learned his job well. In addition to grappling with Sade's assortment of pitches, he could snap a throw to second or third base in an instant. He taught base runners to stay close to the bag and give up any notions of trying to steal. He had a knack for blocking home plate. In skirmishes at the plate, Mosher used his legs and hips to deflect sliding runners away before applying the tag. During the 1949 season, he tagged out nine would-be scorers. On many Sunday afternoons he went home bruised and lame and sore without having once ventured into fair territory, except perhaps to run the bases.

But Mosher never wavered, never asked out. He was the Townies' catcher, asked to play the position by Boyce, and he wouldn't think of quitting. Asked once if Sade was hard to catch, he answered, "It was easier when he was sober," and laughed. "Gawd," he recalled, "if he'd been drinkin', you never knew where the ball was goin'. I'd hafta take him out back of the dugout between innings and make him throw and work it off. After two, maybe three, innings he'd straighten out. But it was fun," he said. "I loved the playing."

Mosher is batting .417 when he steps in against McPherson in the bottom of the sixth, bases loaded. McPherson delivers a pitch over the plate, and Mosher slaps it into right field. Two more runs come home while right fielder Philbrick chases the ball, and another roar goes up behind the Townies' dugout. Mosher races to second base. Mitchell stops at third.

Townies' fans keep up their thunderous cheering for Bruce Mosher, who is the next batter. McPherson is coming undone. He kicks the dirt, tugs on his cap, and squints at his catcher for a sign. His first pitch plunks Mosher in the rib cage, and the howling behind the Townies' dugout goes up another notch while Mosher trots to first base. The Townies' jump up in the dugout and shout a chorus at McPherson as well, "Hey, there, sonny boy, no more of that!" and "What's the matter, sonny boy, can't you take it?" The game is delayed while an exchange of hollering takes place. Then Hellgren swings under a McPherson fastball for strike three to end the rally. Boyce nods at Sade and says, "Nine more outs, Sade." The Townies lead 7–5.

It's the top of the seventh. I go to first base and toss warm-up ground balls to the infielders. Sade stands on the mound, rubs the baseball, and watches me finish. "One at a time, Sade," I say. He turns and eyes Mosher for a sign.

Centerfielder Davenport steps to the plate. Sade quickly gets two strikes and then throws the fast drop for strike three. But the pitch breaks wide and sails by Mosher to the backstop. Davenport scampers to first base. Rangeley catcher Eddie West then bounces a slow-roller toward the left side. Fans in the first-base bleacher seats rise in anticipation of trouble, but Bergeron gloves it cleanly and throws to me for the out while Davenport runs to second. Sade settles in. He induces Quimby to loft a fly ball to Mitchell in right, and strikes out Ross with three fastballs. Six outs to go.

Al Bergeron leads off the bottom half. Of the original Townies, only Bergeron had a baseball past. He played shortstop for the high school as a scrawny underweight freshman in 1940. By 1943 his arm had strengthened, and he joined the pitching staff, which also included lefty Bob Parlin, Verne Gray, and Larry Davis, pitchers who, except for Parlin, would later throw for the Farmington Town Team. Following graduation in 1943, teenager Bergeron enlisted in the navy and served on Peleliu and surrounding South Pacific islands as an Aviation Ordnanceman until the end of the war. The navy discharged him in 1946, and he started at shortstop for the Townies in the Independence Day game against East Dixfield.

Life was not easy for Bergeron. He grew up in Temple during the Depression, the second in a family of eight children, the first of four shortstops, all of whom were agile, quick in mind and hand, and competitive, traits probably honed at the dinner table when the pork chops and mashed potatoes—food raised in the back yard—were served.

While the three younger Bergeron shortstops, Gary,

Al Bergeron at Hippach Field c. 1950.

Michael, and Terry, lingered near the Townies' dugout and envisioned themselves someday wearing a Townies' uniform, too, Al played a steady shortstop and earned the respect of his teammates. Quick hands and a strong arm helped him recover from an occasional bobbled bouncer hit his way, and he built a reputation for reliability. He could make all the plays. Boyce put him leadoff in the batting order, where he consistently hit over .350 and reached base on walks more than any other Townies hitter.

Bergeron is one of the straightlaced Townies. Good natured, jovial, friendly, serious in his doings. He doesn't carouse, show up late for games, or drink. He works at being a good ball player. Errors embarrass him. His girlfriend, Audrey, who comes to practices and games, energizes him to achieve, and he behaves himself, lives straight, and will marry Audrey after the 1949 season. Notwithstanding Bergeron's austere lifestyle, his freewheeling, card-playing, cider-drinking teammates have accepted him as one of them.

Bergeron steps in against McPherson, drives his first pitch safely into the gap in right center, and stops at second base. Sade is next. A .352 hitter, Sade has slumped at the plate since the middle of June, about the time the barrel of apple cider in his cellar went empty, going hitless twenty-one consecutive at-bats in one stretch. McPherson is careful with Sade, however, and walks him. Freddy Dunn steps up. The fans cry for the Townies to increase their slim lead.

Dunn looks at Boyce, who is sending signals from the third-base coaching box. Though Boyce doesn't use the bunt often, this is an opportunity to score another run, or perhaps two, and nail down the win right here. Art Mitchell disagrees. "Boyce doesn't like to use the bunt," he says. He predicts Dunn will hit away.

"This is the right spot for a bunt, push the runners along," I answer. But Dunn swings and fouls off the pitch.

"Dunn's a good hitter," Mitchell says. "Boyce thinks he can knock one out of here." But Boyce's bid for a big inning fails: Dunn pops out to the catcher; Blodgett hits a come-backer to McPherson; Al Mitchell taps one to the mound, and the inning is over.

Sade strikes out right fielder Philbrick to start the top of the eighth. Then, in an unexpected move, Rangeley manager Prince Edwards sends a pinch hitter to the box to bat for pitcher Johnny McPherson. McPherson has singled, walked, doubled, and scored two runs in the game, but the high schooler, after plunking Bruce Mosher in the ribs—the third Townies' batter in the game to suffer a McPherson pitch in the torso—is not coming to bat against the fearsome Sade. Sade turns and smiles at the infielders.

"Five outs to go," I tell him.

Sade refocuses and fans the pinch hitter. Then shortstop Barrett bounces one straight back to Sade, and he tosses it to me for the third out. Sade walks to the bench and looks at Boyce, who's grinning at him. "Shee-it!" Sade blurts. "I didn't want to hurt him. I just wanted to make him look a little foolish."

In the top of the ninth, Sade handcuffs the Rangeley hitters again. Novak pops an inside curve to Blodgett at second base. Davenport and West whiff. The Townies win, and we are in the championship game. But the celebration is brief. The game is at four o'clock and Boyce needs to name a starting pitcher. Tyler is ready, but he threw six innings in the first game and will need to loosen again; or strong-armed Sade, who just finished his third inning of the day, can keep going—see how long he can pitch before Boyce will need to call on Tyler.

"What do you think Boyce will do?" Art Mitchell asks.

"Sade," I tell Mitchell. "He'll go to Sade. Sade's his ace. Folks came to see him pitch against Burnham."

"I'm not sure Sade is the best choice," says Mitchell. "Tyler's undefeated—and Sade has time now to sit with his friends."

During the intermission, townsfolk wander. They dole out twenty cents for a hot dog, play a game of beano, or find someone to talk to.

Kids search under bleachers for returnable bottles. Players lounge in the dugout or play a game of catch.

Cal Tyler keeps to himself. A teenager, he doesn't hang out with the raucous Townies. He remains quiet and seeks the company of his school friends in the bleachers. Sade, conversely, is a lightning rod. Folks gravitate his way. The players see him as their last best hope, and indeed he may be. But now, between games, he tells stories, sips from a bottle in a brown paper bag, and stays loose.

The afternoon sun tips toward Day Mountain in Temple.

Boyce waits.

Chapter Nine
SHOWDOWN GAME

S ince April Boyce has not looked back. It has been a succession of tomorrows: tomorrow's players, tomorrow's preparation, tomorrow's game, tomorrow's pitcher. Now there is no tomorrow. The qualifying game is over, and we face our biggest game of the year— again. But regardless of how the championship game turns out, the Townies cannot be denied what we have earned here: we have played to the last. There will be no more. For Boyce, a win will bring the Townies respect. A loss will just bring next year.

Boyce doesn't counsel with either Art Mitchell or me before he writes the lineup in the scorebook. He names Sade starting pitcher. The team was built around Sade. Sade is the star, the marquee, the one player who can put the Townies on par with any team around. He's earned the chance to face the powerful Legionnaires and Boyce knows it. "Get your arm loose," he tells Sade.

Pa shows up at Legion Field before the second game starts. "Couldn't make it this morning," he says. "Had a sick cow to look after."

"Sure," Boyce answers, attending to the score book. "I'm battin' you second in this one. We need some hits early."

"But I haven't hit hardly a thing for the past four, five games," Pa moans. "Just a couple dinky ones off Bucky in East Wilton." Pa batted over .500 in May and June, as high as anyone on the team.

"You're overdue," Boyce tells him. "You'll break out of it."

"I never batted against Burnham, you know."

Bill Burnham consistently overpowers batters with a frightening fastball. Like Sade, Burnham can throw a breaking pitch, too, but a moving fastball is his "out" pitch. At times the pitch rises as it approaches the plate. Other times it dips. An anxious batter who hesitates a bit too long on the ninety-mile-an-hour pitch and swings out of sync will foul it off, beat a piece of it into the ground, pop it straight up, or miss it altogether. And Burnham will tease batters with his fastball, snooker them into swinging uselessly at pitches off the corners of the plate.

Bill Burnham grew up in Phillips. An oversized, barrel-chested giant of a man who, like many of his pitching contemporaries, displayed muscles that came from woodchopping, Burnham relied on pure strength to win ball games. Last year, 1948, Burnham was unbeaten and led Phillips to the North Franklin League championship. Named to the league's all-star team, he pitched against Rumford and narrowly lost to the perennial Andy League powerhouse, 1–0. In the 1948 Labor Day celebration at Kingfield, Burnham out-pitched Kingfield's Milt Simmons to clinch hot-stove league bragging rights in northern Franklin County for the winter.

Burnham and four other Phillips' players—Milt Stinchfield, Theron Stinchfield, Rink Avery, Dexter Merchant—were named to the 1949 North Franklin League all-star team as well. In an all-star game against the Somerset League champion Solon Travelers, Burnham came on in the sixth inning and struck out five in the final four innings. His reputation as a hard-throwing fastballer was well deserved.

* * *

At four-o'clock, the fans turn their attention back to the field. It's a baseball crowd: partisan and full of energy. At two minutes past four, an impatient voice cries out, "C'mon ump! Get it started." Burnham is ready to pitch, and the Townies' shortstop, Bergeron, steps into the box. Bergeron's remarkable ability to get to first base by any means—hit, bunt, walk, hit by a pitch, error—has sparked Townies' rallies throughout the season. His on-base percentage from the lead spot is .610, and the fans remember the ground-ball single he bounced into the outfield in the first game that started the sixth inning game-winning rally. "Get it started, Al," someone yells. He lofts the second pitch of the game toward center field, and Rink Avery makes a running catch for the out. Back in the dugout Boyce asks him, "What'd he throw you, Al?"

"Fast," Bergeron says and sits down.

"Did it move?" Boyce continues.

"I don't know. I barely saw the damned thing."

The jester Hellgren counsels him. "You should move up in the batter's box, Al. Get closer to him, where you can see the ball better."

Bergeron grins. "I got a piece of it," he answers.

Pa walks to the plate. Pa joined the Townies in 1947. He played nine games at first base that year and batted .200. One of the oldest active Townies now, he is not a competitor, has little intensity for baseball, and doesn't always pay attention to game situations. He is inconsistent in the batters box, and hitting slumps have plagued him. He plays first base well, if a bit lackadaisically, and he is accused by some Townies' fans of misplaying too many throws from infielders, of not seeing the ball well on Sunday afternoons. He's mishandled the ball twice at first base this season but, on a team where the infielders juggled the ball thirty-eight times, the two miscues caused little overall damage. Obviously, the concern over whether Pa can see the ball well enough is unfounded. I made three errors at first base myself this year—and I was sober every game I played.

In 1947, Pa finished his first Townies season in a dreadful slump, hitless in his last thirteen times up. In the Andover Fair game he didn't hit the ball out of the infield in five trips to the batter's box. His best game—three hits and three runs scored—came in June against Andover, after pitching hay and drinking hard cider in Howard Mitchell's hayfield all morning.

Pa came home from the war disillusioned. His trucking business had languished and failed. Many of his friends had moved on to new jobs, new girlfriends, and new lives, and he showed no interest in starting over. His closest friends—Sade, Hellgren, and Wirta—played for the Townies and urged him to join in the Sunday entertainment. Reluctant at first, he eventually needed them. Boyce gave him a boost, furnished him a uniform, played him at first base, and batted him high in the order. Pa responded and filled a gap in the team's lineup.

But many times Pa is absent or late. He has missed seven games this season, none of which was caused by a sick cow. I watch him closely every game he plays, disappointed that he can't contact the pitch well. I don't think he takes the game seriously, doesn't work on improving, as Boyce preaches. Just one key hit, delivered in the Rumford Point game, say, when he had a chance to pull it out for the Townies, might have excited him enough to improve his swing and contribute even more.

This year he is at .303, and is in another slump, managing but two hits in his last sixteen at-bats. Boyce thinks he's due to break out of it. But he bounces a Bill Burnham fastball to the right side and second baseman Joe Sala tosses him out. Then Freddy Dunn slices a ground ball into right field and reaches first base safely, but is stranded when switch-hitter Dick Blodgett, batting lefty against the hard-balling right-hander, is late on a fastball and bounces it to third. The Townies fail to score.

Sade walks to the mound rubbing the baseball. He nods to Bill Mosher and throws him warm-ups. Leadoff hitter Dexter Merchant steps in. Sade fires a fastball, spins a slow curve, and then offers another fastball that Merchant, a right-handed batter, reaches for and slaps into right field for a single. Then centerfielder Avery is up. He pushes a ground ball into left field—two runners on base,. no one out.

The game is only a few minutes old and the Townies are in trouble. Sade needs to bear down, or we'll get shoved into a hole right now, play the whole game from behind. This could be the game-breaking moment—and in the first inning.

Small-town baseball teams who scored first on Sunday afternoon usually won. Falling behind early forced the trailing team to play stressful ball. Tension diminished their performance. They lost confidence and spirit. Consequently, they fell further behind and played out the game with no thought of actually winning. In seventeen Townies' games this season, the team that scored first won. Reasons may have included two teams not fairly matched, a pitcher with an off day, or an unexpected error. But in every instance the team that went ahead first won. Energized by their lead, they concentrated and hustled and came out ahead.

Burnham comes to the plate and flexes his Popeye-size biceps. He hit .340 this year. Legionnaires' manager Fillmore Harnden sends signals from the third-base coach's box. On the first pitch, Burnham turns and bunts. The ball rolls toward Dunn, who charges in from third, gloves the ball, and flips it to Pa at first in time for the out. Merchant advances to third and Avery to second.

First baseman Milt Stinchfield comes to the plate. A fan yells, "Two big ones out there, Milt." Sade throws the drop, a pitch he uses for outs when he can control it. It doesn't drop and Stinchfield taps it straight back to the mound. Sade holds the runner at third and tosses the ball to Pa. Two outs. The runners hang close to the bases, and the Townies foresee getting out of the inning unhurt. But then .375 hitter Adley drives a Sade fastball into center, where it drops in front of Hellgren for a single. Two runners cross the plate. Joe Sala follows with another single. But Toothaker ends the inning with a ground ball to

Blodgett, who tosses it to Pa for the third out. The Townies trail, 2–0, after one inning.

I look at Art Mitchell. "Not all games are won in the first inning," I say. "Burnham has more work to win this one."

Burnham puts the Townies' down in order in the top of the second; right fielder Al Mitchell grounds the ball to shortstop; catcher Bill Mosher strikes out on a Burnham fastball; and left-fielder Bruce Mosher taps a Burnham speedball back to the mound to close out the inning.

Boyce stops Sade on his way to the mound. "Sade," he murmurs, "throw the drop more. The're makin' contact with the fastball."

"I dunno, boss," Sade answers. "It wa'n't working in the first. I couldn't get it over. They laid off it."

"Well, they slapped your fastball all over the place. Keep workin' on the drop. It'll come."

Sade liked big games and big crowds. At the opening of Temple's new ball field in 1946, in front of what might still be our biggest crowd ever, he pitched a shutout against East Dixfield. He followed that with victories over Norridgewock and Jay and since then has thrown four shutouts, a no-hitter, and struck out as many as twenty batters in a game.

But at times, the opponents inexplicably score a big inning on him early, put a crooked number on the scoreboard, as if he were a high school freshman in his first start. In a 1946 game against the Hard Cider Boys, Sade gave up six runs in the second inning, and if Bob Stevens, who played first base for the Hard Cider Boys and later said that Sade was the toughest pitcher he faced in a long baseball career, hadn't struck out twice in the inning, the shiretowners might have batted around again. Sade gave up two hits and one run the rest of the way. In a game at Hippach Field in 1947 against the Hard Cider Boys, by then called by some the over-the-hill gang, Sade gave up eleven runs in the first inning, righted himself, and then threw a two-run ball game.

Townsfolk explained Sade's inconsistency as caused by a "small drinking situation" that affected his ability not only to throw but to see. Sade drank. Drinking was characteristic of most men I knew in Temple. Sade, whom I suspected also drank as a woodchopper and infantryman, seemed unaffected by it, took it in stride. Drinking was a lifestyle. But his drinking unnerved catcher Bill Mosher on more than one Sunday. "Sade would show up with his cronies," Mosher said years later, "slightly out of kilter, particularly if they had some distance to travel, and it would take an inning or two to work out the fuzziness." Mosher would take Sade behind the dugout between the early innings and keep him throwing until the fuzziness wore off. Sometimes it would take two or three sessions.

This is too important a game for Sade to fool around with an elixir—and he's been playing since one o'clock. "Hell," Art Mitchell says on the bench, "he's only given up two runs. That won't amount to nothing."

In the second inning, Mosher calls for the drop. Sade throws it, and Mosher calls for it again. Phillips' batter Wing trickles a ground ball to Blodgett at second for an out. Mosher keeps calling for the drop, and Sade throws third-strike drops by right-fielder Ross and third baseman Merchant. Art Mitchell looks at Boyce, "Good advice there," he says.

"Eyesight probably clearin' up some," Boyce answers.

"But we still have the problem of the two runs," I moan to Mitchell.

Boyce tries to rouse his hitters. "He's throwing hard, but it's straight," he tells Hellgren, leading off the top of the third. "Jes' put some wood on it, Put it in play." But the Townies again go down in order. Hellgren bounces a pitch to Merchant at third. Sade strikes out. Then Bergeron brings the Townies' fans to their feet with a drive toward right field, but the Legionnaires' Ross makes a running catch to end the inning.

The game moves into the bottom of the third. Sade goes to the mound determined. His arm is strong; the drop is working; he has retired four consecutive Legionnaires. Rink Avery leads off and pulls a pitch toward third base. The sure-handed Dunn can't pick it up, a rare error, and Avery reaches first. Bill Burnham also bounces a pitch toward Dunn, and rushing to erase the previous miscue with a double play, he mishandles this one, too. Sade, peeved by the two errors, stomps his feet, kicks the dirt, and glares at the Townies' bench. Boyce goes to the mound. "Gawdammit, he shoulda had it," Sade pouts. "It was a double-play for sure."

"Settle down," Boyce tells him. "Milt Stinchfield's up. Pitch him low an' he'll hit another one on the ground. We'll get the double play yet."

Sade throws low fastballs to clean-up hitter Stinchfield, and he slaps a ground ball to Bergeron at shortstop. Bergeron tosses the ball to Blodgett at second for a force-out on Burnham, but Blodgett's throw to Pa at first is late. Now, with runners at first and third and one out, the Legionnaires are poised to do some more damage. Sade throws the drop. Adley hits it on the ground to Bergeron—the third double-play ball of the inning—and Bergeron throws it past Blodgett and into right field. The Legionnaires score, and Stinchfield races to third. On the next pitch, Adley goes for second and Joe Sala drives a Sade fastball by the outstretched gloves of Bergeron and Dunn into left field. The score is now 5–0, sapping the energy out of the Townies' fans. The next two hitters, Toothaker and Wing, ground to Blodgett, ending the inning.

Sade scowls in the dugout. "Gawdammit, I threw the fastball low like you said, threw the drop when Mosher wanted it, and the gawdamm hitters beat the ball into the ground like you wanted. An' it's five to nothing. Now what?" He sits sullen, but Boyce is calm.

*   *   *

Over the past three years, the Phillips Legionnaires have won the big games. The Legionnaires comprise strong-armed pitching, potent bats, and a baseball-savvy manager, Fillmore Harnden. And they expect to win. They will have it no other way. In 1946 the Legionnaires battled the Farmington Town Team all summer for the North Franklin League championship and in August beat the shiretowners in the showdown game behind Larry Sanders' superior pitching and third baseman Bill Burnham's clutch hitting. No one was surprised. The following year it was the same: a winner-take-all game with Farmington that Bill Burnham pitched and won, benefiting from the lusty hitting of sluggers Rink Avery and Milt Stinchfield. In 1948 Bill Burnham's pitching put down Farmington—now called the Flyers— again in a crucial North Franklin League game for the league lead. And in Kingfield on Labor Day that year, they bested a brawny host club to win the holiday tournament as well. So the Legionnaires came to Strong in 1949 no strangers to winning big games.

But losing is not part of Boyce's vocabulary either. He knows, of course, that he can lose—will lose—but he doesn't talk about it, doesn't dwell on it. In his view, dwelling on losing is for losers. He will put the Townies up against anyone, and he accepts being beaten. He knows that baseball teaches many of life's hard lessons. He is a forward looker who learns from his experiences, then puts the past aside. All the time, bit by bit, he reaches toward being his best.

When the Townies come off the field to start the fourth inning, the game's outcome, in the minds of many, has already been decided. Boyce, undaunted, looks at Pa. "Wait for a strike, Monty." Pa goes to the plate and waits for a Burnham strike. He pops it up over Joe Sala's head at second base. One out. Freddy Dunn, who punched out a single in the first for the Townies only hit, is next. He steps into the box, drives the pitch deep into the left field gap beyond the outfielders, and pulls into second base ahead of Adley's throw. The fans behind the

Townies' dugout shout their approval. Dunn has broken the Townies' hit draught. Blodgett then pokes a ground ball toward shortstop that gets away from Toothaker. Dunn stops at third, Blodgett at first. Boyce is presented with the precise situation he asked for, two runners on base and only one out. Al Mitchell strides to the plate.

Mitchell first played for the Townies in 1948 when Boyce, who saw his potential as a future regular, used him as a backup third baseman to build his experience and bolster his confidence. He responded to Boyce's mentoring by hitting .296 and in 1949 became the Townies' regular right fielder. He is hitting .292 and has played errorless right field.

Mitchell possesses the strongest arm of the Townies' outfielders, perhaps even of the Townies' team. Twice against the South China Clippers, who had not been privy to the well-known strength of his arm, Mitchell threw out runners trying to score from third base after fly ball outs. On two other occasions he caught a low liner hit to right and doubled up a runner on first. His arm has earned a reputation. Runners now keep a cautious rein on their ambitions when a ball is hit to right field.

Boyce knows about Mitchell's arm, of course. He learned the year before when he subbed him at third base and watched in awe as his throws to first nearly tore Pa's mitt off. "That kid," Boyce said then, "that kid is somethin', that arm of his. I never saw the likes of it—an' he's just in high school!"

Boyce also knows firsthand that Mitchell can hit. On two occasions in the village school yard, eighth-grader Mitchell, swinging a cracked and dented bat held together with maybe a half-mile of black bicycle tape, drove a weathered and worn baseball, equally wrapped in black tape, across the school yard, the road, Aunt Marion's lawn, and up against her house. The second time, the ball flew through the front window into Aunt Marion's parlor—more than two hundred feet away. After Boyce had replaced the window pane, Aunt Marion, a dite too gratuitous the first time the ball careened off her home, remarked at the supper table, "I'm going to speak to Mrs. Stolt."

Schoolmarm Stolt announced the next day just before recess that we must post an outfielder in front of Aunt Marion's windows whenever Mitchell batted. "Mrs. Boyce told me she thought boys should play baseball, she didn't want to stop the games, but it shouldn't be necessary for Mr. Boyce to fix broken window panes." We heeded her advice. Mitchell continued to hone his thunderous swing but with an outfielder standing in front of Aunt Marion's parlor window.

Mitchell lettered in baseball his first three years at Farmington High School. Thankfully he was there when I joined the team in 1949 or I'd still be there in the locker room trying to put on the uniform Coach Carlson handed me. I had never worn a baseball uniform and didn't know how to dress in one: the sequence of knickers, knee-length socks, and sliding pads. It was too much for me, who'd worn only shorts in the hayfield games, to figure out. I peeked at teammates in the crowded locker room who were somehow arranging everything to fit. *What are these things,* I wondered. *How do I attach the stockings to the knickers, what should I put on first?* I looked for Al Mitchell.

"They're sliding pads," he told me. "Tie them around your waist before you put your pants on."

"Why?" I asked.

"Damned if I know," Mitchell answered. "Just let the pads hang down over your hips like six-guns. They're supposed to keep you from getting a razzberry on your arse when you slide into second."

"Then what?"

He laughed. "Pull your stockings all the way up over the knee before you pull on your britches. Then pull the britches up until the elastic leg bottoms are snug under your knees, drop the trouser tops back down around your feet leaving the leg bottoms up, and roll the tops of your stockings down over the leg bottoms. That'll hold the stockings up—an' don't forget to pull your britches back up around your waist."

At Legion Field now, Mitchell hitches up his britches and waggles his bat at Bill Burnham, anxious to make contact with the ball. He slices a Burnham fastball toward shortstop, and when the ball skips through Toothaker's legs, Dunn scores from third base with the Townies first run. With Mitchell on first and Blodgett on second, Bill Mosher bounces another pitch toward Toothaker, but third baseman Merchant darts in front of the error-prone shortstop, snags the ball, and throws Mosher out at first. Both runners advance, and Bruce Mosher, batting .067 in his last five games, comes to the plate with two runners in position to score. The hopeful behind me cross their fingers. "Poke it out there, Bruce," they yell.

Mosher takes an awkward stance at the plate: slightly bowlegged, a small paunch jutting over his belt, leaning heavy on his right leg, and brandishing the bat behind and below his right hip like you'd hold a broom if you wanted to swat a horse on the ass. He makes contact with Burnham's second pitch and drives the ball into left field. It falls safely, and Blodgett trots home. Mitchell holds at third when the charging Adley comes up with the ball cleanly and throws it home. On the throw Mosher races into second.

Hellgren is next. "Two ducks on the pond," someone yells. Hellgren swings under a Burnham fastball for strike three and leaves both runners stranded. But the Townies are back in the game.

I'm excited. The deficit is cut to three, and perhaps the Townies have solved Bill Burnham's forceful pitching and are ready to challenge the Legionnaires' supposed superiority. Sade goes to the mound in the fourth looking for a zero. Merchant leads off and hits a sharp grounder toward Pa at first. The ball ricochets off Pa's leg into right field, and Merchant dashes safely across the base. *Pa should have snagged it,* I think, and Sade surely thinks so too, but he doesn't fume or pout or kick the mound. He glares at Rink Avery in the batter's box. Then he fans Avery with a drop, induces Bill Burnham to hit a weak one-hopper back to the mound, and whiffs Milt Stinchfield with another drop. *This is the Sade I know,* I think. Safely back on the bench, he leans over to Pa. "I had to get four outs that inning, Monty. Mebbe you should ask your kid someday how to snag those things."

"Huh? The damned thing hit a rock. You saw it for cripes' sake. Hit me right in the shin," Pa wails. "I'll be sore for a week."

I can hear the ball pop in catcher Wing's mitt as Burnham warms up for the top of the fifth. Burnham wants command of the game back and Sade steps up to the plate. The infielders chatter at Burnham, rallying him with the noisome babble found in small-town ball games. "C'mon, big Bill. Take it to him, babe." I don't like infield chatter. The chatterer's attention is on his talk and not on preparing for the next pitch. And the chatter distracts the pitcher's concentration, as well. Though I prefer to simply mutter expletives to myself, I participate in the chattering when I'm out at first base as a show of loyalty to Sade. But I don't have a large chattering repertoire. "C'mon, Sade," is usually the limit.

But the Legionnaire infielders don't see it like I do. They prattle profusely at Burnham—"You-d'babee, you-d'boy; come-babee, babee, babeee; you-d'boy, you-d'boy, you-d'boy; bring-it-to-'em, bring-itto-'em, bring-it-to-'em; you-d'boy, you-d'babee, babee, babeee. Letitallout, letitallout, Billyboy," they prate as Sade drives a fastball on a low line that handcuffs shortstop Toothaker and drifts into short left field. The chatter stops while Toothaker retrieves the ball and then starts again. "C'mon, babeebabeebabee. Get-two, get-twooo. You-d'boy."

But Sade is stranded on first as Burnham puts the Townies down in order in the fifth. It is the same in the sixth. Burnham has found his rhythm, and, as quickly as a Townies' hitter appears at the plate, Burnham frustrates him with his hopping fastball. The Townies are impotent, intimidated by Burnham's hulking presence on the mound. The square-jawed Boyce sits quietly as Burnham hypnotizes his team. In the seventh, they leave a runner at third when Dunn grounds weakly to Sala.

Meanwhile the Legionnaires break the game open again. In the bottom of the sixth, Rink Avery singles into center driving home two base runners and pushing the score to 7–2. They put up another run in the seventh. Lead-off hitter Joe Sala drives a Sade fastball beyond the reach of Al Mitchell in right field and then challenges Mitchell's throwing arm in a daring race with the ball for third base. Mitchell's throw comes in on target to cutoff man Blodgett, who relays the ball to Dunn at third. But Sala, hat flying, skids into third base an instant ahead of the ball. Then Toothaker comes up and slaps a single into center field, driving Sala home. The Legionnaires lead, 8–2. The Townies need a miracle.

When they come in to the dugout, Boyce heartens his team, "We've six outs left, boys. Let's make the most of 'em. Who knows what'll happen?"

If Bill Burnham continues to pitch like he has, I muse, *everyone knows what will happen.*

It's nearing six o'clock, and the ending seems no longer in doubt. The sun slants through the trees, and shadows creep onto Legion Field. The air takes on a foreboding chill. Fans begin to wander away. They are tired or hungry or have drunk all they can hold. They gather up their belongings and traipse toward the exits—except for the persistent Townies fans, who huddle in the seats behind me, steadfast to see the end. Townies' fans will stay as long as their team is here.

The Townies start the eighth in the middle of the batting order. Dick Blodgett, the staunch second baseman, steps up to the plate and strikes out. Just like that, before the Townies have settled on the dugout bench, before Sade has lit a cigarette, before Al Mitchell has picked up a bat and moved to the on-deck circle, Blodgett strikes out. Bizarre.

Dick Blodgett is a small man, lean, and strong. Too small, and perhaps too shy, to play baseball, football, or hockey in school; he ran cross-country and track instead and avoided the turbulent sports until the Townies came along. In his youth he worked on his father's farm: ploughed, cut hay, pulled a crosscut saw, and drove a logging truck. At twenty-three, when World War II broke out, Blodgett left Temple for the only time in his life and served as a private, a maintenance man, in the Army Air Corps. After the war, he came back to the family farm, married Helen, joined the Congregational Church, politicked for selectman, and earned a meager living building kitchen cabinets and bookcases for townsfolk, and remodeling farmhouse ells into something more utilitarian.

Blodgett is brainy. No subject is beyond his imagination. He can design kitchens, read—and draw—blueprints, and discuss the intricate rules of land surveying. He knows geometry and trigonometry and can describe the forces that keep aircraft in the air. I picked up a national magazine once on a cross-country flight, and inside was an article in which Dick Blodgett debated the ecological virtues of beaver dams.

Like a few other Townies, Blodgett probably drinks too much— hard cider and vodka are plentiful in Temple. Many townsfolk remember the Sunday morning in 1947 when the Townies met in Howard Mitchell's field to put in his hay. Blodgett was there and, perhaps a dite more than the others, quenched his hayfield thirst with Mitchell's fermented hard cider, by then packing enough wallop to floor a kangaroo. That afternoon, in a two o'clock contest with Andover, Blodgett came out of his shell a bit, stroked several hits, played errorless defense at second base, and laughed and promoted the use of hard cider in the dugout—"fill up the water cooler with it," he declared. Still, Blodgett is a personable player who speaks softly, causes no commotion, and seems embarrassed to talk about his hitting or even to send someone a modest invoice for a piece of quality-built cabinetry.

He is most proud of his fielding. He played shortstop in the first Townies game in 1946, and stayed there until Al Bergeron arrived home from the war. Then Boyce switched him to second base. After fourteen consecutive errorless games at second base, Blodgett knew he could handle a glove, but he never claimed to be a strong hitter. "I get a single or two once in a while," he'd say. Boyce moved him to fourth in the batting order this year. And he hasn't struck out all day. He's whiffed only four times this year. Not since July has he fanned, twenty-eight consecutive times at bat without striking out. No one expects Blodgett to whiff. He's the team's surest hitter. He batted .413 during the season and led the team in extra base hits. But in the eighth inning at Legion Field, he inexplicably fans.

Then Al Mitchell steps into the box, drives a liner over Sala's head into right field, and stops at first base. Bill Mosher is next. Mosher is tired, plodding to the plate. He aches and is sore—so sore that years later he will still remember the details:

"Gosh," he says, "We'd been playin' since noontime. An' I'd been catchin' Sade for four hours, Tyler before that. I felt like I'd been beaten up for good. I was ready for supper and some rest."

"Was Sade hard to catch that day?"

"You never knew where Sade's pitches were goin'; could go any-place. An' Sade's drop was always hard to catch, bouncin' at you all over the place. Give you bruises all over. He had good stuff that day, but I chased it a lot."

"You had a long day?"

He paused. "Gosh, you could get plumb worn out catchin' Sade just one game. That day there was *two*."

"Was he sober?"

Mosher laughed. "I think so. He might have had a drink between games, but he seemed okay. He was tired at the end, too. Gawd, we all were. Those two games in Strong, they were *hard*."

Mosher gets the second out when he swings under a Burnham fastball for strike three. Bruce Mosher comes up then and singles to right field. Mitchell eases into second. The crowd begins to stir at the first Townies threat since the fourth inning. Hellgren swings a bat in the on-deck circle. Boyce comes in from third and counsels him. "Jes' put some wood on it. Try to keep this thing goin'."

A thin wiry man, a logger who takes a twenty-pound chain saw into the woods every day, Hellgren played center field in the first Townies game in 1946 and has become a sociable fixture here, often chatting with outfielders Bruce Mosher and Al Mitchell and yelling advice to his friend Sade.

Hellgren was born in Temple in 1920 of Finnish immigrants. His Finnish steam bath, nestled in the woods behind his bungalow, was the Saturday-night bath of choice for Ma and Pa. We went there often before the war, and Hellgren and Pa drank home brew, laughed at jokes I didn't understand, and talked of the woods and how hard they struggled to eke out a living in Temple. Hellgren's sense of humor bolstered him then: when he lugged his crosscut into the woods for the day, or loaded icy birch logs onto Pa's truck by hand in a cold rain, or came to our kitchen on Sunday with a bag of beer to play poker and worry about the looming war.

Hellgren and teammate Elmer Wirta served in an anti-aircraft artillery battalion in Iceland and later in Brussels, Belgium, launching 120-mm shells at German bombers and V-1 rockets streaking toward Antwerp and London. After the war, Hellgren married Bertha, swapped his bucksaw and crosscut for a new chain saw, bought forest land in the Temple outback, and spent his weekdays logging.

Sade and Wirta played for the Townies then, and, though Hellgren lacked any previous baseball experience, he joined in. He could throw and catch a ball, and Boyce taught him how to play center field, how to position himself for lefties and righties, where to throw the ball when it came to him. And gave him plenty of practice in the batter's box.

Hellgren played a pivotal role in the first Andover Fair game in 1946. In the fourth inning, the Townies leading 3–1 and three runners on base, he stroked a two-out single into left field that scored two runs and pushed the lead to 5–1. As he skipped down the first-base line, he likely figured his hit gave the Townies a little breathing room, but it carried more weight than even he thought. The single proved to be the deciding hit when Rumford Point rallied in the bottom of the ninth inning and forced Sade to strike out the last batter with the winning run on base, preserving a 5–4 win.

But Hellgren was never sure the center field job was his. He seemed insecure and worried at times that Larry Barker, John Hardy, or some young upstart like Al Mitchell, would take the job away from him. He didn't believe he could hit well enough and thought his throwing arm was too weak. But he took extra batting practice and offset his shaky arm by playing shallow in center field, a technique that warned runners not to try advancing an extra base on balls hit to center. He knew few hitters had ever hit a Sade pitch over a center fielder's head and played the odds. He worked hard, and he kept his center field job.

Hellgren's extra work at batting practice paid off. In 1946 he hit .408, the next year .327. In 1948 his .448 hitting average and eight doubles led the team. But this year his average has trailed off to .259, and Boyce has dropped him to eighth in the batting order. And he's having a frustrating day against Bill Burnham: a groundout to third and a swinging strikeout so far. Now, with two strikes and two runners in scoring position, he swings and misses a fastball, Burnham's third strikeout of the inning.

The Legionnaires go quickly in the bottom of the eighth, as though they are trying to finish an already-decided game and scurry home for chores before dark. Avery grounds a Sade pitch to Pa at first. Burnham strikes out; Milt Stinchfield bounces one to shortstop Al Bergeron; and the Townies take their gloves with them into the dugout as the shadow of Spruce Mountain crawls onto the playing field.

Infantryman Sade is angry. He looks out at the pitchers mound and sees the enemy. "C'mon," he says, "let's show these sunsabitches what we can do. Who the hell do they think they are? Getting off so easy." He picks up a bat, looks at Pa, and grins. "I'm gonna show that sonavabitch Burnham right where the sun sets. You watch."

"You show him, Sade," Hellgren twits. "You show him."

Boyce appeals for one hit at a time, "We need a base runner, Sade. Pick out a good pitch."

Sade doesn't dawdle. Burnham puts a fastball over the plate, and Sade hits it into center field where it bounces in front of Rink Avery. He stands on first base and grins at Pa on the bench. Bergeron comes up and puts a Burnham fastball hard on the ground. Stinchfield backhands it at first and throws to Toothaker at second, forcing Sade out. Bergeron is on at first.

"Hit one out, Monty," Sade urges Pa. "He's throwing nothing."

The aura that surrounds Sade inspires Pa. They both campaigned under General Patton in World War II, and Pa wants to stay in Sade's adventurous shadow. He grits, swings at the fastball, and bloops a single, a Texas leaguer, into right field. Boyce holds Bergeron at second base. The Townies are on their feet in the dugout. The crowd cheers. Pa looks at Sade and winks.

"What's he throwing out there?" Dunn asks Sade.

"He's tuckered," Sade answers. "He's got nothing."

"Didn't he throw anything crooked at all?" Dunn asks.

"Not to me, he didn't," Sade answers. "I hit the first pitch that looked like a strike."

Dunn hits a liner that bounces in front of Adley in left field. Bergeron rounds third and legs it toward the plate, but Boyce, coaching at third base, puts up the stop sign. I look at Art Mitchell beside me. "He coulda made it," I say.

"Sure," Mitchell answers. "But we don't need a run; we need six runs." *Three hits in the inning*, I think, *and we don't have a run yet.*

Blodgett comes up with the bases loaded. The bleacher-seat crowd is on its feet and the players are standing in the dugout. "Keep it going, Dick," someone yells." The hits keep coming. Blodgett drills a single into right field, and Bergeron comes home, the first Townies run since the fourth inning. Up steps Al Mitchell.

Boyce paces back and forth behind third base. He raises one finger and chatters to the runners. He shouts instructions to Mitchell. Mitchell waggles the bat at Burnham. On the bench, Art Mitchell murmurs, "Be confident."

It's a hard spot for a high school kid, I think.

Burnham takes a deep breath, pauses, frowns, grips the ball, twists and strains through his characteristic windup, then hurls the ball toward his catcher. Mitchell passes it up. The next pitch is over the plate, and Mitchell drives it into right field as though Aunt Marion's parlor window were perched out there for him to aim at, and pulls up at first base when Boyce holds the runner at third. Now the score is 8–4, the bases full of runners. Bill Mosher comes to the batter's box. I look at Art Mitchell. "Mosher's the tying run if he gets around. What a game."

Mosher drove in the winning runs in the first game with a single. But he has struggled at the plate since. Now he faces Burnham with the game on the line. It's a classic matchup: the unfocused and besieged fastballer, Burnham, who's given up five hits in the inning, and the exhausted .400 hitter, Mosher, who has struck out twice and is hitless in the game. Boyce prods him. "Pick out a good one, Bill."

Mosher is the unheralded on-field leader of the Townies. Since Boyce handed him the catching tools last season, he has excelled. He is a consistent threat in the batter's box and has led the team in batting average over the past two seasons. He has earned the highest regard from his teammates. But he wants no more than to help the Townies win. There could be no more satisfying place for him right now than standing in the batter's box at Legion Field facing Bill Burnham with the bases loaded in the ninth inning.

What a glorious season this has been, I think. A long winning streak, the struggle to recover from a devastating slump, and now these climactic games at Legion Field. The stands are quiet for the confrontation. Mosher steps in.

It's a battle of dragons in slow motion. Burnham stares toward the outfield, scuffs at the pitchers rubber, calms his mind, turns and glares at Mosher. When he's ready, he hitches his pants, tugs on his cap, and squints to Wing for a sign. Mosher dries his hands on his uniform, massages the bat handle, steps into the box, and cocks the bat. "Stay on top of his fastball; stay on top of it," someone pleads. Then Burnham throws.

Burnham wins. Mosher passes up pitches outside the zone and fouls off several fastballs but eventually, after perhaps nine pitches, he swings by a fastball for strike three. "Damn!" I say. "That shouldn't happen to Mosher. Why him?"

There's one out left. Bruce Mosher comes up. Boyce stands in the third base coaches box holding up two fingers to the three runners on base; Hellgren stands in the on-deck circle swinging two bats; players stand in the dugout; the crowd stands on the bleacher seats. Mosher has been on base six times today, two hits off Burnham in this game. Out of his slump, he's likely to keep the rally going. He goes into his awkward crouch, waggles his bat somewhere behind his right hip, and waits. But Burnham is confident now. He squints at Wing, then toes the rubber and delivers a pitch wide of the plate. Burnham avoids the middle of the strike zone, and eventually Mosher swings and sends a weak ground ball to shortstop Toothaker. Just like that, the game is over. The bleacher fans are silent. Boyce walks to the Phillips' dugout. The Townies stuff their bats, balls, and other baseball dunnage into an old army duffel bag.

The games at Legion Field were characteristic of the Townies' year: promising, yet disappointing in the end. One or two timely hits off Burnham might have salvaged the game and an auspicious season, but the exemplary Burnham refused to yield the crucial hits, and the Legionnaires' potent bats took the game out of reach.

Now we are quiet. This loss doesn't feel like other losses. It seems as though we never had a chance against the highly-touted Phillips' ace. But tomorrow, the veterans will go to work and the high school kids to school. As for me, I will be back on Lake Avenue. I will start my sophomore year at Farmington High School, no longer an unknown Temple kid. And on Saturdays, I will smile and take pies and cakes and home-style bread to a hundred waiting customers along Highway 4 in Farmington, Strong, and Phillips.

Chapter Ten

PA RETIRES FROM BASEBALL

I t is May 1950. The Boston Red Sox trade for Clyde Vollmer and bring up slugger Walt Dropo from Louisville. Rutgers baseball stars Jim Monahan, Dudley Eppel, and Rudy Stanzel sign on with the Farmington Flyers. Pa retires from the Temple Townies, and Boyce searches for a first baseman. With his fortieth birthday coming up, Pa is the oldest of the war veterans. Since his divorce from Ma, life has been difficult: he doesn't keep a home in Temple; he rooms at Uncle Phil's in Farmington, or someplace else in town within walking distance of the liquor store. His life lacks order and stability; his interest in baseball has disappeared. Boyce appeals to him, but Pa doesn't waver. "I've had enough," he says. "I'm gonna hang 'em up." And he does. It's the first crack in the Townies original makeup, one that will have to be repaired.

The candidates to replace Pa at first base are few. John Hardy, who appeared at first a few games in 1946 between umpiring chores, is not available. Nor is Pa's part-time backup, Granville Knowles, who graduated from high school and left for an out-of-town job. Boyce knows—and I know, too—that I'm not ready to step in as the regular first baseman. Boyce needs more hitting than I, or any of the other high

Bob Parlin, with Bruce Mosher in the background. Hippach Field, 1950.

schoolers, can provide now. But Boyce knows that baseball in Temple is too important to let the team disintegrate. He goes to Fairbanks and calls on Bob Parlin.

Parlin pitched four years for the Farmington High School Greyhounds —Lefty Parlin, Coach Clarence Gould dubbed him. But Coach Gould also kept him in the lineup when Larry Davis, Verne Gray, or Al Bergeron took a turn on the mound, and his slugging produced four of the Greyhounds' best years. After graduation in 1943 he enlisted in the navy and served on board a Landing Craft, Tank (LCT) in the South Pacific during the final months of World War II. Gunner's Mate Parlin and the LCT delivered troops and armament to South Pacific islands in support of the island-to-island thrust toward the Japanese homeland. "We had a ring of destroyers around us at sea," Parlin said years later, "and only once did a Jap Zero get through the ring and take a shot at us." The Zero missed; Parlin came home to New Vineyard after the war and put on his baseball glove again.

Parlin played for New Vineyard in the North Franklin League, an eight-team loop of up-country teams comprising Rangeley, Stratton,

Kingfield, New Portland, Phillips, Strong, New Vineyard, and the first-edition Farmington Flyers, and earned a fearful reputation as a preeminent hitter, accumulating a large number of doubles and homers each season. In the North Franklin League he first faced Phillips' fastballer Bill Burnham. "Fastest I've ever seen," Parlin said when I asked about Burnham, "I couldn't hit him. He was the best."

"Maybe you had a bad day," I suggested.

"I sure as hell did, had several of them." Parlin said, chuckling.

The Townies played New Vineyard twice when Parlin was there, losing once 6–3 in a New Vineyard hayfield when Sade fell behind in the middle innings and Boyce called on untested Cal Tyler to pitch the rest of the way. We redeemed ourselves later at Temple, when Sade's arm toughened as the game moved along and the hitters came back from an early three-run deficit to win, 14–4. Parlin played in both games and hit safely four times.

In 1949, as Parlin tells it, the undefeated Farmington Flyers hosted the New Vineyards in a league game at Hippach Field. After six innings, the New Vineyards, on the strength of Parlin's double and a couple of other timely hits, and bolstered by the shutout pitching of crafty Elwyn McAllister, led the doughty Flyers 3–0. But by then, Parlin bemoans, the Flyers had solved the mystery of McAllister's junky pitching and went on to topple the upstart cellar-dwellers, 7–3.

Following the 1949 season, the New Vineyard baseball team folded; the following spring Parlin and his bride moved to Fairbanks. It's a May Saturday when Boyce stops the bakery truck at Parlin's new house and knocks on the door carrying an armful of breads and cakes. He comes out a half-hour later smiling. "We've got a new customer, Johnny. And a new first baseman, too," he adds.

Boyce is jubilant that Parlin will wear a Townies uniform. "He was looking for a chance to play for us," he exclaims. "He'll fit into our infield nicely. We'll be a threat to anyone now, even to the Clippers!" *Parlin's bat will be welcome in the Townies lineup,* I muse, but I'm disappointed such a drastic move is necessary. I would likely be ready to take Pa's place in a year or two—if I can learn to hit. But Parlin will help the Townies now. It is a bold move by Boyce. He has looked farther into the future than two years. He knows the war veterans—seven of the original Townies—will disappear from the lineup soon, and he cannot replace them with youngsters he has watched play across the street in the school yard, not yet.

Larry Barker also retires, the first of what will perhaps be three times. Barker, the team rogue, keeps his teammates loose with good-natured teasing and willingly does anything Boyce asks—except sit on the bench. He was the regular left fielder in 1947 and '48, replacing the injured Howard Mitchell, and he pitched in spots when Boyce asked. He even filled in once at first base.

But Barker is a perfectionist, a craftsman. An expert operator of a hand-fed letter press, his work day holds no slack, no place for a false start or a waiting period. Idle time frustrates him, immobilizes him. And he can't take it on the Townies' bench. He needs to be engaged. He played in four games in 1949: on the mound in a six-inning victory over Callahan's Hard Cider Boys to stretch a win streak to five games, and three times a substitute when Boyce needed a rangy outfielder. He managed two hits in the four games and felt not playing regularly was costing more in frustration than he wanted to spend. To fill Barker's uniform, Boyce chooses Keith Porter, a high schooler who has played no baseball outside the school yard, and sits him on the bench in Barker's spot.

On opening day we travel to Kingfield. Boyce puts Parlin in the lineup at first base, names Cal Tyler the opening-day pitcher, and sits Sade on the bench with Porter and me. Sade is unaccustomed to such treatment, and I expect to hear some discourse on the circumstances that put him here, but he is quiet. Perhaps he's pouting.

Sitting on the bench is customary for me. I'm thankful I can sit on the Townies' bench; I know that Boyce will occasionally put me in for an inning or two. But bench warming for the high school this year frustrated me. I didn't get off. Not once. Coach Carlson sat me there all season without using me in a single inning. I know my weakness—Coach Carlson knows it, too. I can't hit. At least not well enough for Carlson to have any confidence in me. I thought he might teach me a technique or show me a swing that would help me work out of a lifelong hitting slump, but he showed no interest in reworking my crude batting stroke. He knows my skill with a glove, too, but he showed no interest in using my defensive skills in the infield for an inning or so, either. I sat on the bench. The entire season. I watched my teammates make as many as nine errors in a game. It seemed to me that my weak bat could have been tolerated in a lineup of such potent hitters as Al Mitchell, Billy Linscott, Joe Green, and Dick Beedy, who battered our opponents for as many as twelve runs in a game—and still didn't win. Perhaps my glove could have prevented a run or two here and there, but Coach Carlson didn't see it that way. Boyce, however, will find a place to use me. And the Townies bench is comfortable. I'm willing to wait with Sade.

In the second inning, Parlin drives the ball into left field for his first Townies hit, a single that scores Blodgett. He tallies his first run a few minutes later to cap a five-run uprising that puts the Townies in the lead, 5–4. Tyler doesn't hold onto the lead though. The Kingies strike back, and Boyce calls on Sade in the fourth. He puts me in the game in the seventh, and I watch the last three innings from left field. The Townies come back for a one-run victory. Boyce is pleased.

"You surprised us, boss," Al Bergeron says, looking up at Boyce as he removes his spikes. "Putting Tyler on the mound at the start like that. We didn't expect it, 'specially in the opening game."

"Tyler was ready." Boyce answers. "I didn't think Sade was in shape."

Tyler was jittery, too, and an error at third base cost him four runs. "Tyler was anxious," Boyce goes on, "and he had some bad luck. Who knows what mighta happened without the error at third? Maybe Sade woulda sat on the bench all day. As it turned out, Tyler had a chance to start, Parlin hit like we expected, and Sade earned a win in relief. Even Johnny here helped out a couple of innings. The team's goin' home happy—and we're goin' to West Peru next week undefeated."

Tyler starts again at West Peru, and Sade watches from the bench. Tyler is solid from the start. He pitches the first six innings and yields a hit and a run. Sade finishes, and we have our second win, 15–1. "You're a genius," Bergeron says to Boyce after the game.

The streak reaches three before we go to South China—Parlin hits his first home run, and Sade earns a win in an 11–1 romp at Strong— and after two years of losing to the Clippers, we feel ready. Boyce remains confident, too—and hopeful—that someday, somehow, we will outscore the Clippers. Thus, he keeps the sixty-mile drive and the annual hunt for the Erskine Academy baseball field on the schedule.

Sade starts and the game moves along quickly. When the Clippers come to bat in the bottom of the fourth, the score is 1–1. Parlin's first-inning single drove in a run for the Townies; Sade has fanned five and limited the Clippers to two dinky singles and a run-scoring double. But in the bottom of the fourth two unfortunate miscues cost Sade his concentration—his composure, too—and the Clippers bang him around for five runs, and then two more in the fifth. After the first four Clippers reach base in the seventh, including a two-run triple by center fielder Joslyn, Boyce calls on Tyler, who limits the Clippers to two hits the rest of the way. But the game is lost. The winning streak is over. Final score: 13–3.

We come home and win the next two games to run our record to 5–1. Then it's two games with the Farmington Jewels, successors to the defunct Farmington Town Team and Farmington's new entry in the North Franklin League. The Farmington Flyers, benefiting from Cash Clark's Coca Cola sponsorship, have moved up a notch, recruited college players from Rutgers, Seton Hall, Colby, and Farmington State

The Townies at Hippach Field, c. 1950.

Teachers College, and joined the semipro Down East League. The Jewels comprise a mixture of the former Town Team, cast-off former Flyers, and high school stalwarts out to prove their worthiness. Boyce, still seeking a Townies victory over a creditable Farmington team, knows that he will face a formidable challenge in the Jewels. He welcomes it.

But the Townies fail to put up a creditable challenge of their own. The Jewels' Holman Davis, a chunky fastballer who has pitched for the Flyers the past two seasons, starts and wins both games. In the first, a twilight affair at Temple, Sade starts on the mound and trails 9–1 after four innings. Tyler finishes up the five-inning game. The following Wednesday Boyce starts Sade again. He moves Al Mitchell to center field—Hellgren is in the woods with his chain saw—and starts me in right. After three innings the score stands at 2–2. Then the Jewels score in every inning. I am in the game just long enough to strike out twice on Davis' fastballs, and then Boyce, looking for a stronger bat, mercifully puts me on the bench and sends Keith Porter to right field. Sitting in the dugout, Art Mitchell leans over and asks, "How was the fastball?"

"You saw it," I say. "What do you think?"

"I think you didn't see it," he answers and I laugh.

"Why in hell," Mitchell whispers to me, "do we even play these guys?"

"Boyce thinks we can win," I say. "He never talks about losing. Accept it, he says, and go on."

"You mean, it's okay to lose?"

"It's not okay. Boyce doesn't like to lose. He just accepts it, doesn't whine over it—as long as we play our best. You know," I continue, "we might win this one yet. We're only a run behind, and Porter hasn't been up yet. Maybe he'll start a rally."

Porter doesn't start a rally. Al Mitchell and Bob Parlin hit back-to-back doubles in the ninth for two runs to make the game close again. But it's not enough. We go home 8–6 losers, our record at 5–3.

Boyce is not troubled by the loss. "Be at practice next week," he tells us. "We play North Jay next, an' then the Clippers are comin' up here."

We are confident we can outscore the North Jays. Boyce starts Sade, and he baffles them for six innings, striking out eight. The Townies score six in the first inning on six hits, two by Blodgett. Al Bergeron has five hits in the game, scores four runs, and is thrown out at the plate trying to stretch the lead. A rested Cal Tyler comes on in the seventh, and Boyce, with the Townies leading 16–0, and knowing that North Jay hasn't hit one beyond the infield all day, puts Porter in left field, Art Mitchell in center, and me in right. Tyler fans six of the ten batters he faces and gives up one hit. The outfield, thankfully, is quiet. Final score 17–0.

"We're ready for the Clippers, boys," Boyce announces after the game.

How can we possibly be ready for the Clippers, I wonder. The Clippers are a powerful team. They play Randolph, Farmingdale, and Pittston, teams that compete for championships. Last year they upended the Farmington Flyers, who are made up of college players seeking a spot in professional baseball. I suspect they've also taken on the Augusta Millionnaires, who feature all-Americans Harry Agannis and Ted Lepcio. And they've beaten us five straight. Putting Bob Parlin in our lineup can't make that much difference.

Boyce knows what we're thinking and he smiles. "The lesson of baseball," he says, "is to keep on playing. Maybe we'll figure out a way to win," Preparation is important to Boyce: be ready, he said once, for the next at-bat, the next game, the next season.

On Sunday, Boyce surprises us. He starts Tyler. "Cal's earned a chance," he tells us. "I'm gonna give him one."

Tyler has not been beaten in two years. He pitched four victories last year without losing, the fourth a win over Rangeley at the Labor Day festival. This year, he's pitched a six-inning one-hitter against West Peru and a complete-game win against Callahan's Hard Cider Boys. And he's pitched in relief of Sade three times, one of them at South China, and not given up a run.

Boyce is risking a dream. The stunned players take the field and leave a gloomy Sade in the dugout. The bleacher-seat townsfolk cross their fingers as Boyce counsels Tyler on his way to the mound. "You're good enough to win, Cal. Jes' relax." Tyler is a gamer. He hasn't been beaten in a Townies uniform. He has a big-game win behind him, and he's strong—he can throw the ball hard. "I'll throw it up there the best I can," he likely thinks, "and see what happens."

The answer comes at once. The first batter hits Tyler's fastball over Al Mitchell's head in right field. Only Mitchell's strong throw keeps him from scoring. Tyler strikes out the next batter with a curveball, but Mosher can't hang on to the pitch. He chases it, collars it, and throws the batter out at first. The next batter singles, the next doubles, and then Sade is up and throwing to Keith Porter behind the dugout. The home folks sit in quiet hope. Tyler walks a batter, then Harris Plaisted singles in the fourth Clipper run, and Boyce walks to the mound. "Maybe I asked for too much, Cal."

Sade pitches to six more batters before the inning ends. The Clippers lead 7–0. "Now it's our turn to bat," says Al Bergeron. The Townies manage one hit in the inning and then are back on the clay. Not until the third inning do we score—Hellgren triples and comes home on a wild pitch—and our final run comes in the fourth when Hellgren's drive into center brings Bill Mosher around. Final score: 14–2.

The loss at the Temple ball field was the Townies sixth loss to the Clippers in three years. By then Boyce had satisfied his desire, once expressed over lunch at Dowe's Diner, to test the Townies against the South China Clippers. He deemed the sixth consecutive loss convincing evidence of the Clippers' superiority. They would not appear on the Townies' schedule again. Ironically, Boyce's best chance to win, perhaps his only realistic chance, came in the first game, when the Clippers' talents were virtually unknown to the Townies.

Sade pitched a masterful game that first day at Erskine Academy—a one-hitter, twelve strikeouts, and no earned runs—for eight innings. Leading 4–1 in the ninth, the Townies, who had played virtually flawless defense all day, were poised to finish off the game. But in just minutes they were beaten. They never recovered from the shock. Though a Clippers curse was never alleged by Boyce or the townsfolk, after the sixth loss I was convinced that the curse had been present at every Clippers game since the deal in the diner. We had been playing without any chance of winning.

*   *   *

We go to Hippach Field for our third matchup against the Farmington Jewels. The Townies win easily behind Sade's three-hit pitching, his fifth win of the season. Sade decides the game himself in the sixth with a base-clearing clout that skids between outfielders into left center and puts the game out of reach. The Townies' defense is errorless in a demonstration of what Boyce yearned for the previous week. He is smiling again.

We follow the Jewels win with consecutive wins over East Wilton behind Cal Tyler, who improves his season record to 4–1. In the second game, Tyler whiffs fifteen, and Boyce, who also catches the last four innings in an unlikely appearance of his 46-year-old legs, doubles and walks in two trips to the batter's box. "I don't think I could do that every day," he comments. "I just wanted to see some of Tyler's stuff up close."

The victory brings the Townies' record to nine wins and four losses, and Boyce, who looks to even-up the season's four games with the Jewels next week, announces that Sade will be on the mound at Hippach Field. "Mebbe you can throw another three-hitter," he says to Sade.

The Jewels start new phenom Billy Linscott—who shined for the high school team in the spring as the freshman shortstop and hit safely six times in his opening game—on the mound. The Townies manage eleven hits off Linscott, but do nothing with them. The Jewels score a run in each of the first three innings and lead 3–0 after four. In the fifth, a Linscott double followed by three singles and manager Paul Richardson's double increase the margin to 7–0. Parlin ignites a Townies' attempt to rally in the sixth, but it is too little, and we fall farther behind. Tyler comes on in the ninth and fans two of the three batters he faces.

"Tyler's throwin' well. As good as I've seen," Boyce says after the game. "His windup baffles 'em. Can't tell where the ball's comin' from. And his fastball surprises 'em. Seems like neither Tyler nor the batter knows where it's goin'. I'm lookin' forward to what he can do for us next year." Final score: 14–4.

*   *   *

Then it's Labor Day and we're in Kingfield, back where we started in May. It's our fifth festival appearance in five years. It's raining—the weather in Kingfield doesn't change, it's always miserable. The game is called off, and Boyce and Harvey Boynton, the Kingfield manager, reschedule for Thursday at Hippach Field.

On Thursday afternoon, Sade pitches a powerful game: a three-hitter with eleven strikeouts. At the end of eight innings, the Townies lead 5–4 on a three-run rally in the second inning featuring singles by Bob Parlin and substitute shortstop Keith Porter. Porter singles again in the sixth, and Al Mitchell drives him home for the fifth run. In the ninth, Sade walks lead-off hitter Morrell, and two groundouts tie the score 5–5. With two outs, he walks pinch hitter Logo. On the next three pitches, Logo steals second, steals third, then scores on a wild pitch, the final letdown in a frustrating season. "No good comes from bases on balls." Boyce iterates after the game.

At the close of the season, Sade had pitched close to one hundred innings. He seemed fatigued. He had reached the age of thirty. Losing had become easier for him. His passion to win had left him. His 1950 record, accumulated against the best of the Townies' opponents, was a mediocre five wins and five losses, the third consecutive year of losing at least as many as he won. But he didn't show any outward frustration. Either he had learned from Boyce to accept his losses, or he was tired. It was a surprise, however, that he could put up with losing without kicking something.

The 1950 season did bring encouraging developments, however, the most promising being Boyce's responses to the loss of Pa and Larry Barker. Boyce had found new talent and made changes intended to inspire and develop the youngsters. And the changes had worked well. Parlin led the team in hitting, as Boyce had predicted, with a .397

average and three home runs—a Townies record. Al Mitchell, who played regularly in right field, emerged as a bona fide threat at the plate and hit .389 with one homer. Cal Tyler earned four wins on the mound and looked ready to pitch regularly. Apprentice Keith Porter learned the vagaries of playing infield and hit .296. In all, the Townies experienced growth in 1950. But consecutive losses to the Jewels and the ignominious first inning against South China after a sparkling streak at the beginning of the season dampened our spirit during the final weeks.

Boyce increased my playing time, as well, and I played errorless defense in eight games, all but one in the outfield. He praised my performances, but my hitting was still lousy, ugly. I went to bat twelve times without a hit. "It'll come," he said. *Always the future,* I think. *He's always in the future.*

We finished the year with nine wins and six losses.

Chapter Eleven

OGUNQUIT

F|olks who purchased *The Franklin Journal* on March 20, 1951
read on the front page the first report of the 1951 baseball
season: Farmington High School coach Howard Crozier had started
baseball drills in the Community Center gymnasium. *The Journal*, following the popularization of local-area baseball after World War II, reported baseball news on the front page. Twice each week, readers could
see at a glance—on the front page, above the fold—such newsworthy
headlines as "Farmington Townies to Entertain Turner at Hippach
Field Sunday" and "Monahan Homers for 5–3 Win Over ASAS." And
not only did the front page include a local baseball story, The Journal
reported the action in the North Franklin League as well, and results
of games in the Timber League, and doings of the Temple Townies,
Callahan's Hard Cider Boys, and other independent nines. Loggers
came out of the woods on Friday afternoons, bought a *Franklin Journal*
at the local general store, and caught up on the baseball scene without
turning a page. Seldom, except perhaps during the dead of winter, did
local drama force baseball off the front page of *The Franklin Journal*.

I am among the infield candidates being watched by new coach
Crozier, one of thirty candidates that year working out on the gymna-

sium's hardwood floor, listening to Crozier preach baseball philosophy, and speculating on prospects for the coming season. But the *Journal* does not report that I have lost enthusiasm for high-school baseball. I still suffer from the belittling experience of not playing a single inning my sophomore year. I suppose I should put the humiliation behind me, but it gnaws on me that Coach Carlson ignored me. Though I needed experience and learning, he refused to put me in the lineup for even a half-inning. I question now whether I belong on the high school team, and after a few sessions with a rubber ball in the gymnasium, my emotions overtake my reasoning. I go to Crozier. "I'm going to take the year off," I say."

"Are you sure?" he asks.

I'm still angry, distracted by the past. But I'd changed a bit that year, too: begun to reason independently and socialized more—I was the class treasurer, performed in a one-act play, went to the junior prom, all that. I'd improved in schoolwork, too, and made new friends. "I'm sure," I say to Crozier. "I don't want to spend another year on the bench."

John Ayer returned to Farmington High School that year. A senior, now, he had moved down east to Sullivan after his freshman year at Farmington. Ayer is a boy-giant, a foot taller than me and more than a hundred pounds heavier. He played football as a freshman and is now the biggest person in our school. His friends call him Big John. He doesn't meet a strict interpretation of Aunt Marion's criteria for righteousness; she would likely cast him out at first glance, but behind his bulky décor is a gentle person with a goodness that I like. We become friends.

I carouse with Big John on Saturday nights. We sit in his rusty pickup truck and sip from brown bottles and talk. We stand on dance-floor sidelines in Chesterville, Fairfield Center, and Bean's Corner and watch girls in tight sweaters and flowery skirts. The music is loud, and

I feel conspicuous. But good-natured Big John likes me, and I am set loose. Though he exposes me to a somewhat risqué society, he is a mentor—of a sort. He cautions me to polish the rougher edges of my demeanor. "Tone down the language a little," he murmurs to me after hearing a somewhat raucous outpouring of colorful dialectics. "Girls don't like those words."

Big John likes to talk. He talks about the football team, his shot-putting skill, the fishermen in Sullivan. He describes his summer job to me—he was a cook in a resort hotel. He reveals his dreams, says he's going to Arizona next winter to cook in a hotel there. He'll travel the West, drink tequila with pretty girls, and come back to Maine in the summertime. I smile at his stories, and I envy him a bit. To me he is the archetypal youth: an athlete, a worker, a dreamer. He has money and wheels and the art of gab. He's visionary, independent, and his optimism surpasses that of any kid I know. I'm eager to tell stories, too, but I have none to tell, so I grin and sip and listen to Big John. "Maybe," he says to me one night, "maybe I can get you a job next summer working with me in the hotel. You interested? What do you think?"

I have no experience living in the world: I don't know how to talk to people. I don't cross Farmington's town line alone. I've been chaperoned to Fenway Park twice and spent a summer in Kennebunk during World War II under the piercing control of Grandma Watson. I don't know how to buy a bus ticket, or tie a necktie, or order a meal in a restaurant. I don't know how to dress. I don't have a girlfriend, and I don't dare find one. I am a stranger everywhere. Every day I figuratively dress up for freshman initiation. I am two feet tall. And after three years on the bakery truck, I have grown weary of knocking on ladies' doors and smiling all the time. Big John's stories spark a yearning. "I might," I answer. "I'd like that—I think."

A few days later, he sees me in the hallway between classes, and as bells ring and kids chatter, he hands me a piece of paper. "Richie—

Richie's the chef," he says. "Richie sent me this. He says he don't have an assistant for the vegetable cook yet. Sign this contract, and you've got a job."

Contract? Contracts are for business deals and insurance policies, not for a job. I didn't sign a contract with Uncle Lawrence to work on the bakery truck. Why do I need sign a contract to work in a summer hotel? "What's the contract for?" I ask.

"It jes' says you agree to work and he agrees to pay you a figger he wrote in here. Here, you read it."

"You gonna be the vegetable cook? I ask.

"Yeah. I was the assistant last year," he says. "You jes' have to keep me supplied with peeled potatoes and chopped onions and eggplants, things like that. Nothing to it."

I know that if I take the contract home for advice, Aunt Marion will read it, and I'll be back on the bakery truck. So I read it myself—and read it again. I read every word, and if I don't know the meaning of a word, I look for it in a dictionary. When I finish, I judge the contract to read as Big John has described: I work, they pay.

I sign it and take it back to him.

"You gotta job," he exclaims.

I announce my new job at the supper table.

"Summer job? Ogunquit?" Aunt Marion queries.

"Yes. I signed a contract."

"You *what?* A contract! Who read it?" she cries out.

"I did."

"*You* did! I mean who else."

"No one."

She goes on. "Oh my Lord! You should *never* . . . "

"Well, it only said that I agree to work and they agree to pay me. Seemed pretty clear to me."

"Contracts are never clear. How much is the pay?"

"Ninety dollars a month, plus a room to live in, and my meals."

"Harrumph! You can make that much in a lot of places right around here. My Lord, I don't know why you want to go a hundred miles away."

Uncle Lawrence is calm, as he is prone to be when Aunt Marion asserts herself. Later, at the first sign of spring, he asks, "Are you giving up baseball?"

"No," I answer. "But I'm not going to play for the high school this year. I don't think Crozier likes me."

"Baseball's too important to let some stranger persuade you not to play," he tells me. "There's a lot of learning on a baseball field."

"I'd like to play for the Townies," I answer, "until school closes and I leave for Ogunquit."

He doesn't mention my going again; he knows why I'm going. And the Townies demand his attention.

The Townies lose seven players in 1951. First, as expected, Sade retires. He has pitched since the Independence Day home-field opener in 1946, when he struck out ten East Dixfielders in a shutout performance. For four years, he has pitched against the best opposition Boyce can supply, and much of that time he was the only reliable pitcher on the team. He threw hard and played intensely, and his exciting performances attracted spectators from all over the county. Though young by many standards—he had passed his thirtieth birthday in 1950—his run-down arm and abused body, victims of a stressful year as an infantryman on the European battlefield and too much alcohol since, tell him no more baseball. "I'll miss him for sure," Boyce moans when he hears the news.

I admired Sade most for his World War II adventures, but I respected him as a pitcher. He was the best around during the years he threw for the Townies, and whenever I faced him in batting practice, I tiptoed into the batter's box. But I often thought his demeanor too intense for a Sunday afternoon social affair. Underneath the Townies' nonchalance, Sade harbored a competitive vein, an intensity and pride that belied his seeming indifference toward the game. Though he knew mistakes were inevitable, it riled him when his teammates made them. He expected—demanded—too much from us. I suspect that, in his view, to lose a harmless baseball game might lessen the invincibility he had earned in the war.

Sade viewed hitters as the enemy. More than six feet tall, square and strong as an oak, well endowed with the ability to overpower hitters, he relished standing on the mound a few inches higher than home plate and glaring down at the batter while Boyce, behind the plate, squatted and signaled a pitch. His competitive posture commanded the batter's mind, and he knew it. Perhaps he acquired the attitude as a squad leader in an infantry platoon. Or maybe from the discipline required to earn a living cutting logs in the Temple outback. Regardless, Sade *needed* to win, and when he commanded the mound he used all of his weapons, even on the weakest hitters. He intimidated batters, tied them in knots. He threw a fastball likely ninety miles an hour and a breaking pitch that broke sharply down and in on a left-handed batter, jamming him and taking away the fat part of his bat.

Hitters who faced Sade never forgot him. More than fifty years later, Bob Stevens, who played for Callahan's Hard Cider Boys and struck out twice against Sade in one inning in a game at Temple, described what it was like.

"Hit?" Stevens exclaimed laughing. "I never hit against Sade. I batted against him a lot of times—but I never hit. Couldn't. He threw air."

Galen Sayward, who played for various Farmington teams, including the Flyers, and who would eventually be inducted into the Maine Baseball Hall of Fame, managed one hit in thirteen at-bats against Sade, a .077 batting average. Years later he recalled those long-ago days. "Sade? Yeah, I remember the sonavagun. He . . ." Sayward scowled and his voice disappeared into an unpleasant memory.

Sade demanded a strong defense. In a 1949 game at Farmington,

I was in right field with Sade on the mound. With runners on first and second, a liner came over Blodgett's head at me. I eased up and caught it on the bounce rather than attempt a shoestring catch and risk a big inning should the ball get by me and roll to the fence. A run scored on the play. At the close of the inning, Sade stalked into the dugout, threw his glove in a corner, and glared at me, a fourteen-year-old right fielder who had made a decision that cost a single run. "You shoulda caught the gawdamm thing," he scolded. "Stay awake out there, for chrissakes." In another instance, after an infielder had kicked a ground ball around, Sade glared at him, stalked him, and when about thirty feet away, fired the ball at him in an obvious attempt to deliver some kind of harmful message. The fielder snagged the ball, walked toward Sade and tossed it to him. No words were spoken, but Sade's message that he wanted an errorless defense was clear.

But Sade will be missed by us, by Boyce most of all. He was tough and a fierce competitor when the game meant everything, Farmington or South China or Phillips, say. He was the team's center; some called him our franchise player. He worked hard at being the best, drew crowds to big games, and many times rose to his acme performance when the going was toughest.

And not only is Sade gone, but the sociable and smiling Hellgren goes with him, making this the first season since before the war that Boyce has fielded a team without a Finn in the lineup. Al Bergeron leaves, too. The Korean War has broken out, and he is ordered to Naval Air Station Whidbey Island, Washington, as an aviation ordnanceman in support of aircraft participating in the war. Word comes back to Temple that he will miss the entire season. Boyce, pining over Sade's exit, now moans over huge losses in center field and at shortstop, where Hellgren and Bergeron anchor the defense. Then he discovers his third baseman missing.

Freddy Dunn had come to Temple in 1949. No one knew exactly where from. Some said Buckfield; some thought Augusta. And as long as Dunn lived in Temple, he never let on to the townsmen exactly where his roots were. He came with a wife and a number of daughters, perhaps three, and moved into the old and dilapidated C.T. Hodgkins place in the village, a place so run down no respectable native-born Temple kid would dare be seen there. Most folks in our town lived in the same house for years, or generations, and kept it fixed up and livable, at least reasonably so. But those who lived in C.T.'s ramshackle house on the corner next to the bridge seemed to be rootless, just passing through—what Dr. Pierce called in his *History of Temple, Maine* part of a shifting population that lives in one place "just so long as the rent can be evaded." C.T. didn't own the house then. He had sold it to Walter McCoy, a local real estate speculator and self-trained entrepreneur, when the mills went bankrupt, and escaped downstate—a precursor to McCoy's later tenants. Dunn and his family lived there during what turned out to be his two-year career with the Townies. The Dunns were pleasant and made friends in town, and most—Boyce included—thought Freddy would be a permanent piece of the summer entertainment at the baseball field.

But in the middle of the night sometime in winter or early spring 1951, Dunn and his family left town as mysteriously as they had arrived. Up and flew. The rent, as Pierce had put it, could no longer be avoided. Boyce will miss him when it comes time to make out the lineup. And storekeeper Uncle Austin, who permitted Dunn generous credit and even cosigned for a loan at the bank to enable him to "get back on his feet," will miss him, too; and perhaps a couple of townsmen's wives, as the story was told, will also miss him. But no one in Temple knew his whereabouts, and I suspect no one there heard from him again. (Years later, one of Dunn's daughters, Diane, will emerge at Morse High School in Bath, where she is courted by an acquaintance of mine. She eventually drops him, however, and marries Bill Cohen of Brewer, later U.S. Senator and Secretary of Defense.)

Boyce will also confront three additional vacancies in the lineup at the close of the high school term: Al and Art Mitchell will leave for summer jobs at Kingsbury School in West Hartford, Connecticut, and I will fulfill my contract at the Sparhawk Hall summer resort in Ogunquit.

Temple has run out of ballplayers. The schoolyard can't produce enough to refill the holes. Boyce needs pitchers and infielders and out-fielders, and all he has left on the bench is part-time third baseman Keith Porter and a tall stack of empty uniforms. But he refuses to abandon baseball. The townsfolk voted at town meeting for Sunday baseball games, and he is not one to disappoint. He will provide them. He hunts for ballplayers willing to wear *Temple* on their shirtfronts. And he puts together one of the most successful teams in the history of the Townies.

First, he calls Lyle Hall in East Wilton. Hall, a pitcher for the East Wilton team before it folded, has pitched against the Townies twice in the past, giving up nineteen runs in one game and twenty-one in the other. But Boyce isn't looking for Hall to replace Sade. "Can you play infield?" Boyce asks, "I need an infielder." Hall says he's played third base, and Boyce fits him to a uniform. And Ray Leach, an outfielder who played with Hall in East Wilton, also comes along, available whenever juggler Boyce has a vacant spot in the outfield.

Next, Boyce looks for a pitcher. "We gotta have another pitcher," he moans. "Tyler's not strong enough yet to pitch every game. He's gotta have help." He reads in *The Franklin Journal* that high-school senior Paul Heath from New Vineyard is the mainstay of the Greyhounds' pitching staff. "Think Heath would pitch for us?" he asks.

Heath has pitched for the high school the past three years and is leading them to an unusual winning season this year. His classmates have dubbed him a future Red Sox star. He pitched for the American Legion team in Farmington and appeared a few times in the New Vineyard outfield before that. The Farmington Jewels liked him enough to put him on their roster in 1950, and he threw a complete-game victory against Stratton in a North Franklin League game, his only start. Boyce calls him and Heath, a lanky and likeable upbeat boy who wears a grin most of the time, agrees to join the Townies. "With you here, we might not notice Sade's gone," Boyce teases him.

"The batters will," Heath quips. "I went to bat against Sade when I played for New Vineyard. Most miserable day of my life—struck me out three times."

His pitching set for the season, Boyce drives up the Intervale Road and calls on horseshoe-thrower Charlie Bennett and asks him if he can fit a few Sunday afternoon outfield appearances into his busy tournament schedule. Bennett agrees to help when it won't interfere with the defense of his state horseshoe championship, and Boyce is set to start the season.

On opening day West Peru comes to town looking to settle up for the shellacking the Townies handed them last year on their home field. Bob Parlin misses the game, and Boyce, racked by absences all over the field, starts me at first base. "I need you today," he says. Keith Porter is at third, Lyle Hall at shortstop, and the Mitchell brothers in the outfield. Tyler starts on the mound.

I haven't played a baseball game yet this year. I handle eight chances around first base flawlessly and do no harm in four trips to bat, grounding out twice, walking twice, and scoring a run on an Art Mitchell single. It is my only game of the season; my disgraceful batting average remains stuck at .000 for the second consecutive year—a Townies record that likely still stands—though my fielding average over the same two years is 1.000. Obviously, the oft-used baseball descriptor "good-field-no-hit" was created for me. Boyce doesn't delve into such trivia, however. "Well done," he says to me after the game, and I am gone.

Al Mitchell, the high school's most potent hitter that spring, and his brother Art, who played well enough in high school to be named captain of next year's team, are in the Townies lineup on opening day, as well. They produce five hits and five runs in the 8–5 victory over West Peru. Tyler is the winning pitcher. The following week Al triples and singles twice, and Art doubles before they leave for the Kingsbury School. Tyler is the winning pitcher again, 13–4 over West Sumner. Boyce, it seems, is finding the help he needs. By the time Independence Day rolls around, the Townies' record is 6–1.

The fast start belonged to pitchers Cal Tyler and Paul Heath, and the hitting of Bob Parlin. Tyler was outstanding, five wins in his first six starts, and Heath won his Townies debut Independence Day at Strong's Legion Field in relief of Tyler, throwing four innings of shutout baseball while the Townies rallied to win. Parlin led the hitting. He doubled home two runs in the romp over West Sumner in June, and homered, tripled, and singled twice in the Independence Day victory.

Newcomer Lyle Hall, who played flawless defense at third base over the stretch of early games, showed Boyce that he could hit, too, contributing a three-run homer in the celebratory Independence Day game in Strong. Blodgett and Bill Mosher hit well, and the Townies defense averaged less than two misplays per game. They lost at Thomaston—most teams who went there succumbed to the talented outlaws that made up the prison nine—but they came home strong and confident, a remarkable attitude given that they were scheduled to travel to Phillips the following Sunday and face Bill Burnham. But they upended Phillips—and Burnham, too—to begin a streak of wins that would take them to the end of the season.

Next they entertained West Sumner at the Temple ball field in a match that created national publicity. When Boyce arrived at the field for the game, he found blank spaces where home plate and the pitchers rubber had been spiked into the ground in May. "What the hell?" he muttered. "Where did *they* go? Is this a joke—or what?"

It was no joke. The game waited, and the West Sumners dawdled, while Boyce searched for a plate and a pitchers toepiece. Somehow he came up with a dusty set in time to squeeze in a game before darkness came on. Paul Heath shut out the West Sumners over the last five innings and Bob Parlin drove home the winning run in the twelfth with his third double of the afternoon for a 6–5 victory. Starter Tyler gave up three hits.

The missing home plate and pitchers slab were never found. Boyce conducted a national search. News of the missing equipment came to Ogunquit via *The Franklin Journal* and *The Boston Globe*. *The Hartford Courant* and *The New York Times* also reported the story. Boyce appealed to the guilty party to return the plate and rubber to the Townies' dugout. "The unkind act will simply be recorded as an error," *The Franklin Journal* quoted him.

Following a midweek twilight game at West Peru, a team calling itself the Farmington Old-timers, comprising such displaced former Farmington Flyers as Vint Davis, Stoogie Whittier, Stan Robash, and Guadacanal-veteran Eddie Callahan, came to Temple. Callahan started on the mound for the Old-timers, gave up six runs in the second inning and then gave way to fastballer Vint Davis. The Townies coasted to victory, 13–7 on Cal Tyler's four singles and Parlin's homer.

Tyler struck out ten for his seventh win. In Ogunquit, I kept a close eye on *The Franklin Journal*'s front

l. to r.: Art Mitchell, Bruce Mosher, Larry Barker, and Al Mitchell, c. 1951. (Temple Historical Society)

page. The Townies were accomplishing the unthinkable.

The sixth win of the streak came against Kingfield at the Temple ball field. The *Journal* called it a thriller. The Townies led 3–0 in the ninth when the Kingies rallied for three runs to tie the score. But in the bottom of the ninth, the Townies' Charlie Bennett singled, stole second, and scored on Ray Leach's long double to left field. Paul Heath, who relieved Tyler and snuffed out the Kingfield rally in the ninth, was the winning pitcher, running his season record to 5–1.

After a Labor Day rainout, the Townies go to Kingfield for the final game of the season. A large crowd of Temple folks follow. The players take their families and girlfriends. Some take their wives. Aunt Marion comes. The high schoolers and kids from the village school yard are there. Townsfolk out on a Sunday drive loop by Kingfield. They come to help extend the streak. Home from Ogunquit, I go to watch. "You probably won't play this one," Boyce tells me before we leave home. "The streak belongs to the fellas that been playin' it."

Tyler starts and throws a see-saw game. The lead changes hands four times, and after six innings, the Townies trail, 7–5. Boyce brings in Paul Heath for the final innings. In the top of the eighth, the Townies rally for three runs to go ahead. The home folks yell and honk and boost up the charging Townies. In the top of the ninth, the Townies' hitters scramble for two more and turn a three-run lead over to Heath. Heath shuts the Kingies down in the bottom of the ninth for the Townies seventh consecutive victory, challenging the 1947 streak of nine straight. "We'll jes' have to keep it goin' next year," Boyce tells his team. And he praises them. "You played under tough circumstances," he says. "So many players comin' and goin'. But you never gave in." I want to be on the receiving side of his comments, but while the talented Townies were scratching out their best record in history, fourteen wins and three losses, I was engaged in a full-time job—seven days a week.

*   *   *

It is June 1951. Aunt Marion and Uncle Lawrence have driven me
here to Sparhawk Hall in Ogunquit in her Chevy. In the bunkhouse, I
toss my suitcase on a bed amid a group of gossiping college students
from Harvard and Northeastern and introduce myself. "I work in the
kitchen," I say. Curious then, I walk five minutes down Shore Road to
view the confines of the summer job I have contracted for—Sparhawk
Hall and the Sparhawk kitchen.

Sparhawk Hall sits on a ledgy bluff overlooking the Ogunquit
River on the outskirts of the village. It is a three-story, brown-shingled,
wooden assemblage of eaves, gables, mansards, porticos, and stoas en-
closing nearly two hundred rooms. It commands the coastline.
Ogunquit beach stretches east toward the sunrise. To the west,
Marginal Way, a fashionable walking path, meanders along a one-mile
headland above the Atlantic Ocean. The resort entertains moneyed
summer folks from away, folks from suburban America who frolick
here in white sport coats, long dresses, and gaudy hats until Labor Day.
They gambol on the beach, stroll on Marginal Way, and shop in dainty
curio shops and boutiques in Ogunquit village. In the evenings, they
don floor-length dresses and coats and ties for dinner in the Sparhawk
dining room and troupe weekly to first-night productions at the summer playhouse out on Highway 1.

I peel potatoes in the kitchen—for two hundred sixty guests. I cut
asparagus, snip green beans, slice carrots, and tip red beets. I peel
Spanish onions under a cold-water faucet and dunk freshly-peeled eggplants into a cold-water bath, all for the two hundred sixty guests.
When Big John Ayer, the vegetable cook and my drinking pal, wants
more, I cut or snip or slice or peel until he stops me. He teaches me
how to use the pressure steamers, then extends his instructions to filling serving bowls for the pretty waitresses at the counter. I help him
prepare on-order hot breakfasts, too, and by midsummer I can flip a

frying egg three feet into the air and land it back in the frying pan—upright.

At five o'clock each morning, the kitchen crew—Big John, second-cook Big Al, a baker whose name I forget and who carried a Shakespearean classic to read during quiet moments, and me—show up in the kitchen to start the day. When we arrive, chef Richard Schoonmaker—folks who know him well enough can call him Richie—who lives on Florida's Ormond Beach in the winter, comes out of his office, where he has been for an hour, and hands each of us the day's menu. I first notice the house count—never below two hundred fifty—penciled onto the margin, and then I read the lunch and dinner vegetable selections: two steamed vegetables, at least two variations of potato, and always steamed rice. The first stint lasts through lunch. Shortly after one o'clock, the waitresses stop coming to the counter with empty serving bowls, and we take an afternoon break.

During the break, a few of us swim across the river to the beach and soak up sun on the sand, splash in the surf, or breaststroke out to deeper water and fight the undertow back to the beach. The waitresses and busboys split into small groups, separated either by school or gender or romantic interest, and compete to tell earthy back-home gossip. Big Al and Big John don't gambol on the beach, nor does Shakespeare. I sit alone on the edge of the dining-room crowd and listen to the gossip. Occasionally John Brine or Moe Mahoney, Harvard boys who have spent other summers at Sparhawk, engage me in a baseball conversation, but I can see they're just humoring me, a misplaced bumpkin right off the bus from Dogpatch. I connect with the experience, but I don't submit to pampering.

At four o'clock I traipse back to the kitchen for the dinner meal, and at eight-thirty to the bunkhouse for the night. "Going out tonight?" folks ask.

"No," I answer. Seldom do I go out after work.

Big John doesn't fool with the beach at all. A veteran of a previous

Sparhawk summer, he looks old enough to visit even the most raucous roadhouse. He and Big Al, I envision, find entertainment similar to what Big John and I found when we weaved to Bean's Corner and back in his rusty pickup last winter and arrived home late enough to sleep until nearly noon on Sunday. But Sunday at Sparhawk is just another workday, and whenever Big John is late to the kitchen on Sunday mornings, I look after his hot breakfast orders: fried eggs and bacon, boiled oatmeal, or perhaps an omelet, and pass them to the pretty wait-resses at the counter. The waitresses and I talk. And once when Big John is absent, one comes to the counter smiling, "This is for you," she says, handing me a dollar bill. "The lady said to tell you the raisin oat-meal is superb."

One Sunday in early July, Big John stumbles into the kitchen around seven o'clock, half asleep and suffering from a hangover. Schoonmaker calls him into his office. I envision their conversation going something like this:

Schoonmaker: "You're late again, John."

Big John: "Sorry, boss. I'll do better."

Schoonmaker: "You're fired, John. You can leave now. Pick up your check at the front desk."

Big John comes to see me at the potato peeler on his way out. "I'm going home," he says.

I sadden a bit. I'll miss Big John. "Thanks for helping me out," I whisper. "I'll see you when I get home." But I won't see him at home, nor will I see him again. I suspect he did not go back to Farmington, nor did he follow the resort-hotel trail to Florida and Arizona and back to Maine. (Years later, a field engineer working for me at the Highway Department will bring a message to my office in Augusta from a tran-sit-mix truck driver delivering concrete to a bridge construction site in Eastern Maine. "Greetings from John Ayer," it reads.)

Schoonmaker comes to the potato peeler after Ayer leaves. "Think ya'll can do the job?" he drawls.

I ponder his question: What if I can't? What if I fail, too? What if he should tell me to pick up my check at the front desk? I couldn't stand the shame of being fired. "I think I can, Mr. Schoonmaker," I answer.

"That's good," he says. "Ya'll got the job."

But there is no one to carry on my peeling chore, and Schoonmaker expects me to carry both ends of the mission, which includes the hot-breakfast work as well. With so much to do, I won't be able to fill the serving bowls on time, and the pretty waitresses will get upset. I'll surely be fired then. "Do I get paid for both jobs?" I ask Schoonmaker.

"I can't do that," he answers, "but I can pay ya'll for the cook's job. It'll be a nice raise for ya," he says in his best drippy voice.

Money was not the issue. I didn't actually get any money at Sparhawk Hall. It was kept in what they called a drawing account, for me as well as for the others, and I could request a spot of cash to spend whenever my billfold needed it. But I didn't draw any money all summer. Didn't need to. My contract called for payment of the balance in my account at the end of the summer, and I looked forward to showing off a big check to doubter Aunt Marion. So, unbeknown to Schoonmaker, I was happy with more money, even though I would work two jobs to get it.

Mindful that my contract requires that I work and he pay, I look up at Schoonmaker standing there in his white frock and creased pants and say, "But I gotta keep peeling these potatoes and all the other work I been doing, too. That's two jobs."

He doesn't yield. But he surprises me. "I'll help," he drawls. "I'll peel the potatoes for ya." And for the remainder of the summer, Chef Schoonmaker is my potato peeler.

I work seventy-one straight days, finishing on Labor Day when the house-count drops to nil. Aunt Marion comes alone in the Chevy, a rainy day. "The Townies are supposed to play today," she says.

Schoonmaker sees me off. "You did a fine job for me, John. I'll be in touch with ya'll in the winter. Like to have you back in the kitchen next summer. Think about it."

"I got my summer's pay today," I tell Aunt Marion on the way home. "Three hundred and nine dollars."

"Is that all?" She answers. "You could have made that much at home."

"I don't think so," I retort. "Besides, I still have it all—and a one-dollar tip."

"Are you ready for school tomorrow?" she asks.

Chapter Twelve

A MENTOR

Aunt Marion says we will go to Temple for Thanksgiving dinner, to Aunt Viola's. "I'm going to Ma's," I tell her, "with Pa."

She is upset, and tries to hide it, but it shows in her eyes. Her chin juts out just a bit. "That's too bad," she says. "Viola will be disappointed."

"I'll speak to her," I answer. "I didn't know." Aunt Marion dislikes Ma, disliked her when she lived in Temple, and dislikes her now. She never mentions Ma at all, hasn't since I moved here. Any discussion with me of Ma, or her life in Temple with Pa before their divorce, is not on Aunt Marion's list of things to talk about. And I sense it won't be. She doesn't tell me why and I don't ask. I don't talk to her about Ma.

I don't spend time with my father. He lives at his brother's place in town and has his own life. He works some of the time; other times he just disappears. He looks me up occasionally and we go to Temple to fish, or to Hippach Field for a Flyers' game, or perhaps, on a holiday, to Kennebunk to see Ma and my sisters. I am a victim of outside forces pushing me first one way, then another. My life is not shaped. My days are not in rhythm. I eat and go to school and work and play, but my thoughts are not centered. I feel stretched between Pa's presence and Aunt Marion's care. They do not ever come together—and certainly won't at Aunt Viola's Thanksgiving dinner. I tell Aunt Viola I am going to Ma's. She smiles and excuses me and wishes me a Happy Thanksgiving.

The winter is cold, teeth-chattering cold. One Saturday Uncle Lawrence knocks on my bedroom door at five a.m. I am sick, congested, a cold in my chest. It is dark, below zero, and I can hear the wind howling outside the bedroom window. We must walk uptown to retrieve the van from a heated garage. I can't bring myself to tell him I'm sick, so I get up and dress to go: sweater, parka, hood, and boots. We walk in the street between rows of shadowy Queen Annes, the snow crunching underfoot. I bend into the fierce wind, crouch to drive off the cold. It's a half-mile, and I resist every step. At the garage he fumbles for the door key. The van starts on the first turn. He points it toward Dryden. I trudge to the first farmhouse door as the sun comes up. In evening darkness I knock on the last.

I try out for the high school basketball team again. I'm a senior and it's my time to be on the team. When Coach Crozier announces the final cut, I have made the varsity—at guard. Crozier sends me into the Madison game, the second game of the year, in the fourth quarter. I'm on the floor for two minutes and score four points—an average of two points per minute played, likely still a Farmington High School all-time career scoring record. We win by forty-two. But my effort is not enough to preserve a spot on the team. Classmates Ted Bradley and Clare Greenlaw are also cut. "Crozier's getting rid of non-starting seniors," Greenlaw tells us. "Gonna give the underclassmen playing time." We've been downgraded to a seat in the bleachers.

At the supper table, Uncle Lawrence reacts with disgust. "We'll see about that," he grunts, and goes next door to talk to Dave Smith. He returns wearing a grin. "Dave doesn't like it neither. He'll help us. He's downright mad. Says we can put together a team of seniors that can play as well as that Crozier bunch any day of the week, maybe better."

Smith was a straightaway man, a bit chesty, weathered face, with a balding forehead. He greeted me the day we moved to Lake Avenue in 1948, squeezed my hand, and said, "My name's Dave Smith. What's yours?"

"John," I murmured.

"Squeeze a little harder, Son," he added and thrust his hand at Uncle Lawrence.

Some called him gruff. He spoke with assertiveness and animation, like a man more accustomed to doing than saying, and often shook the crooked little finger on his left hand for emphasis. But his gruffness was a facade, his frankness sincere. He was full of goodness. He became a friend, a mentor, a counselor. He embraced me, encouraged me, cared about me. "Join up," he said many times. "Don't be left out."

I went with Smith and his son, Allan, to Flyers' games in the summer at Hippach Field and for an ice cream afterward. On hot days when they went for a swim after work, I went along, too. He endured baseballs careening up against his granite steps during my evening solo practice sessions. He found space for me in his Dodge when he traveled to Allan's high school basketball games. He tagged me with a nickname, told me silly jokes, urged me to relax and smile. He loaned me Allan's baseball glove, and I used it for years.

Once he asked me to ride out to the baseball field in Temple with him. Boyce was holding practice there, and Smith had agreed to measure the distances along the left and right field foul lines to the woods. He set his surveyor's transit at home plate and asked me to hold a 12-foot leveling rod at the edge of the woods. "Hold it upright," he said. "I'll measure the distance." I followed his instructions, but I was puzzled. I saw no measuring tape, no visible means of determining distance. "How did you do that?" I asked when I came in.

He said something about lines inside the eyepiece and let me look through it. "It's not a secret," he said. "But you have to study it and learn the theory before you can understand it." He made me curious.

I gave little thought those days to what I would do after high school. From time to time Aunt Marion would mention college, but her remarks were more conclusive than exploratory. "Of course, you're going to college," she'd say, but the discussion ended there. The high school's guidance counselor, whose job it was to open my eyes to a future I could succeed at, tried to cull some talents or skills out of the customary aptitude testing, but he told me that the results showed nothing illuminating or calling. "You seem to have a leaning toward math," he said. "Perhaps you could learn bookkeeping." But I felt no sense of direction. I needed a vision or a dream.

Then Smith asked for help again—washing his car. I grabbed the hose. "Don't hose it," he told me. "Wait." He washed his Dodge from the bottom up with soapy water and a wet sponge. "If the car's wet, I can't tell where I haven't sponged," he explained. "This way I don't miss anything." I followed him with the hose while he loosened dust and grime—and queried me. "What about after high school?" he asked. "Any ideas yet? College? Work? Any plans at all?"

"No," I stammered. "Aunt Marion expects me to go to college—somewhere. But she was a teacher, and I don't want to teach. Mr. Reed at the high school said I could learn bookkeeping, but I don't have any interest in bookkeeping. I just don't know." I paused a moment while he sponged the top of the car. "How am I supposed to know what I want to do anyway?"

Smith often planted a thought in my mind, a problem I would have to solve or a joke I would have to figure out. He thought about my question a few moments, and I prepared to listen for words I could use. Then he described his own work to me—engineering: surveying, designing, managing construction. He was passionate about his job, working with instruments, measuring and computing, scrutinizing, analyzing, reasoning, and working outdoors. "It will be your decision, Son," he said while I rinsed the last of the car. "Think about it. You can do anything you want to do, be anything you want to be, but you'll have to work for it—and you'll have to do the work yourself." I wasn't sure I could be anything I wanted to be. But what he said about work stuck with me.

A few days later he found me lolling in Magoni's soda shop on Broadway, sipping a lemon coke and listening to whomever. "I've got a little measuring job up on Strong Road," he said, "and I'm working alone. Can you give me a hand?"

On the way he briefed me. "A new house has been built up there. I need to show it on my plans. We need to find points in the road and measure from them to the house."

He parked beside the road, fetched a roll of blueprints from the trunk, and spread them on the hood. He turned the pages until he found what he wanted. "Right here," he said, pointing at the plans. "We're parked right here by this tree. The house is over there, 'cross the road." I noticed the house was new. "We need to find two nails," Smith said, walking into the road. We measured to the corners of the house from each nail, and then the dimensions of the house. He showed me the blank space on the plan where he would plot the house, then we were done.

He invited me to visit his office in Augusta. "If your civics class takes a field trip to the legislature, come see me. I work right next door to the capitol." Later, when I made that trip, I found him in an old wooden building, working at a drafting table in a huge room at the top of a stairway. Fluorescent lights cast a blue tint into cigarette-smoke haze drifting over a dozen or more tables. At each table, men in white shirts and neckties worked over rolls, strips, and single large sheets of paper.

Smith squeezed my hand and pointed to his drawings. "We're designing new highways. You're in the highway design office," he said. "We're putting together plans for road-building projects this summer." He turned a few pages. The sheet with the house was there, and he explained how he transferred the measurements in Strong to the plans in Augusta. He leafed through several other pages of drawings: earth cuts and fills, drainage culverts, roadway dimensions. He showed me his tools: flat plastic triangles, measuring scale, hand-cranked calculator, and drawing instruments. He introduced me to other engineers working on their own plans, and they showed me features of their designs as well. I spent fifteen minutes there. When he finished, I knew more about civil engineering than any other kid in the high school.

Boyce and Smith invite eight high school seniors—Art Mitchell, Vern Hodgkins, Ted Bradley, Don Turner, Clare Greenlaw, Alan Smith, Art Lambert and me—to a meeting in the barn at Lake Avenue. It's a full three-bay barn, a hayloft on either side and a center aisle where hay, in the distant past, was lifted to the lofts. The center aisle allows for throwing a basketball up to a hoop hung on a beam. We can practice our shooting eyes here, foul shots, set shots, hook shots. "Where we going to play," someone asks.

Smith tells us they'll arrange games in nearby towns, take us there, and coach us. "But you'll have to practice on your own," Boyce says. "Be in shape, sharpen your shooting eye."

The barn defines our world. I am there every afternoon. Art Mitchell is there; Don Turner walks there from around the corner. Bradley comes. At times Pa and Uncle Lawrence come to throw up foul shots and watch. We play one-on-one, two-on-two, and toss up long shots from the driveway outside the sliding barn door. We create simple plays and use the side-beams under the lofts to carom the ball to a teammate. We drill in foul shooting and backhanded layups. We dribble behind our backs, and Greenlaw perfects his hook shot.

Globetrotters they call us. We barnstorm all winter, much like the Townies or Mack's All Stars do in the summer. We travel upriver to North Anson and downriver to North Jay. We go to North New Portland and East Wilton, to Strong, and to the YMCA tournament in Auburn. We play in Grange halls, dance halls, and old gymnasiums. At North New Portland, Greenlaw's arcing hook shot caroms off the ceiling back to the floor, and the referees rule the ball still in play. We win most of our games, and Boyce and Smith, who are having as much fun boasting about our exploits as we are on the floor, applaud us.

The Globetrotters accrue local fame as well. Basketball fans in Farmington notice us, and though the high school team is putting together a winning record and will close out the season claiming the Franklin County championship, a few wonder why some of us are not playing with Crozier's gang. After the county tournament, Boyce and Smith arrange with local sports promoter Jack Callahan to show off the Globetrotters, who had edged his old timers in an earlier game. "Bring the Cider Boys to the Community Center for another matchup with our Globetrotters," Boyce asks Callahan. *The Franklin Journal* reports that the return contest between the Globetrotters and the basketball version of the Cider Boys is scheduled as the preliminary game of a benefit doubleheader at the Community Center. We practice in the barn every day. There will be a large crowd at the game, we speculate, and we want to play well, look polished against the older and rougher Hard Cider Boys.

But the much-touted Hard Cider Boys are a ruse. Callahan has no intention of exposing his celebrated baseballers to the threat of humiliation on the basketball floor in front of a crowd. Instead, he beguiles the high school varsity into settling the controversy with the Globetrotters. On Tuesday night, the varsity players show up at the Community Center. They come with their high scorers, defensive whizzes, and the skills Coach Crozier has painstakingly taught them. They come, of course, without Crozier, who folks say is busy planning

Player stats from The Franklin Journal, *March 1952.*

Globetrotters (42)	G	Fg	Pts
J. Hodgkins, lf	2	0	4
Turner, lf	4	0	8
V. Hodgkins, rf	1	0	2
Bradley, rf	0	0	0
Greenlaw, c	7	1	15
Lambert, lg	1	0	2
Smith, rg	1	1	3
Mitchell, rg	4	0	8
Totals	20	2	42
Junior Aces (29)	**G**	**Fg**	**Pts**
Magno, lf	2	0	4
Tyler, rf	1	0	2
Waldon, rf	1	0	2
Huart, c	1	0	2
Diehl, lg	4	0	8
McCormack, rg	3	1	7
Roux, rg	2	0	4
Totals	14	1	29
Globetrotters	13	22	36	42
Junior Aces	10	12	16	29

Referees, Green and J. Linscott. Time, 4-8's.

for the baseball season, and without the two starting seniors, who choose not to play against their class-mates.

At courtside before the tip-off, Boyce leans into our circle, "Well, boys," he says, "here's what you've been waiting for."

Greenlaw's hook shot is accurate. Bradley scores from the corners. Mitchell smothers the Greyhound scorers along the baseline. I and the others plug their access to the basket from outside and toss in a few points at the other end as well. When the fracas is over, we have outscored them 42–29. Bradley sums it up. "We made our point," he puns.

I apply for admission into the civil engineering curriculum at the University of Maine. Dave Smith, who comes to the parlor many evenings and talks the language of road building with Boyce— macadam surfaces, asphalt emulsions, superelevations, watersheds— provides the inspiration. Later a small envelope arrives in the mail from the university. "It is a pleasure to send you your certificate of admission

My scholarship announcement,
The Franklin Journal *April 1952.*

to the freshman class," the letter reads. I am in.

I don't have any money. I don't have a job. Aunt Marion has not revealed a plan to me, but I will have to rely on her if I can't come up with enough money to pay the bills at the university. A scholarship from the university will pay my tuition. A summer job, if I can find one, will go a ways toward paying the rest of my bills: dormitory, dining room, football games, and all that. I need a summer job. The bakery van is out. No new money there.

Schoonmaker writes and offers me the cooking job at Sparhawk Hall, but I turn him down. Cooking is not for me. "I'm taking a college education in civil engineering," I write him. Then Dave Smith brings word to Lake Avenue that the highway department needs engineering students to fill summer jobs. I write to Mr. Ernest Merrill in Augusta, who Smith says is head of the highway department. "I'm taking engineering at the university," I write. "I need a summer job."

179

*   *   *

Deep snow falls on Farmington that winter. In February the streets plug under a forty-inch blizzard. Lake Avenue folks wallow in the middle of High Street uptown to fetch a newspaper and cigarettes at Barton's and a quart of milk at the A&P. Sportswriter Cliff Gove writes in his weekly *Franklin Journal* column that Hippach Field is buried under tons of snow and the baseball season will be a long time coming. When April arrives, Hippach Field is still blanketed. But high school coach Crozier is undaunted. He issues the call for baseball candidates and extends the indoor workouts indefinitely. "The snow will melt," he tells us. "We'll wait inside."

"I'm coming out for the team," I tell Crozier. "I'll do the best I can." He tells Gove that he expects me to help the team. "He's baseball wise," Crozier comments. Journal sportswriter Stew Goodwin is a touch wordier. "The 1952 team," he writes, "will include Hodgkins, a senior, fancy fielder, and left-handed swinger, at the initial sack."

Art Tyler reports to Crozier, too. I sense Tyler, a pitcher like his older brother Cal, is looking to impress Townies' manager Boyce enough to earn a spot on the Townies' staff. Art Tyler is a quiet boy, soft spoken and polite, perhaps a tad shy. He has grown up in the shadow of his well-known brother who replaced Sade as the Townies' pitching ace. But Art is determined to succeed as well. Unlike Cal, who focuses exclusively on baseball, Art spreads his athletic skills around. He plays tackle for the high school football Greyhounds and substitutes at guard for the varsity basketball team. He may be the best all-round Temple athlete ever. He earns a spot on Crozier's pitching staff.

The season opens at Phillips on April 29. Art Tyler is on the bench, and senior George Pillsbury is on the mound. It is a frigid day; the diamond is wet. A sharp wind blows off snowy Saddleback Mountain and rattles our uniforms, conditions similar to what we customarily find in Rangeley or Kingfield, and more suited to rugby or

The Farmington High School baseball team, the Greyhounds, and Coach Howard Crozier (l.), 1952.

football than baseball. But we warm our bats on mediocre Phillips pitching and rout them, 17–4. We lose the Sandy-Andy League opener, however, 3–1 at Wilton and our home-field opener to Jay, 8–7, when, in the bottom of the ninth after the Jay pitcher plunks Bernie Rackliffe in the ribs with a fastball and walks Bill Diehl and Gearry Ranger, I strike out on fastballs to end the game. The word is out. My weakness is a pitch right down the middle of the plate—or anywhere else for that matter.

Coach Crozier reacts. He drops me from second to eighth in the batting order. "He'll strike out less there," he probably thinks.

We are 0–2 and in the Sandy-Andy League cellar. Livermore Falls comes to Hippach Field for what many folks will later recall is the most unforgettable game in Greyhound baseball history. Crozier surprises everyone and starts junior Art Tyler on the mound—perhaps to shake Pillsbury up a bit. With the ball in his hand, Tyler is a paradigm of perpetual motion. He paces and fiddles and kicks the pitching rubber. He tugs on his cap and tightens his shoelaces and massages the ball. But he pitches a masterful game, nine strikeouts, five Falls' hits, no runs. In the bottom of the eleventh inning, with the score 0–0, we load the bases on a Ross McCormick double and walks to right fielder George Pillsbury and team captain Art Mitchell. Tyler comes to bat, pulls his cap down tight, hitches up his pants, and squeezes McCormick home with a perfect bunt along the first-base line. Game over.

Tyler's masterpiece is our only league victory. We lose the remaining three games of an uneventful season and stay where we started: last in the Sandy-Andy League. We close out my fractured high school career under the lights at Hippach Field, losing to New Hampshire's Faye High School, 11–5. My final high school season is over. I earn a letter and an invitation to the Townies' workouts. Boyce says he is working on a surprise for us.

Chapter Thirteen

MURDER AT THE MAINE STATE PRISON

S pring 1952, and the townsfolk are excited. Never before have they been as keyed up. The Townies are strong and full of success. Their 14–3 win-loss record during the turbulent '51 season—their best ever—left a seven-game winning streak on the line. Townsfolk are eager to see it extended. And when spring baseball workouts begin, they learn that Boyce has decided to move the Townies up a level, to put us into a league, and to play for a championship.

Since the end of World War II, when Boyce reinvigorated the town team and called it the Townies, they have played independent, non-league baseball. Independent ball has worked well for the sociable and freewheeling Townies, and Boyce, though he occasionally arranged a contest against a league team with an open date on its schedule, had no interest in playing league baseball. He favored independent teams, teams who year after year likewise played sociable ball—until 1952. This year the Townies are forced to give up independent baseball. Boyce, who manages one of only two independent teams still playing in the area—the other Callahan's Hard Cider Boys—can't come up with a schedule of games against independent teams. His former opponents have either abandoned baseball or joined a league.

Abandoning baseball does not occur to Boyce. Small-town baseball teams are now playing for league titles, state playoffs, and national tournaments. Independent teams are disappearing. Organized amateur baseball is opening outward: the Farmington Flyers compete in the new semipro Down East League; Wilton, Dixfield, and Rumford play in the Timber Loop; Strong, Phillips, and Kingfield, and the new Farmington Jewels compete in the North Franklin League; North Jay has gone a ways south to play in the Lakes Region League. The Townies want a league. We are a team without a schedule.

Boyce puts us in the Lakes Region League. Organized in 1949, the Lakes Region League comprises teams from Kennebec, Androscoggin, and Franklin Counties. Farmingdale, Pittston, Monmouth, Litchfield, Tri-corner, Wayne, North Jay, and now the Townies play in the Lakes Region League. Except for North Jay, they will be new faces for us. "It'll be a change," Boyce tells us at the first spring workout behind the high school in Farmington, "but we'll hold our own against these teams." *Sure*, I think, *just like we did against South China*.

He must have read my mind. "These teams don't stand up well against the likes of South China, either," he continues. "And we'll be all right here. We've got reliable pitchin' now, what with Tyler and Heath—and Collis Ames has pitched three years of high school ball. He may come over to pitch for us, too."

"But I heard that Monmouth is a powerhouse. Blow your jock right off," someone says.

Ignoring the remark about Monmouth, Boyce tells us he's been named to the board of directors for the Yankee Amateur Baseball Congress, the overseer of amateur baseball in Maine and an affiliate of the American Baseball Congress. "An' we'll be playin' for the championships," he goes on. "The Lakes Region League champion qualifies for the Yankee Amateur Baseball Congress state tournament—and the national championship, too. Who knows? We'll see what we can do."

But Boyce does not have a full team. Al Mitchell has left for the

Kingston School again, and Art Mitchell will follow, leaving a blank spot in the outfield. *He could fill it with me,* I think. *I could handle right field for sure. At least he could try me against the Cider Boys. See what I can do. I'm having a good year with the glove for the high school.* But Larry Barker comes out of retirement to play left field, and Bruce Mosher will platoon with him. Dick Blodgett decides to play second base for one more year, and Al Bergeron comes home from the Korean War to play shortstop.

Then, at the last moment, Boyce moves Bergeron to center field. "He will help us in center," Boyce remarks. "He's rangy, can see well enough to track the flight of the ball, and he throws well." Boyce likes the versatile Bergeron. He also likes, I notice, having his best defensive players in the middle of the field—catcher, pitcher, shortstop, second base, and center field—and the good hitters, usually weaker defensively, on the edges. He puts me at shortstop.

He also recruits Roger Parlin, who has caught three years for the high school and will catch one more. Parlin will back up Bill Mosher behind the plate and substitute in the outfield.

The Korean War claimed Roger Parlin out of high school after his junior year. He and two classmates, Collis Ames and Bernard Davis, who will also eventually join the Townies, trained with the U.S. Marine Reserve in Augusta. In the summer of 1950, shortly after the outbreak of the war, their unit, an anti-aircraft artillery battalion, was called to active duty and shipped to South Korea as part of the First Provisional Marine Brigade, and arrived in Pusan early in August. They were immediately thrust into action along the Pusan Perimeter, a shrinking defensive line around Pusan, while General MacArthur organized the Inchon landings. Asked the role of his battalion on the Perimeter, Parlin answered, "We threw 90-mm shrapnel shells into the sky over South Korea as fast as we could." Reservists Parlin, Davis, and Ames came home in 1952 in time for the summer baseball season. Parlin, brother of Townies' first baseman Bob Parlin, and Ames, a high school right-hander before he left for Korea, joined the Townies in time for the opening game.

Paul Heath opens our season on the mound in an exhibition game with Callahan's Hard Cider Boys. We beat them handily, our eighth consecutive win going back to last season. But Boyce isn't satisfied. "I need a shortstop," he moans. "Johnny doesn't have the arm yet to play shortstop, and neither does Blodgett."

The following week, a stranger walks into our practice session behind the high school. He carries a glove and baseball shoes and is chewing on a spear of grass he probably found sprouting up in the neighborhood between the sidewalk and the street. "My name's Danforth," he tells Boyce, "an' I'm looking for a chance to play baseball."

"What position you play?" Boyce asks.

Ernie Danforth, until the end of the '51 season, played shortstop for Litchfield in the Lakes Region League. But he owns a road grader, and when a grader-job opened up with the State Highway Department in Farmington, he moved. Out for a walk after supper, he discovered the Townies practicing in his new neighborhood and went home for his glove and spikes. "I'm a shortstop, never played any other position," he tells Boyce, "but I'm willing to try anything for the chance to play."

Boyce smiles. "Welcome to the Townies," he answers. "I think I can use you," his shortstop problem now just a memory.

Boyce intensifies preparations for Memorial Day and the opening of the Lakes Region League. He drills us in fundamentals every night that week, and is elated when he sees Danforth's considerable skill at shortstop. "Looks like we're coming together at last," he announces on Friday. "We play a tune-up with the state prison nine Sunday."

"Where we playing?" someone asks and then laughs.

"We'll play 'em down there, boys—they won't be comin' here."

Most small-town baseballers in Maine know the prison team well. Out of three hundred-some inmates, they field a superb nine and seldom lose to any adventurous outsiders that go there. Boyce answered an advertisement in *The Lewiston Daily Sun* the previous year, and while I was in Ogunquit, he took the team there, losing 7–3. Treated well and able to bring all his players back home, he joked, he's giving the prisoners another try, an unconventional sort of away-and-away series.

On Sunday morning I ride to Thomaston in Boyce's car. On the drive to the coast, players compete for the funniest joke: "They have it too easy," someone says, "playing at home all the time."

"I should think they would be good. They practice all day—every day."

"Is it legal to steal second base down there?"

"Or home plate?"

Boyce never has found the missing Townies' home plate. "Be on the watch for our plate, boys. Maybe they'll be usin' it."

"Maybe Gallagher stole it and took it there with him."

"Is Gallagher still there?" comes a voice from the back seat.

"Who's Gallagher?" I ask.

Boyce tells the story. In 1936 Robert Croswell inherited the family general store in Farmington Falls, the fourth generation Croswell to operate what was in 1816 named The Old Country Store but later called simply "Croswell's Store." A no-nonsense Yankee businessman who had owned a hardware store in Hartford, Connecticut, Croswell came to the family store after his father died, moved into the next-door homestead, and continued the family legacy: providing sundries and necessaries to folks in Farmington Falls out of the longest-running family business in Franklin County.

At 2:00 a.m. one hot August night in 1948, twelve years after

Croswell had arrived in Farmington Falls, a self-made burglar alarm fashioned from a trip wire and buzzer running from Croswell's Store to the homestead sounded in Croswell's bedroom. He awoke immediately and, while he pulled on his trousers, directed Mrs. Croswell to phone Sheriff Earl Hawkins. "Come quick," she shouted into the mouthpiece. "Robbery at Croswell's Store!"

Croswell snatched his wire-rimmed eyeglasses from the night-stand, grabbed a 12-gauge shotgun from the closet, and dashed outside. As he approached the store, he saw two shadowy figures, alerted now to trouble outside, attempting to escape out a side window. "Stop, you barstards," Croswell yelled. Someone yelled something back, and Croswell fired at the fleeing burglars, knocking the lead one down. The second figure dashed into the woods behind the store.

Sheriff Hawkins, who had ordered deputies Ken French and Leo Hewey to the scene, was out of his patrol car by then and saw the wounded burglar crawling for a pistol lying just out of his reach. He yelled at Deputy French, "Get him, Ken! Get him 'fore he gets the gun!"

French leaped onto the burglar's back, pinned him to the ground, and held him while Deputy Hewey scooped up the gun and what *The Franklin Journal* would later report a set of modern burglar tools: an electric drill and a sledgehammer. Sheriff Hawkins quickly set up roadblocks on the village's perimeter, organized a foot-posse of nearby neighbors, and ordered the posse to track and capture the accomplice in the woods. He then called for an ambulance to attend to a bleeding Andrew Gallagher.

Croswell, in trousers and pajama tops, and armed with the loaded 12-gauge, commanded the nighttime scene like a Revolutionary War Minuteman. When Vint Davis, ambulance driver, undertaker, and right-handed long-ball slugger for Callahan's Hard Cider Boys, approached in the ambulance, Croswell brought the shotgun to the ready and shouted, "Dim them lights, Vint. This is still a battleground heah."

Davis assisted burglar Gallagher, bleeding from several wounds in his torso, to a seat in the ambulance and drove off under the cover of darkness. The accomplice was never found. At the hospital, the night nurse removed Gallagher's bloody shirt and, as she held it up for the police to observe, remarked, "This thing looks like a sieve."

Later, while Gallagher's wounds healed in the hospital, his wife drove from Brewer to pick up $200 found in Gallagher's pocket. "It's not mine," Croswell told Sheriff Hawkins. "I don't keep money in the safe overnight." In October, barely two months after the break-in, Andrew Gallagher was sentenced to five to ten years of hard labor at the state prison in Thomaston.

Boyce ponders the question asked from the back seat "I suspect he's still in the prison," he answers. "It's only been a little over three years."

We enter the prison in a line, a warden counting us as we file in. I am last, number twelve. It occurs to me that if a prisoner should somehow put on street clothes and walk midway in our line on the way out, I would be number thirteen—of only twelve who came in. Years later, teammate Bob Parlin will remember the counting, too. "I made up my mind on the way in," he will say, "that I'd be up front on the way out."

We pass through the kitchen where prisoners with long shiny knives peel and chop and slice in the streaming sunlight. The ball field comes into view out a window: a quarry some thirty feet deep hacked out of bedrock with sledgehammers and chisels by prisoners carrying out what Maine judges call hard labor. The bottom is leveled and smoothed and a sandy baseball diamond—ninety feet between the corners—is squeezed between its rock faces.

A scoreboard sits propped on a wooden frame behind the visitors' bench. A wire screen hangs on iron posts behind home plate and catches errant pitches before they can careen off the fractured rock. Players' benches sit in the open on each side of the infield. The right-field foul line runs along the bottom of an improvised wall more than three hundred feet to a foul pole at the base of a cell block. The left-field foul line runs only about thirty feet beyond third base. There, a jagged yellow paint line runs up the splintered wall signifying the end of the field. If I can just pop a pitch over the third baseman's head, I muse, the ball will bounce around on that broken-rock face all afternoon.

Boyce sees the game as preparation for the rugged competition he expects in the Lakes Region League. He starts Tyler on the mound. Tyler hasn't pitched since September last year, and the prisoners hit him hard, scoring six runs early in the game. We're impotent in the batter's box against the prison right-hander. He methodically works his way through our nine batters and retires all of us one after the other. Tyler, who fans in his only at-bat, returns to the bench and blames the strikeout on the catcher. "I think that damned Gallagher's catching," he tells us.

Gallagher? I thought.

"How do you know?" someone asks.

"He asked me if Temple was anywhere near Farmington," Tyler answers. "Wants me to take a package to his friend up there, Sheriff Hawkins." Tyler laughs.

"What'd you tell him?"

"Told him he'd hafta see Boyce. 'Boyce who?' he asked, and before I could answer, I'd struck out," Tyler moans.

Paul Heath comes on to relieve Tyler and tries to keep the game close. He pitches around the first few batters and stays out of trouble, but when Gallagher comes to bat, he rattles and accidentally plunks him in the ribs with his fastball. "My gosh," Heath will say later, "I didn't know what to do. I was concerned that he would think I hit him intentionally, he being penned up for a local robbery and all, so I walked over to the line and apologized, 'I didn't do it on purpose' I told him. He nodded to me, but I thought I shoulda been more careful."

The incident flusters Heath. He can't regain his concentration, and the prison team hits him often and runs up the score. "I didn't want to start a bean-ball contest, so I was more careful than usual, I guess. Kept gettin' it out over the plate," he related later with the same concerned look on his face he likely wore that day in Thomaston. "And then," he said, chuckling, "the next time Gallagher came to the plate, I'll be damned if I didn't hit him again. He had quite a stern look on his face when he went to first base that time. Gosh, I thought I'd die—right there on the mound."

An inning later, I come to bat for the second time and eye the left field broken-rock wall butting up against third base. I set my feet in the batter's box and cock the bat. Just as the right-hander goes into his windup, Gallagher asks, "What do you suppose that pitcher out there is in prison for?"

"I dunno," I answer, and duck an inside fastball.

"Murder," I hear Gallagher drawl. "Murdered his wife. He's gonna be here all his life—so it don't make no matter to him where his fast-ball goes when he fires it in here, now does it?"

I edge back from the plate, and the next pitch sails over the outside corner for a strike, a perfect pitch to knock onto the broken rock behind third base.

"An' you know," Gallagher goes on, "he don't have no thumb on his pitchin' hand neither. Maybe you noticed that."

"No, I didn't," I mutter."

"Well, he don't. An' better if he don't. Without that thumb, he can make the ball spin so's it'll drop like it fell right off a table when it gets here. Wanna see it?"

"No," I say. "I'll take a straight one—over the plate."

"You wanna straight one? Okay—I'll get you a straight one. Watch this."

He throws me the tabletop drop—and then strikes me out on a straight one that misses the plate outside.

"Nice talkin' to you, kid," Gallagher says.

We are no match for the prison nine. Losers, 14–2, we feast on a turkey dinner in the dining room and then file out of the lockup for home. I go through the gate number seven in line, right behind Bob Parlin, who has jockeyed his way to sixth. He looks back at me and grins. He had doubled and singled twice, once off the rocky wall.

On Memorial Day, Tri-corner comes to Temple for the Lakes Region League opener. There's still snow in the woods in left field, but the playing surface is clear. Temple furnishes a crowd for the game. They sit in the bleachers in shirtsleeves, relieved that their onerous winter—the Temple postmaster skied to Farmington twice in February in snow too deep to plow to fetch a sack of mail and a half-dozen news-papers back to the village—is finally over. Though the winning streak ended in Thomaston, the home-town crowd comes filled with hope for the new venture into league play. They watch curiously while the Tri-corners warm up, perhaps uneasy that Boyce has stepped up to tougher competition. The Townies are accustomed to winning, however, and notwithstanding the debacle in Thomaston the week before, Boyce has us ready. Tyler is on the mound, newcomer Danforth at shortstop, and Al Bergeron in center field. I sit on the bench with Art Mitchell, back-up catcher Roger Parlin, and relief pitcher Paul Heath.

The Townies are in untrodden territory, however. No single team is expected to dominate the Lakes Region League. Boyce tells us be-fore the game that each of the first three years of league play has pro-duced a different champion. Fayette the first year, Readfield the second, and Monmouth have each competed in the state playoffs for the Maine Amateur Baseball Championship. Boyce says 1952 is anybody's guess. We look to be as strong as anyone else before the season opens. "Perhaps we'll be a contender," he says. Some see the chase for the flag coming down to the Monmouth Ms and the Tri-corners. Others favor the Ms and their ace pitcher, lefty Dick Grondin. "Personally, I like Tyler's pitching," Boyce remarks. "Let's wait and see what happens."

Boyce's optimism suffers when we lose the opener in front of the home-town crowd. And we lose the next game, as well, to North Jay and left-hander Don Oakes's curveball. The following week, in a contest of winless teams, we travel to Litchfield and face Frank Webster. "Webster's crafty," Danforth warns us. "Don't let him fool you. Be patient up there." We commit eight errors that afternoon but manage to offset the porous fielding with nineteen hits off Webster and a string of Litchfield relievers. In the end we are ahead, 19–13.

"There's number one," Boyce sighs, relieved that we have somehow won a game. He starts pitcher Paul Heath the next week against the defending champion Monmouth Ms. Heath gives up nine runs before Tyler comes on in the seventh and finishes. Monmouth left-hander Dick Grondin holds the Townies to five hits, and the Ms claim their third straight win, 9–1.

"You pitched well," Boyce tells Tyler, who held the Ms to one hit in the final three innings. "We jes' needed to get you some runs. An' we will. I'm not givin' up, not yet."

But after four weeks all signs point to the Townies being out of contention. Undefeated Tri-corner leads the league with four consecutive wins behind Earl Tibbetts's pitching. Monmouth and North Jay are head-to-head in second place, both with 3–1 records. The Townies are in sixth behind perennial loser Wayne and the unknown Pittston Ramblers, who we haven't played yet and are one game ahead of us in the standings, with an ignominious 1–3 record. The season looks lost. We need a game or two against Callahan's Hard Cider Boys to reclaim our spirit.

"So who's pitching next week against the Pittston Ramblers?" I ask Boyce on the way home from Monmouth. I get the long answer.

"Well," he says, "first, someone *has* to pitch. I'll pick Tyler, but that's not all I have to do. He has to *believe* he can win, and I need to work at that—at practices and whenever we talk. I have to build his self-confidence, coax him into believing he is good enough to win."

"Is he?"

"I think so."

"We've started out slow."

"I know. But we play 'em just one game at a time. Next week is Pittston."

"I wish I could come to practice," I tell Boyce. "I need to swing more." My summer job has kept me away from the weekday workouts. Mr. Merrill, head of the highway department, sent me to Dave Smith, but I worked nearby for only a day or two, and then he sent me to a shorthanded survey crew on new-road construction in Solon, fifty miles away. After work in Solon each day, my boss dropped me at a rooming house in Madison, where I rinsed off the dust and walked along Main Street until I found a tempting restaurant. But nowhere on Main Street, nor anywhere in Madison, could I find a place to practice my swing.

"Swing whenever you can," Boyce tells me. "It'll come."

We beat the Pittston Ramblers, 13–3. Tyler pitches a complete game and strikes out thirteen. I play a few innings at second beside shortstop Ernie Danforth and knock out a three-bagger for the Townies' only extra base hit. Boyce smiles. "Felt good, didn't it?" he says.

Next North Jay comes to Temple expecting to win. A loss to Monmouth has dropped them into third place, and they need a victory to stay close to the leaders. But our two wins have brought us to within a game of the North Jays, and we're excited about our own prospects. Perhaps we can finally earn some respect in the league.

Dick Blodgett calls the outcome a slaughter. *The Franklin Journal's* Tuesday edition will call it a trouncing. Tyler's confidence, boosted by the thirteen strikeouts against Pittston, peaks for this game. He goes all the way and fans thirteen again. Our hitters—Bob Parlin, Hall, Bill Mosher, and more—are relentless. We score thirty-three runs, the most since the war, and jump into a third-place tie with North Jay.

Bill Mosher and Boyce, c. 1952.
(Temple Historical Society)

We are smiling again, and so are our fans. Folks discard their forecasts of collapse. Boyce reinvigorates his talk of contending for the pennant. We follow up the North Jay massacre with wins over Wayne and the Farmingdale Chiefs. We have somehow come alive and pulled into contention for the top spot. We lose to Litchfield—Frank Webster's tantalizing junk ball paralyzes our hitters and causes Boyce to express his displeasure by kicking all the dirt out of the third base coaches box—but we remain three games behind league-leading Tri-corner and trail the second-place Monmouth Ms by two. With five games left on the schedule, Tyler has run his record to 4–1, and our big hitters relax, knowing now that they can hit the best pitching in the league. "The hits will keep coming," Danforth says. We feel no fear when powerful Monmouth comes to the Townies' ball field.

The Townies cowered when we faced the Ms earlier in Monmouth, and except for a close loss to rampaging Tri-corner, the Ms have continued to come out on top. Champions in 1951 and contenders for two years previously, they have built a reputation that belies the casual and lackadaisical personality of small-town baseball teams.

The Ms and their fans treat the game seriously. They see winning as important. Dick Grondin is undefeated on the mound, and the team's top batters, Bob Anderson and Wes Johnson, regularly produce long hits. Only undefeated Tri-corner, one slim game in front of the Ms, stands between them and the sunspot when they come to Temple. "Monmouth is as good a team as the league has," Boyce says before the Townies take the field. "I expect them to be there at the end. Let's see if we can stay with 'em."

The Townies eke out a 6–5 extra-inning victory in front of a high-spirited home-field crowd. Though Tyler is plagued by wild pitches, hitters Ernie Danforth and Bob Parlin keep the crowd on their feet and the game close. In the tenth inning, the Townies score the winning run on a costly Monmouth error and pull to within two games of the league leaders. At the all-star break, we stand alone in third place. "We've played the best baseball in the league since the first week," Boyce declares.

It's August, midway through the season, and the Lakes Region League all-star team gathers at Farmington's Hippach Field. The league has voted four Townies all-stars—Tyler, Bob Parlin, Danforth, and Bergeron. The league office votes Boyce manager. For the contest with the North Franklin League all-stars, Boyce will choose either Cal Tyler, who leads the Lakes Region League pitchers in strikeouts, or undefeated Mommouth Ms ace Dick Grondin, to pitch. In a surprise move, the North Franklins put Lefty Gomez, former New York Yankees' pitching ace who is vacationing in Rangeley, on the mound to face Boyce's Lakers.

"This is the big leagues, Cal," I whisper to Tyler, who is sitting in the Hippach Field dugout. "Maybe it'll be Tyler versus Gomez." Tyler chuckles and starts to pace.

Vernon Gomez won 189 major league games for the New York Yankees in the 1930s. Four times a twenty-game winner, he led the

American League in strikeouts three times and pitched in seven all-star games, four as the starter. His undefeated 6–0 World Series record is the best in major league history. A baseball zany—he credits his pitching success to clean living and a fast Yankees' outfield—Gomez retired from the Yankees in 1943, and when asked in an interview by a prospective business employer why he left his last position, he answered, "I couldn't get the side out."

Boyce chooses the Monmouth Ms left-hander Grondin to be starting pitcher and the Townies' speedy Al Bergeron to bat leadoff and play center field for the Lakers. When Gomez goes to the mound, Bergeron, who is swinging two bats in the on-deck circle, asks, "What now, boss?"

"Go up there and get on base. That's what," Boyce answers. "He don't throw as hard as he used to."

But Gomez is a puzzle to Bergeron and the rest of the Lakes Region League's all-star lineup. He throws a major-league fastball that wanders, and the hitters are jittery and fail to make solid contact. Gomez pitches two innings and doesn't give up a hit. He yields five walks and two runs, however, and when he leaves the game the North Franklin stars trail Boyce's Lakers 2–1. "That's enough for me," Gomez tells *The Franklin Journal* as he heads back to Rangeley and his fly rod, "I jes' needed a little limbering up before the old-timers game next week in Yankee Stadium."

With Gomez on his way to Rangeley, Boyce's all-star hitters— Monmouth's Bob Anderson and Wes Johnson, Farmingdale's Bud Ochmanski, Tri-corner's Jimmy Mulherin and Arnie Crocker, North Jay's Mel Pomeroy, the Townies' Bob Parlin and Ernie Danforth, and others—break the game open. By the sixth inning, they have gone through Gomez and four more up-country pitchers, and a fifth one is trudging in from the bullpen when umpire George Cobb, undoubtedly fatigued by the parade of runners crossing the plate in front of him, mercifully calls time out and announces the game is over. "Enough is enough," he shouts. The score is 23–6. "Thank gawd," the new relief pitcher mutters as he runs off the field.

"You win, Cal," I say to Tyler, who pitched the last three innings and held the North Franklins scoreless.

The Townies refocus on the pennant race. In third place, two games out, we travel to Pittston on a lowery, threatening day. The rain holds off long enough for Tyler to strike out twelve Ramblers before the game is called in the seventh inning—his sixth win. Danforth and Larry Barker lead the hitting, which produces eighteen runs. Then the Farmingdale Chiefs, who had upset the Tri-corners the week before, come to Temple. *The Franklin Journal* calls it the feature game of the week: "the rising Farmingdale Chiefs against the powerful Temple Townies." It's a seesaw game that takes all afternoon and tests the crowd's patience. Tyler whiffs nine while the hitters—Bergeron, Bob Parlin, Hall, and Dick Blodgett—produce just enough runs to squeeze past the Chiefs, 9–8, and stay in the chase. Meanwhile, Monmouth's Dick Grondin shuts out Tri-corner to take over first place as Boyce predicted. We end the day one game out of second place and two away from the sunspot.

The remainder of the schedule frustrates Boyce. We need help if we are to

Cal Tyler, Bill Mosher, and Paul Heath in 1952. Tyler struck out 100 batters in the Lakes Region League that year—a league record. (Temple Historical Society)

close on Monmouth. We pick up an automatic win over Wayne, which has withdrawn from the league and forfeited its remaining games. But Monmouth wins as well, 7–3, over Farmingdale, sinking the Chiefs into fifth place and mathematically eliminating the Townies from the pennant chase. "We go to Tri-corner next week," Boyce announces, "and play for second place."

Years later, Cal Tyler showed me the ball and glove he used in the final game at the Leeds ball field. Written on the ball are the names of the 1952 Townies and the game's final score: Tri-corner 5, Townies 1. Tyler struck out eleven Tri-corners that day. I asked him what he remembered.

"I rode down to Leeds with Bill Mosher in his new Mercury," he told me. "We talked: who the good hitters were, what I'd throw. You know, what a pitcher and his catcher talk about before a big game."

"Did you have a plan?" I asked.

"Tri-corner had a good team. They were out of the gate with eight wins, then slumped. But they were up for us that last day. They still had a mathematical shot at the pennant. And the Tri-corner pitching was tough to hit that day."

"You pitched well," I reminded him.

"I pitched, I think, as well as I could pitch. But there was a lot of bickering. The umpiring was bad—at least we thought it was bad—so bad, Boyce protested the game . . . but nothing ever came of it."

"*The Franklin Journal* called the game a melee," I told him.

"I didn't feel so bad about the loss," Tyler went on. "Tri-corner had whaled us on Memorial Day, hit everything I threw. Heath relieved, and they hit him, too. Their big outfielders, Jimmy Mulherin and Marshall Pratt, could both hit the cover off the ball. So I thought I did well. Pitched as good as I could."

*   *   *

Cal Tyler set a Lakes Region League strikeout record that year. In seventy-one innings pitched, he fanned one hundred batters, the first time—and likely the last—in the history of the league. And in a league that featured such stalwarts as Dick Grondin, Don Oakes, and Frank Webster. He won seven games and lost two for the third-place Townies in our first attempt at league baseball. Boyce was not surprised. "He's shown the makings of a good pitcher all along," Boyce reacted. "This year he came out not just a good pitcher but a power pitcher, as good as Sade. I'm looking forward to him being around a long time."

After the season, Cal Tyler and Paul Heath are both drafted into the army. For two years they have been our pitching staff, accumulating twenty-five wins against nine losses and threatening to capture the Lakes Region League championship in the Townies' first try. Heath will not pitch again. Tyler will pitch one more time, a futile start against North Anson in 1955. The Townies' future without either one looks troublesome.

In October, a week before Heath will board the train for Fort Dix, and five months before Cal Tyler will follow him, the Townies and their exuberant fans gather for an evening in the Grange Hall, Temple's version of a public hall, where town meetings, potlucks, and entertainments are held. Boyce brings a jumbo-size "Good Luck" cake from his bakery van, and Aunt Marion brings card tables. We play cards and eat cake and ice cream and reminisce and laugh. Boyce presents baseballs signed by the 1952 team to Tyler and Heath and thanks them for their first-rate exploits on the pitcher's mound.

"It was a fun evening," Heath will remember years later. "I loved the Townies. They'd encourage you, pat you on the back—and they had a sense of humor, too. A great bunch."

Chapter Fourteen

CHASING DREAMS

T he campus impresses me. It is all grass and brick and lush landscape. It is archetypal construction sitting under huge oak and elm trees. It is spacious grassy slopes, a central quad, and athletic fields. It is old—and new, too. Uncle Lawrence drives Pa and me along its near-empty central road perhaps a mile to the north end of campus, where we find Dunn Hall, a classic residence hall named in memory of Maine's Chief Justice John Dunn. It's one of the first buildings to be built of brick at the university following World War II. I will learn later that it was constructed during a post-war steel strike; the builders substituted a structural concrete frame for the intended steel, the first example of such framing on the campus.

In the third floor hallway, I find a door with my name posted on it. Inside, my roommate—Hugh Gates from someplace in upstate Vermont—is asleep on a bunk. Pa and I and Uncle Lawrence carry suitcases, boxes, and a mass of high school academic paraphernalia up two flights of stairs to the room and place it on the floor. I say my good-byes in the parking lot. No moralizing. No pep talk. Just a handshake. Then they are gone.

Gates wakes up when I return and looks at his watch. "Gosh," he exclaims. "I gotta take a test!" and he disappears out the door before I can tell him who I am. Later, after I have filled a closet with the contents of my suitcases and written my name on my possessions, Gates, a somewhat meek-looking, sober boy of middling proportions, returns. We chat. "I'm temporary here," he tells me.

So am I, I think, *only four years.* I question him.

"Yeah," he answers. "I've been accepted at the Naval Academy, but I need another course in English composition before I can start there."

He came to the University of Maine, I muse, *to prepare for the Naval Academy? He must know something about this school I don't.* "Is English tough here?" I ask, a bit apprehensive.

"I hope not," he answers.

I seldom see Gates after our first meeting. He sleeps in the room, but I don't know where he is when he's awake. Then, one day in midwinter, I come back to the room, and his things are gone. I wonder where he went, whether he made it to the Naval Academy on the strength of University of Maine English Composition. (Sixty-some years later, I will read a piece in a Maine newspaper featuring Hugh Gates, owner and president of America's last hand-crank telephone company. I write a note on a Christmas card and send it to him at the company headquarters in upstate Vermont, but he doesn't answer.)

I have no time anyway at the university to pursue a friendship with Gates. I am overwhelmed by the academic intensity. Though my classes are simply higher-level variations of familiar high school work, I study five hours each night, go to bed after midnight, and wake up ten minutes before an eight-o'clock class in trigonometry. Physics, chemistry, and English composition lectures fill out the days; afternoon science labs run into darkness; reading and writing occupy the time I'm not horsing around between dinner and sleep. Professors show no tendency to fuss over students. In chemistry and physics lectures, I am a number on a seatback, and I could fill my chair seat with a mannequin or scarecrow—or Gates, for that matter—and be counted present. Professors establish expectations, what physics Professor Bennett, a wiry-haired, kinetic classroom performer who has authored our textbook, calls "my goals for you," and there is no compromise. I struggle. My fall semester's disappointing grade point average energizes me a bit. But I worry that I will fail, like Ayer did at Sparhawk Hall. I have no place to go. Fear motivates me to work harder, study more, go to class on time.

My second semester curricula is tougher, and I show no improved performance over the fall. Obviously, I reason, I am not assured of success. Lack of self-discipline threatens my existence at Orono. I change tactics, organize my time: I write four crucial daily activities on a piece of paper—class time, study time, work time, rest time—and schedule daily hours for each. I concentrate on learning rather than just using up available time reading and writing. I set my alarm to wake me in time for breakfast and a bit of energizing food. Evenings, aside from a part-time job flipping hamburgers in the Dunn Hall canteen, I avoid temptation: no diversions, no horsing around.

Fraternity rush takes place in the spring. Allan Smith, my Lake Avenue pal, has joined Phi Kappa Sigma, and he introduces me to the brothers there. It seems a place I can find the friendships Aunt Marion warrants for me. And the collection of engineering files in the attic—copies of previous exams, English essays, and technical lab reports created by a succession of civil engineering students who have passed through Phi Kappa Sig before me—will be helpful, too. Though Smith is in the graduating class and I will face the ordeal of pledging and Hell Week without his reassurance, I agree to accept the invitation and join a group comprising mostly strangers, though likeable strangers. I reason the pledge class will come together as friends and allies long before Hell Week.

My spring semester final grades border on dismissal. English composition has dragged me down. I suspect my preparation for college

English was inadequate. My teachers in the Village School, Stolt and Josselyn, introduced me to the fundamentals years ago, taught me the prerequisite grammar—primary school then was called grammar school for just that purpose—parts of a sentence, basic punctuation, and the common rules of capitalization. Unfortunately, I didn't take my grammar school instruction seriously. At the high school, I endured Marion Bryant's English lessons, just as Pa had years before me, but I don't recall her instruction being presented in a logical or analytical style that I could retain. Consequently, I failed to grasp how to create a readable sentence or construct a thoughtful paragraph. I had no under-standing of independent clauses or adverb phrases, various applications of verb tense, or parallel construction. My college essays, which clearly lack evidence of constructive writing, validate my learning there. English composition, I will slowly but eventually determine, is a man-agement problem; the solution a process, a series of steps that lead to a coherent outcome. Mrs. Bryant, as beloved and enduring as she may have been, didn't see English composition in that context.

Though aware in the spring of 1953 of how close I have come to glaring and total failure, I am confident. I have survived a year in col-lege. I have discovered a new group of friends, friends who will support my attempts at progress and not tempt me with pizza and beer at Pat's downtown pub. I have discovered new resources in the Phi Kappa Sigma attic. I can relax. School is closed, and I know what I will face in the fall. I hurry home to Temple for Townies workouts in advance of the Memorial Day opening game.

With no reason to live there any longer, Aunt Marion left Lake Avenue after I left for the university. She proclaimed that Christine had broken their agreement and raised the rent, and she refused to pay it. Plus, she had come into an available house on Cummings Hill Road in Temple, across from the ash-filled, rock-lined cellar hole of her for-mer home.

My great-great Grandfather Alpheus Hodgkins, the first Hodgkins to settle in Temple, built the house about 1840 so I was told, and it had passed through several generations of Hodgkinses since, eventually to Grandpa C.F. But two years past, in 1950, Grandpa C.F. died of a heart attack walking to Uncle Phil's after a Flyers' night game at Hippach Field, and the house had landed in Grandma Luna's lap. So as soon as I left for the university, Aunt Marion seized the opportunity to relieve Christine of her burden of trying to collect the rent. With me no longer underfoot, she and Uncle Lawrence and new-home-owner Grandma Luna hied back to Cummings Hill Road.

The house was empty—and it was a wreck. Grandpa C.F. had rented it occasionally to local indigents looking for a place to live where rent could be avoided and drinking either unnoticed or accepted, and the upkeep of the place had been ignored. Aunt Marion and Uncle Lawrence—and Dick Blodgett, as well, whom Aunt Marion persuaded to come to Cummings Hill Road with his hammers and saws and renovate the living space—went to work to make the small Cape Cod suitable for habitation. When they were done, it fit the family perfectly. Two bedrooms on the ground floor—a master, and a small one for aging Grandma Luna—and two bedrooms at the top of the central stairs, one for me and a spare for houseguests. The shed provided shelter in winter for the walk from the house to the barn, where the car was kept, and ample storage for Uncle Lawrence's baseball equipment. Aunt Marion's Chevrolet fit nicely behind the barn's sliding door. And the land offered space for a large vegetable garden.

Boyce gave up the bakery route in fall 1952, as well. "Too much work for what I get out of it," he said then, and I was reminded of the many times I'd watched him count a bagful of nickels, dimes, and quarters, the proceeds of knocking on farmhouse doors for a week, and take them to the bank. He became a painter, an interior decorator. Folks in the family and in the village kept him busy reenergizing their parlors and upstairs bedrooms. Occasionally, he painted a building's exterior to the extent he could reach without a two-story ladder, but he shied away from heights. He set his own working hours and at the end of the week took paper money to the bank. For the first time since I'd met him, he took Saturdays off. The extra time went into keeping the baseball team credible. He re-graded and reseeded the field, bought new uniforms, and searched for players that could face up to the competition in the Lakes Region League. He seemed happier.

After Christmas, he went to Florida with Aunt Marion, the first time I had known him to take more than four days off at once. For six weeks, he picked his breakfast orange just outside the kitchen door; he climbed Citrus Tower and toured Busch Gardens with Aunt Marion; he took a part-time job in his landlord's paint crew and renewed a faded house in Saint Cloud; and he watched a session of major league spring training in Sarasota. In late February he and Aunt Marion drove back to Temple, where he spent another six weeks shoveling snow out of the driveway waiting for the grass to appear at the ball field.

In March, snowstorms refilled the roads in Temple, and low temperatures froze the drifts in place. Snowbanks reached into the low limbs of roadside maples. The town was dormant. Yet the optimistic and passionate townsfolk, as they had done since World War II, voted at town meeting to allow Sunday baseball during the coming year. But the days stretched into April before any sign of the cold earth appeared at the baseball field—or anyplace else in town—and May before Boyce could call the Townies to pre-season workouts.

I find Boyce busy retrofitting the team. Second baseman Dick Blodgett, a regular since the Townies opened the 1946 season, has retired from baseball. Larry Barker, too—for the second time. Starting pitcher Cal Tyler has boarded a train for Fort Dix, New Jersey. And relief pitcher Paul Heath is clerking in a U.S. Army post office in Berlin. "You'll be playing second base this year," Boyce tells me at the supper table the day I arrive. "Danforth will be at shortstop again, and the two of you will work together in the middle of the infield."

Most young baseball players have a role model, a player who inspires them, who leaves an imprint. In my case it is Ernie Danforth. I was seventeen years old when I met him at a Pratt Field practice session behind the high school in Farmington. I watched him intently during his first season with the Townies. Danforth was an unassuming man whose demeanor exuded confidence but who lacked any semblance of braggadocio and spoke of his own baseball ability only with his glove and bat. He owned the shortstop position. Lithe, rangy, and relaxed, flawless with his glove, he made the hard plays look easy. He was best gliding to his right into the hole, stabbing a ground ball, and then overhanding it to first base ahead of the runner. He teamed well with Blodgett at second, getting the ball to him quickly and accurately on double plays, and covering the bag on throws from Mosher. Like Bergeron before him, Danforth was the leader, the anchor, of our infield.

Offensively, Danforth was not an exceptional hitter. But Boyce, who knew him as well as anyone, put him third in the batting order ahead of Bob Parlin. He rewarded Boyce's confidence by hitting over .300, a good number of his singles and doubles turned into runs when Parlin came to bat.

Danforth impressed me with his quiet ability and his optimistic outlook. He didn't complain. He didn't get down on himself when the opposing pitcher struck him out or when he booted a ground ball. He relaxed and enjoyed the game. "Those things will happen," he told me. "Don't let them ruin your fun." Now, a year later, we are the second-base combination in the middle of the Townies' infield, and I'm excited.

"The hitting will come, "Boyce counsels me. "Don't worry about it. The job is yours even if you don't hit. We need your defense. I picked up a new sinker-ball pitcher to replace Tyler and Heath. Should keep the infield busy."

Larry Davis, a Flyers' castoff who has pitched for the Farmington Town Team the past few years and throws a mean curveball, will be wearing a Townies' uniform. Six-and-a-half feet tall, the lanky, long-armed Davis has a reputation for keeping hitters edgy and off balance with a variety of deliveries, but his sinking curveball is his "out" pitch. Batters react late, and if they happen to contact a piece of the ball, they beat it into the ground. Davis is baseball-wise as well. He has pitched for the high school, the Town Team, the Flyers, and the Jewels. His record also includes one game against the Townies in 1951. He started for the Farmington Jewels in a season-ending feature against us under the lights at Hippach Field, a game that he finished and won. Undoubtedly, Davis' impressive win against the Townies was still on Boyce's mind a year later when he went looking for a capable pitcher.

"What about some relief pitching?" I ask.

"Larry Davis is a complete-game pitcher," Boyce answers. "He's tough. But if the game gets out of control, or Davis' arm gets sore, I can bring in Lyle Hall for an inning or two. He pitched some when he was in East Wilton."

Boyce sounds confident, but he is taking a chance with Hall. "Davis can handle it," he avows. "His record shows he can."

Boyce talks on at the supper table. "And it looks like Al Mitchell will be leavin'," he says, "so I got another hitter comin' too, an outfielder, Bernard Davis from the high school team. He'll play right field and bat in the middle of the lineup someplace. Hits a long ball—so don't worry about your hitting. We got plenty of hitting—we'll be a contender."

On Memorial Day in Temple, Larry Davis bears out Boyce's appraisal. He throws an eleven-inning victory over Tri-corner, striking out nine. Though he trails after five innings, he pitches shutout ball for the last six and retires the Tri-corners in order in the tenth and eleventh. Meanwhile, the Townies nibble at the Tri-corner lead and tie the game in the ninth when I single through the right side of the infield to advance Art Mitchell to third, and a Bill Mosher fly ball scores Mitchell. With one out in the bottom of the eleventh, I single again to right; and singles by Bill Mosher, Vern Hodgkins, and Al Bergeron end the game. *Maybe Boyce is right,* I think, *just let it happen.*

We outscore independent Buckfield in an exhibition on an open date and then travel to Pittston for our second league game. At Pittston we have no inkling of what to expect. The Ramblers have pummeled Litchfield, yet they have been upended by the Farmingdale Chiefs, a weaker team by all accounts. Davis starts, and the Ramblers score early. After seven innings they're still in front by three. But the Townies rally: I lead off the top of the eighth, plunk an outside pitch down along the third-base line, and leg it across the first base bag ahead of the throw. I have started something. The next six batters single, too, and, with two outs, I come up again. Mindful of my unsettling bunt earlier, right-hander White keeps his pitches off the plate. I can hear Boyce yelling. "Make him throw it over the plate." But White refuses to bring his fastball in, and I walk. We score nine runs in the inning and take command of the game. Davis fans four of the last six Rambler batters for an 18–9 win. The Townies are off to a fast start: two wins, no losses, just a half-game behind the first-place Randolph VFW, a powerful new team in the Lakes Region League.

Boyce is in a good mood after the Pittston game. Davis has pitched well. Our hitters have been explosive in the batter's box, including my four hits in the two games. "We're strong up the middle." Boyce remarks, "If Davis can get his arm loose a little earlier, maybe we can stay in the thick of things."

It is not Davis' stiff throwing arm, however, that handicaps the Townies. It is shabby baseball. At Monmouth the following Sunday, though we're handcuffed by strong-armed ace Dud Holland, we hand the Ms an easy win: Davis kicks around a Monmouth bunt on the mound while an Ms runner scampers to first. Mosher throws a pitch into center field trying to nab a thief at second. Hall ducks an errant throw and loses it in the bushes behind the third base dugout while a runner rounds third and scores. We commit eight blunders, and Boyce is beside himself. "This is ridiculous," he mutters, pacing back and forth in front of our bench. "They're not beating us; we're throwing it away." The final score is Monmouth 7, Townies 0. Sadly, the sloppy exhibition is a precursor of more trouble to come.

Boyce stews over the defense. He drills us into the darkness at weeknight practices. He lectures us, "Make the routine play, the easy play, every time," he emphasizes. "The easy play should always be an out. Errors can come on the hard ones."

But we prove to be slow learners. We commit eight more errors against the undefeated Farmingdale Chiefs and drop behind early, 10–6. A rally in the seventh inning ties the game, and Boyce smiles for a moment, but the Chiefs put over another run to win the ragged scuffle, 11–10. With eleven strikeouts and ten Farmingdale hits, Larry Davis pitches well enough to win, and he pounds out a fourth-inning home run as well. But the Chiefs play errorless ball and knock us into fourth place.

The Townies are in a funk, a defensive funk. We are trying too hard, playing the game all tightened up. We are afraid to make an error for fear the game will be lost. We go to our positions hesitant and wait for the next miscue. The opponents see our fear and run on us, forcing us to throw the ball. It's an old trick. Boyce taught it to the Townies in the beginning. "Pressure the defense," he told them. Now Monmouth and Farmingdale have turned the tables—and the pressure shows.

Much of the Townies' success over the years came from reckless baseball, playing free and easy, having fun. They beat most teams easily just letting the game unwind, playing like kids in a pasture. When they played for a jug of cider, rather than a championship, they laughed. The hits came freely, and the throws were accurate. If someone bobbled a ground ball, he smiled and said, "Hit me another one—if you dare." Playing high-end teams with a league championship in the mix has stressed us. The throws are tentative. No one wants to be guilty of the next error. Everyone is off balance, out of sync. Boyce will have to loosen us up, put some fun back into the game—somehow.

We travel to Litchfield. Their grassy field behind the town hall is smooth and true. We play errorless ball on a park-like surface and trounce the home team, 9–3. Davis commands the game with his sinking curveball and strikes out ten. Lyle Hall bangs out four hits, and center fielder Al Bergeron makes two long-run catches and throws out two runners at home plate. I single once and on my next at bat drive a pitch deep into right field that brings Boyce to his feet, but he sits down quickly when Blaine Linton makes a running catch in the corner. "Think we're ready for Randolph, boss?" Bergeron asks after the game.

New-entry Randolph VFW is the team to beat in the Lakes Region League. Led by ace pitcher Bill Verhille and long-ball hitters Don Thibeau, Arthur Benner, and Wally Spear, they opened the season with five straight wins. They look unbeatable. The Townies' record stands at 3–2 when the VFW come to Temple, and the game will either keep us in contention or relegate us to mucking around with Tricorner and Farmingdale in the middle of the standings.

Larry Davis matches up with Verhille in a classic pitcher's duel. The Townies score first, a single run in the fifth inning knocked across the plate by Lyle Hall's double. In the sixth, Vern Lee smacks a double off Davis that scores two, and the VFW take the lead. Verhille shuts us down the rest of the way, and the VFW go home with their sixth consecutive win. We play, arguably, our best game of the season. Davis strikes out fifteen, and the defense, carefree again after an errorless game at Litchfield and Boyce's desertion of late-evening drills, commits only two harmless bobbles. But our four hits—I am hitless against Verhille—are not enough. "Randolph's sure the class of this league,"

Boyce observes after the game. "We played our best game of the year and never had a chance." Final score: VFW 4, Townies 1.

Phinney Field in Leeds. The Townies are weak in the middle again. Danforth, Bergeron, and Larry Davis are unable to play. Boyce starts Lyle Hall on the mound and the Tri-corners predictably nick him for sixteen hits. When it's over we drop into a fourth place tie with the Tri-corners and retreat to Temple. We need a restart. We're in a muddle. I wonder whether Boyce can disentangle us.

For years Boyce recruited, experimented, and juggled players to keep pace with the competition. When Sade retired, when the navy recalled Bergeron, when Hellgren left, and when Boyce himself was forced to the bench by age and injuries, he recruited and patched together a competitive lineup, put together a team that, for the most part, produced a winning record, a team that excited the townsfolk and kept their interest and support. This year Blodgett retired, Al Mitchell left town to work, and the army drafted the pitching staff, Tyler and Heath. But Boyce cobbled together a potpourri of odds and ends: locals, out-of-towners, kids, and veterans, into a competent team. And he is satisfied with it. He knows, however, that we are thin: our bench is weak, there's no relief pitcher, no fill-in infielders, no pinch hitters; he cannot adequately fill a hole caused by a Sunday afternoon absence. He's frustrated.

I feel the pressure. I'm a four-year veteran with the Townies, and I'm frightened. I'm a regular, but I'm fearful of failure in the batter's box and the pressure spills over to my defense around second base. Danforth helps. He compliments me and calms me. "I'm tickled to be playing beside you," he tells me. He makes me feel as though I belong here, that we are a pair. Boyce bolsters me as well, tells me not to worry about the hitting. He needs defense. Maybe he's right.

The Lakes Region League has turned out to be tough going for the fragile Townies. We are not a serious threat to the league's elite, of course, but at full strength, we are not pushovers either. Boyce knows it; he tries to keep us relaxed and having fun, keep us whole. He says we're a better team if we're having fun.

It is the mid-season all-star break. Six Townies are elected to the team: players Lyle Hall, who leads the league in batting, Bob Parlin, Ernie Danforth, Al Bergeron, and Larry Davis; and batboy Glen Tyler, Cal's young brother. Only undefeated Randolph suits up as many all-star players as the Townies. The Lakes Region League names Litchfield's Hap Furth its manager and schedules an all-star affair under the lights at Pettingill Park in Auburn against the Twin City League all-stars. The game is expected to settle a controversy over the merits of small-town ball versus semipro urban ball. The country boys prevail, the game's outcome is not reported in the urban newspapers.

August comes. We are tied for fourth place in a seven-team league. Five games left in the season. We split the first two. Korean War veteran Bernard Davis' second homer of the season lifts us to an 11–9 win over the Pittston Ramblers. Larry Davis throws a nineteen hitter—yes, nineteen hits—and strikes out ten for his fourth league win. Then, in front of the same enthusiastic home-town fans, we lose to Monmouth in what *The Franklin Journal* will call a tight battle. Leading 6–4 after eight innings, the Ms score seven ninth-inning runs off Davis' sore arm and loosen the game up a bit. Hall comes in to finish and gives up a long homer to Ms pitcher Don Oakes before getting the third out. Left-hander Oakes, who has moved over to the Ms from North Jay to bolster their pitching staff for the pennant chase with Randolph, holds the Townies to a meager five hits, one a rare home run by singles-hitter Al Bergeron. At the end of the game, the Townies are alone in fourth place, one game behind the Farmingdale Chiefs.

Three games left. We traveled to Togus to confront the third-place Chiefs. Townies pitcher Larry Davis stays home. Boyce has told him to rest his troubled arm. As the season draws down, Davis' arm gives

Boyce fits. Either the arm won't loosen until Davis has yielded a half-dozen runs, or it wears out in the late innings. Boyce needs it for a full game. "I want you ready for Randolph," he tells Davis. "Maybe some rest will help."

"Who's gonna pitch?" Bergeron asks, afraid that Boyce will call on him.

"Hall will," Boyce answers, as though third baseman Hall is part of the pitching staff.

Bergeron smiles. "Maybe I should play a little deeper in center," he quips.

We play at the Veterans Administration Athletic Field. The patients and staff mingle along the foul lines at game time. Most have come to see the Chiefs and Townies battle for third place. But the field is mistakenly reserved for two games at the same time: an Augusta American Legion game and the Townies' third-place battle with the Chiefs. A war veteran in the crowd settles the dispute. "Play the semi-pro game first, he yells. "We came to see the semipros play." I am surprised to learn that he means the Townies. So is Boyce. The officials shorten both games to seven innings, and the American Legion teams wait with the spectators while the semipro Townies and Chiefs reconcile the matter of third place in the Lakes Region League.

In the bottom of the first, Hall takes the mound, throws a half-dozen warm-ups, and nods to Mosher that he is ready. Knowing that two more teams are waiting to play on the same field, he stuns his teammates by facing only twenty-three Chiefs all day, giving up just three singles and winning, 4–0, putting us into a third-place tie. He also leads the Townies in hits, banging out three singles in four at-bats. "Nice call, boss," Bergeron ribs Boyce on the way out. "Hall made it easy for us."

Hall pitches again the following week against Litchfield, and wins again, 6–5. The Chiefs lose to Randolph, and we take sole possession of third place. Davis tells Boyce his arm is ready for the final fracas at

Randolph, but undefeated Randolph has clinched the Lakes Region League title, claimed a spot in the Yankee Amateur Baseball Congress regional tournament, and left for Auburn where the tournament is underway. Boyce makes several futile attempts to reschedule the final game, but the VFW keep winning tournament games and eventually win the regional championship. When they leave for Battle Creek to play for the national championship, the Lakes Region League declares the season over, and the Townies claim third place behind Randolph and Monmouth.

Larry Davis, who pitched his heart out for the Townies over the long season, goes home to rest his aching arm. "I'd like to had another shot at Randolph," a grinning Boyce says later, warming his hands over the wood heater at the general store. "See what we coulda done."

Chapter Fifteen

GILBERT P. LESLIE, JR.

M|ay 1954. I walk onto sunny Hippach Field, where the greening grass is soft underfoot. Boyce is here, and the Townies, readying for another season. "The league has split into two divisions," Boyce tells us. "We're gonna play in the Northern Division. Randolph and Monmouth won't be on our schedule this year. We can go around them to get to the tourney."

"Who'll be in the Northern Division?" someone asks.

"Some good teams will be there," he says. "North Anson's comin' in, and so's Livermore Falls. And Kingfield and Strong out of the North Franklin League. They'll be five of us." He sounds excited. Livermore Falls, which last played in the Lakes Region League in 1951 and is thought to be a contender for the flag in the Northern Division, will likely give us trouble. But the two teams from the North Franklin League will be fun to play.

Boyce spends his May evenings on the telephone. Larry Davis, the Townies' sole pitcher in 1953, is not coming back. He tells Boyce his sore arm has not healed. "I can't get the ball all the way to the plate," he says over the phone. Boyce searches the county for a replacement. Bob Tufts is staying with Kingfield, Farmington's Collis Ames and

Strong's Clyde Pingree are both out. Boyce comes up with Lyle Hall, the Townies third baseman. "It's gonna have to be you, Lyle," Boyce tells him. "You can handle the pitching best of any I can find." A tall, stringy right-hander who has toned his muscles on an East Wilton farm, Hall has all the story-book makings of a country pitcher—sort of a Lil Abner in a baseball uniform—but he has an unsettling history on the pitchers mound, at times giving up as many as twenty runs in a game. But Boyce puts his faith in Hall, and Hall agrees to try his fast-ball on the league's heavy hitters.

Al Bergeron calls Boyce. "I can't make it back to center field this year," he says. "Gotta build a house. Audrey says it's time for her own picket fence and flower garden. You know what I mean. I'll be back next year."

"I'll have a place for you, Al," Boyce answers. "If you need help with the house, mebbe we can put together a roofing session."

Boyce's search for a center fielder lasts only a few minutes. Larry Barker, who retired for the second time a year ago, comes out of his Sunday afternoon chaise lounge and goes back to center field. "There," Boyce exclaims. "We'll have a team yet."

Boyce calls Ike Spencer in Strong and schedules two games. "Ike needs a taste of the Lakes Region League experience before he starts out on a new venture," Boyce tells us. "An' I need to know whether I have a team here or not." We go to Strong, as Boyce says, to loosen our muscles, but I'm certain it is mostly for Boyce to see how Hall matches up against credible hitting, aware that certain pieces of his pitching makeup might be fragile. We lose, 4–3, but Boyce finds plenty to be encouraged about. Hall pitches well. He keeps his tempo under control and his fastball on the corners of the plate. "The pitching and the defense were great," Boyce says after the game. "And I know we'll hit. We're good hitters."

The following Sunday at Hippach Field, Strong's right-hander

Milt Simmons engages Hall in another pitching duel—for five innings. In the sixth, the Townies ahead 2–1, Larry Barker and Bob Parlin connect for run-scoring doubles, and the Townies score five times. Ernie Danforth triples home three more in the seventh. Hall shuts out the Strong batters after the first inning, and the Townies coast, 10–1. Boyce pencils the details into the score book. "The league's opener is Memorial Day," he tells us. "We play Kingfield at home."

On Memorial Day, the Temple ball field is too wet for baseball, so we host Kingfield at Hippach. The Townies tattoo right-hander Marty Sillanpaa, who pitched for the high school during the cold spring and was thought ready for the faster Lakes Region League, for six innings and we lead, 4–0. Hall is surprisingly tough against their robust array of muscle-bound sluggers, who play their best baseball in cold, wet weather. But the Kingies threaten with two runs in the top of the seventh. In the bottom half, the Townies' Bob Parlin and Bernard Davis drive home three more with extra base hits to regain a comfortable lead. Then in the ninth, Kingie slugger Howie Dunham's three-run triple unsettles Hall, and the Kingies push over five runs. The Townies lose, 8–7. "The game was ours," Boyce mutters afterward. "And we let it get away."

"What went wrong, boss?" Parlin asks.

"I think the long game tired Hall out," Boyce answers. "He shut 'em out for six, but then they got to him. The big bats—Dunham, Morrell, Tufts, an' the others—he couldn't keep 'em quiet. Couldn't stop 'em. Too bad. He works so hard." Boyce looks around the field as if he's trying to find someone. "We need another pitcher—somehow."

Oak Hall is one of the original University Maine buildings, dating from 1868, when the land grant college opened for instruction in agriculture and engineering. An archetypically-styled brick four-story residence hall situated on the north end of the old campus, it housed the first classes of civil engineers. A devastating fire destroyed the building in 1936, but the university reconstructed the classic dormitory, and it reopened in 1937 featuring two-room suites.

After the Memorial Day game at Hippach Field, I drive Pa's six-year-old Mercury coupe to the university. My roommate, Gilbert P. Leslie Jr., is waiting for me at Oak Hall. Thirty civil engineering juniors, equipped with slide rules, drawing equipment, and leather boondockers are there for a six-week civil engineering summer camp that will see us apply the practical side—the field work—of civil engineering. Leslie and I share a two-room suite, spacious digs considering we spent the school year wedged into the confines of Phi Kappa Sigma.

Leslie, from Newington, Connecticut, joined the Phi Kappa Sigma fraternity with me in the fall. Together we bore the severity of Hell Week and pledged the oath of brotherhood. We were the only civil engineering students in the fledgling class, and each of us offered considerable assistance to the other throughout the academic year: we exchanged insights into the expectations of professors; collaborated on whether a pop quiz might be imminent; cooperated with each other on our exclusive access to the civil engineering files in the attic; discussed our personal analyses of the results of exams; and, on more than one occasion, strayed downtown together to Pat's pizzeria and pub for late-night dimeys and pickled eggs before retiring to the open-air communal bedroom on the top floor of the frat house. Now best friends, we are partners in summer camp and over the next six weeks will delve into the nuances of what working civil engineers actually do.

"What will you do on weekends?" Leslie asks me.

"I'll go home," I tell him. "I play baseball on Sundays for the Temple Townies."

"Gosh," he answers, "I've played baseball. Maybe I'll go with you."

"Sure," I say. "What position you play?"

"I pitched for Newington High School," he says.

Boyce will be pleased to hear this, I think.

*   *   *

By Friday, however, Boyce and the Townies are in more trouble. Bill Mosher reports that he has retired from baseball. "It's a shocker to me," Boyce exclaims. "It'll sure be different without Bill." A young man, perhaps twenty-nine, Mosher is Mr. Dependable among the Townies. He has been in the starting lineup every game since 1947. With no experience whatsoever, he put on the catching implements in 1948 when Boyce injured his throwing arm and has caught every game since. Some say he was persuaded by wife Natalie to give up the game, that the team frustrated her. No baseball fan herself, the team took away her Sunday afternoon picnics, rides in the country, and trips to the coast for lobster. Bill, in the woods every working day loading six cords of pulpwood onto his stake-bodied truck and delivering it to a mill somewhere, couldn't satisfy both Boyce and Natalie. After seven years, he switched to Natalie.

Boyce's troubles keep coming. Ernie Danforth and his grader have been transferred to the highway department's West Gardiner camp. Danforth's shortstop position will be a troublesome hole to fill. In his two years with the Townies, his all-around play has inspired us to threaten the league leaders for the flag, finishing third twice, a goal that not even Boyce realistically expected to achieve. Not a long-ball hitter, Danforth hit well over .350 for his two years. His defensive play anchored the up-the-middle defense, and his professional demeanor served as a model for teammates. His grader contributed as well. He smoothed our clay infield while he was here and constructed little-league fields for teams in New Sharon and Farmington Falls. And he will not forget us. He will return later with the grader and build baseball fields for kids in Fairbanks and Temple, as well.

And Boyce has even more finagling to do. Larry Barker, his muscles aching after only two games, gives up his second comeback attempt and retires again. "So what are you going to do?" I ask Boyce, as though he has all the answers.

When we arrive at Livermore Falls on Sunday, Boyce is ready. He loans Gil Leslie a glove and a uniform and names him starting pitcher. He moves Lyle Hall back to third base, a position he excels at, and sends me to shortstop. He brings Roger Parlin, who caught four broken-up years for the high school in Farmington, in from right field and puts him behind the plate. Bernard Davis goes to second base, and Bucky Buchanan, a singles hitter from East Wilton brought to the Temple ball field by Lyle Hall, goes to right field. Art Mitchell is in center, and Bob Bell, an acquisition from West Farmington whose baseball experience was with the East Wilton team, goes to left in place of Larry Barker. Finally, Boyce sends Bob Parlin back to first base and says, "I think we're set. We should give 'em a run for their money."

We score three runs before Livermore Falls comes to bat. First-inning singles by me, Hall, Bernard Davis, and Roger Parlin give Leslie a three-run lead before he even throws a pitch. But Leslie is understandably nervous on the mound, with strangers everywhere, and he gives up two quick runs before he settles down. At the end of eight innings, the Townies lead the duel between pitchers Leslie and Larry Lapointe, 4–3. But in the ninth, the Indians score twice, and we're beaten, 5–4. Leslie has thrown a remarkable game against a highly regarded team, striking out fifteen and allowing five hits, but the Townies fail to capitalize. We leave eleven runners stranded. Boyce is a whit irked at the last-minute loss but perks up later. "I think we've found a pitcher," he remarks. "We'll see what that brings."

Leslie smiles. I remind Boyce that I enjoyed a rare, two-hit game myself and was errorless at shortstop.

The university's civil engineering camp fascinates me. Professor Wes Evans, head of the Civil Engineering Department, divides thirty of us into four- and five-person teams and equips each with state-of-the art measuring devices: theodolite, leveling rod, steel chain, and string-suspended plumb bobs. He sends us onto the campus and beyond to apply the principles of geometry and trigonometry in determining the form and position of the landscape.

First comes a geodetic and topographic survey of the hilly north end of campus. We locate and plot—adjusted for the curvature of the earth—such striking campus features as fraternities Beta Theta Pi and Sigma Nu, and the university infirmary. We contour the grassy landscape down and across State Highway 2 to the Stillwater River. We pinpoint the location of walking paths, sign posts, Andrew Carnegie Library, and a Revolutionary War cannon on high ground that once, I presume, defended the campus against an upriver assault by the British.

Next, we move our devices off-campus. We survey, design, and plot an improved roadway plan for a dusty, winding lane through the university's forest in nearby Stillwater village. Professor Frank Taylor cautions us that our designs may not be constructed soon, but "Try to come up with something useful," he says. Last and most intriguing is hydrographic engineering. We determine the volume of Stillwater River water flowing under the bridge in downtown Orono. For this project, Professor Sproul, head of what is called sanitary engineering at the university, furnishes us with a torpedo-like vane attached to a sounding chain that, he tells us, indicates readings of flowing-water velocity on a gauge attached to the vane by a wire. It's an electrical contraption. However, we measure water velocities at one-foot intervals top to bottom, sound the riverbed bank to bank, and apply our slide rules and a little-known formula to the data. No two teams in summer camp come up with the same answer, but Sproul is tolerant of the results. "Close enough," he says.

Summer camp is a delight. I relax in the company of people I've come to know well. And Leslie is a close friend. We meet girls here, flirty professors' daughters, barely old enough to know that civil engineering students come to the campus in summer but who delight in riding in the rumble seat of Pa's Mercury coupe. Evenings we debrief our daily work in Pat's basement pizzeria and pub downtown on Mill

Street. On Fridays, Taylor and Sproul, who have worked us extra hours during the first four days of the week and likely look forward to a weekend plug fishing on Pushaw Pond, release us early. Leslie and I head for Temple—to Aunt Marion's.

We are welcome there, and she feeds us fresh vegetables from her abundant garden and macaroni-and-cheese casseroles from her oven. On Saturday nights she serves us thick sirloins. "These will put strength in your muscles for tomorrow's game," she says. "Nothing like beefsteak to build up the muscles." She loans us her Chevrolet as well, and we cruise to Farmington and look for entertainment there: a baseball game at Hippach Field, a visit to the drive-in movie in Jay, or perhaps the lounge at the Riverside Hotel in Livermore Falls. After the movie or last-call at the Riverside, we entertain local girls at the Chuck Wagon restaurant with tales of college life in Orono. Life is pleasant. Sundays are baseball.

Leslie's second start for the Townies comes against North Anson at the Temple ball field. Though he lost the past week to Livermore Falls, his performance at the Falls has earned him pre-game publicity in *The Franklin Journal*—"Boyce plans to pitch Gil Leslie," the newspaper's Goodwin pens. The townsfolk flock to the ball field in large numbers. Aunt Marion is a Gil Leslie fan and wheedles folks all over town to come to the game, come and see the new college kid pitch the winless Townies back to respectability, she promises.

Leslie doesn't disappoint. After walking the first batter of the game and then giving up a double that scores a North Anson run, he settles down and takes command of the game. He limits the North Ansons to six hits and no more runs, and whiffs ten. And he is at his best when the North Ansons threaten to rally, stranding nine runners on the base paths.

Meanwhile the Townies, led by newcomer Bucky Buchanan's three singles and Bernard Davis' three-run triple, tattoo North Anson's reputed ace, right-hander Ralph Manzer, for twelve runs. Tuesday's

Franklin Journal calls Leslie "master of the situation." He has moved us up a notch—we're no longer cellar-dwellers.

We travel to Kingfield to face the undefeated Legionnaires. Leslie is our starting pitcher. *The Franklin Journal* calls the contest between undefeated league leader Kingfield and the recent cellar-dweller Townies a "trophy fight." Juggler Boyce doesn't boast that his team is in a fight for the pennant, but he does believe we can win. He has replaced retiring war veterans with a mixture of agile and enthusiastic youngsters; he has persuaded proven out-of-towners—some are former opponents—to suit up for the Townies; he has found a solid starting lineup. Now, after the Townies have scalped a presumably stronger North Anson team, he feels that, with Leslie on the mound, we are a match for the league leaders. "The Kingies are strong," he tells us, "but not unbeatable."

We are no match for the Legionnaires. They score early and, led by Marty Sillanpaa and his hard-hitting teammates, keep scoring. They increase their lead as the game moves along, and pitcher Howie Dunham holds the Townies to a meager three runs. In the top of the seventh when the game is no longer in doubt, Boyce lifts pitcher Leslie and brings in Lyle Hall. As the Kingfield lead increases, Boyce becomes uncharacteristically suspicious that the plate umpire's eyesight is failing and officially protests the game. But the final score of 9–3 stands: Squanto Wilson, league president, denies the protest; the Legionnaires' winning streak remains intact; and the Townies' upsurge toward league parity founders.

But the Townies do not fold. We climb to fourth place on the strength of one victory. With four games left on our schedule, second-place Livermore Falls and cellar-dwelling Strong are due in Temple for a rare doubleheader. Though Livermore Falls has beaten us by a run with Leslie on the mound, Boyce thinks we are a better team. "They were damned lucky," he cries of their last-minute win at the high school field in Jay. "The bounces went their way."

And Strong?

"Well, Strong hasn't won a game yet this season."

The Townies have won one. "Should be a piece of cake," someone boasts while we warm up.

I don't recall another doubleheader in Townies history. We frequently played two games in a week: a twilight affair midweek and a Sunday afternoon nine-inning contest. But never two games in a day. "Baseball is supposed to be *fun*," Art Mitchell moans.

"This will be fun," I say. "Hell, if we weren't playing baseball, we'd probably have to pitch hay."

Hall goes to the mound against Livermore Falls in the first game. "Put your fastball over the plate, Lyle," Boyce tells him. "That's all you need to do—over the plate."

Hall could throw a baseball as fast as anyone, but neither he nor anyone else had any idea where it was going. When he let his fastball fly, batters worried for their safety and took cover. But when Hall was missing the strike zone, he slowed his pitches and aimed them toward the plate. And batters rapped the ball into the corners of the field.

The Townies jump into the lead, and for six innings, Hall puts his speed pitch close enough to the plate to stay out of trouble. When the seventh comes, the Townies, who have mustered seven runs mainly on the strength of Roger Parlin's triple and two singles, lead by five. In the top of the seventh inning, Hall comes undone. The Indians rally. Eight batters come to the plate, and seven hit Hall's now slowed fastball into some remote part of the field. With one out, the Indians tie the game, 7–7. Boyce turns to Leslie who is throwing behind the dugout. "You ready?" he asks.

Leslie nods, and Boyce goes to the mound to get Hall.

"Give 'em the curveball," Boyce tells Leslie. "They haven't seen a good curveball all day."

Leslie retires the next two batters.

In the bottom of the seventh, the Townies break the tie with a single run. Leslie then shuts out the Indians in the final two innings for the win, his second of the season.

For twenty minutes while Strong players toss baseballs around the field, Leslie sits in the shade of the dugout. Then he goes to the mound for the second game of the afternoon. For nine innings he handcuffs the Strong batters, yielding just six hits and three runs. At the same time, the Townies, with four hits by Bernard Davis and two doubles by Leslie, blitz pitcher Milton Voter for eighteen hits and thirteen runs to secure Leslie's second win of the day. The final score is 13–3. Leslie comes off the field after the last out, and Boyce smiles. "Big day, Gil. We won't win the flag, but we're in the battle for second place."

We travel to Strong and win a slugfest, 16–13. Leslie starts, but is knocked out in the fourth inning. Edgar Davis, a Farmington boy who pitched for the high school and came to the Townies after graduation, comes on and keeps the Strong score below that of the Townies. Townies Bob Parlin and Leslie each slug four hits in the contest. We end the day alone in second place, half a game ahead of North Anson and a full game ahead of the Livermore Falls Indians. "No game next week," Boyce tells us. "Then we'll travel to North Anson for the final game of the season."

Four Townies are selected to play in the league all-star game. Townies first baseman, Bob Parlin, the only player in either division to be selected for the all-star team three times starts for the Northern Division. Lyle Hall is chosen for the pitching staff—Leslie is unknown to team managers at the time of voting—and second baseman Bernard Davis and left fielder Art Mitchell are picked as reserves. Boyce is made team manager for the second time, and the Townies' Glen Tyler is back as batboy. Six Kingfield Legionnaires are selected, seven if Bob Tufts—picked as a pitcher and third baseman—is counted twice. For the North Ansons, pitcher Ralph Manzer and three outfielders suit up for the game. Manzer will likely pitch against the Townies in the battle for second place next week, but Boyce starts him against the Southern Division all-stars. "Maybe Boyce will pitch Manzer the whole game," Art Mitchell says.

The all-stars play a night game at Hippach Field. The Southern Division lineup features four Monmouth Ms and two Randolph VFW, and the Southerns win handily. Lefty Dick Grondin starts on the mound, backed up by proven winners, Bob Baumer, Bill Verhille, and Johnny McCabe. "We were never in it," Boyce admits after the game. "The Southern Division sure is the class of the league."

"Mebbe, mebbe not," Kingfield's Howie Dunham mutters.

North Anson came into the Northern Division unknown to us. We knew that Madison and Bingham, teams in the same upper Kennebec River Valley, both fielded exemplary nines over the years, and we kept away from them for the most part. But North Anson's reputation was a mystery. We had no trouble beating them earlier in the season in Temple, however, and Boyce drove upriver on the final day brimming with enthusiasm—the Townies led the North Ansons by a full game. Sole possession of second place was at stake. Though a loss would keep us in a second-place tie, not something to be scoffed at, Boyce did not favor a deadlock. And the players knew it. We also knew that he would accept whatever happened and not dwell on it. The pre-game *Franklin Journal* termed it the weekend's featured contest. We hoped to be ahead at the end.

It's a seesaw game. The Townies score first, a run in the top of the second off North Anson starter Winfield Davis, who is making his first league start. North Anson answers with two runs in the bottom of the inning. The Townies regain the lead in the top of the fourth, when Leslie homers over the left field fence for two more runs. But then we come apart. Leslie is not up to snuff. Maybe he ate too much of Aunt Marion's beefsteak the night before, or hit too many golf balls at the Jay

Hill driving range, or stayed too late at the Riverside's lounge. The North Ansons get to him in the fourth inning, and the fifth, and again in the sixth. I crouch at third base during one of these ragged innings while Leslie tries to reckon with a so-so curveball and a porous defense, and I mutter, "Hit it to me; hit it to me," a tactic I felt for most of my baseball career would result in an out. A batter cooperates, hitting a bouncer to my right. I glove it and throw low right by Bob Parlin at first base into the crowd, my only error of the season. A runner scoots by, and then another. Boyce comes out in the seventh and pulls Leslie. Hall comes on.

The Townies battle back. We knock Winfield Davis out, and our bats keep us in North Anson's shadow all afternoon: the Parlins, Bob and Roger, knock run-producing doubles; I hit two singles, and the rest of our lineup chips in generously as well. Runs are plentiful—the Townies score thirteen—but the North Ansons stay just beyond our reach. Boyce is frustrated. He paces, he points, he pleads. At the end he accepts it: the final score is North Anson 17, Townies 13.

It was a season of near misses. The short eight-game schedule put too much pressure on us to be perfect. We lost the first game in an instant when explosive Kingfield scored five in the ninth to win by a run; then Livermore Falls rallied for two in the ninth to edge us by another run. Two blips and we were mired in the cellar. Then we struggled back and contended for outright second place. Last came the telling game at North Anson. *The Franklin Journal* reported it a scuffle, but there was no doubt of the outcome after the fourth inning. Though the second-place deadlock disappointed us, we seemed destined to lose up there, and we lost with emphasis, putting a cloud over our season-long struggle for recognition in the new league. We blew it.

Unbeaten Kingfield claimed the title, and confirmed their claim by continuing to win through three rounds of the Yankee Amateur Baseball Congress tournament at Pettingill Park in Auburn, eventually losing to Vermont champion Barre. That Bob Parlin and three other

Townies had made the all-star team, and Bucky Buchanan, our new right fielder had won the Northern Division batting championship hitting singles, was little consolation for us. Though Boyce had managed us marvelously, blending a variety of skills and ages, men who hardly knew each other, even some with no particular loyalty to Temple except for their love of the game, into a first-rate team, I wondered, after the calamity at North Anson, if we could ever again be as we were.

In July 1954 I report to work at the highway department six weeks late, six weeks after Mr. Merrill has assigned the summer work to a cadre of college students. But he finds work for me, critical work that none of his field staff is available to perform, construction work that must be performed now lest his contractors be delayed completing important projects. Mr. Merrill introduces me to Mr. Arthur, an office-type engineer with an upper-lip moustache and wire-rimmed glasses and whose full name I forget immediately. Arthur is moderate and measured and doesn't carry a suitcase with him as I do. He sleeps at home nights. We travel to the job in the same four-door sedan in which I envision he takes his wife to Sunday church services.

He drives us, my suitcase tucked in the trunk of the sedan, to Rockland. Our job there, a specialty task performed only once on a job—and often not at all on country projects—is to scratch a blue crayon line onto upright stakes standing along the centerline of Main Street, which I notice is gravel now and bustling: men walk around pointing, a truck dumps something, a grader windrows cobblestones to the side. The blue line will be scratched exactly twenty-four inches above the soon-to-be finished new-pavement surface, and will be used as a guide by the fine-grading and black-topping crews that will follow us.

Also tucked in the luggage compartment of the sedan are the instruments of our work—transit, tripod, and leveling rod—instruments I am familiar with. We assemble them and Arthur directs me to hold the leveling rod on the head of a large iron spike driven into a tree root on someone's lawn. Then he somehow computes the various readings that will position the leveling rod at the right elevation against each centerline stake. I hold the rod, or a small portion of it, against each stake and slide it up or down at Arthur's signal until he grunts, "Gud." Then I mark the stake with a knife blade and scratch the knife mark with blue crayon. This routine lasts for about a quarter-mile of U.S. Route 1. At the end of the day, Arthur tucks the instruments into the trunk again, drops me and my suitcase at the Thorndike Hotel in the center of town, and drives home to Augusta

Our work in Rockland lasts for most of a week; then we move to Fairfield, followed by Thomaston, and then Brunswick. Arthur drives home to Augusta every night, and I spend the lonesome weeks in some seedy hotel or rooming house with no car, no telephone, no television, and no one in town that I know. I eat supper in a Main Street diner, sit in the hotel lobby, read local newspapers, and go to movies I haven't seen in some other town. I write an occasional letter to my girlfriend of the moment, but have no hope of receiving a response. I am lonely.

But the work fascinates me. Arthur, normally an office geek who seldom ventures into the bowels of a project, and who has been sent into the field with a moonstruck college kid to keep dusty, dirty road-building projects on schedule, shows me how to come up with the readings that control the height of the rod against the stake and lets me operate the level while he takes a turn with the rod. He explains to me in excruciating detail the construction activities going on around us. Perhaps they are as fascinating to him as they are to me. He treats my transgressions gently, and I correct them. I suspect that Arthur's summer is not turning out as he had hoped: an airy, lighted office in Augusta with time to go out for lunch each day, frequently with Mrs. Arthur. That he is Mr. Merrill's choice to spend the summer in the dust gnaws on him. But he is good to me, and I become accustomed to his eccentricities and grow to like him. I do as he asks, and he, as others have, rewards me with his teachings.

Finally, I leave Arthur and join a crew in coastal Belfast in time to witness destructive Hurricane Carol. The hurricane drives the four of us into the rooming house while it uproots giant elm trees, blows shed roofs onto Route 1, and otherwise wreaks havoc outside our nineteenth-century manor window. I am no longer lonely. We sleep, play poker, and frequently send the rodman out to buy pizza and more beer. At the end of the week, the storm is over, and the summer as well. Aunt Marion meets me in Augusta and drives me to Temple for the three-day Labor Day weekend.

Later, at Phi Kappa Sigma, Leslie and I recount our summer with the Townies. "I'll never forget," he tells me, "the goodness of Lawrence and Marion. How they took me in and fed me and accepted me like I was one of the family. And," he muses, "I pitched and won both games of a doubleheader—in semipro ball, too."

Chapter Sixteen

CHASING MARBLES

T hough Boyce was a man of unyielding optimism, luck was not a frequent companion, no matter how hard he worked. And many times, the harder he worked, the less he seemed to benefit from good fortune. But hope never abandoned him. He never stopped chasing his dreams.

The 1954 baseball season does not discourage him. "After all," he reasons to a crowd one evening at the general store, "we finished in second place. Gosh, we had Kingfield beaten the first game of the season, and we let 'em off the hook. Who woulda thought they'd go undefeated? Of all teams. Heck, if we'd won that one, who knows what woulda happened?"

The lingerers lean forward a mite to hear what Boyce is saying. "Tough competition—teams like Kingfield, Bingham, North Jay—they'll make us a better team. An' Tyler's due home anytime now," he says, "and Heath should show up soon." He lights a cigarette and blows the smoke into the rising air. "And Al Bergeron. He's finished building his house. I expect him back. And Bucky Buchanan, too. I mean he won the battin' title last year. He wants to play. Who knows? We might win somethin'."

"What about Gil Leslie?" someone asks.

"I don't know about Leslie yet," he says. "But he'll be around in the spring, and stay with us until school is out anyway. And I'm expectin' he might stay for the summer."

Evenings at Phi Kappa Sigma, forty of us observe study time. I read structural theory, set up a solution to a water supply problem, or compute the stress in a riveted steel girder oblivious to any chitchat or commotion, and am interrupted only by a visit to the kitchen for a snack or a chat with Matante, our French housemother, or the inevitable nightcap at Pat's downtown pub, which starts for some as early as nine o'clock. The work is more difficult, but more interesting as well. The deeper I get into difficulty the better understanding I have of what it takes to be a civil engineer.

My grade point average improves to a comfortable level. I am confident I can succeed. Boyce and the Townies have changed my outlook. A bad grade doesn't discourage me. It won't mark me for life as a poor student. If I suffer a setback or fall into a losing streak, I am no longer paralyzed by fear. I just keep on struggling. Perhaps the next exam, maybe the next lab report, I'll start a winning streak and move ahead again. I know now that setbacks are inevitable—and temporary. I work harder and occasionally treat myself to some time at Pat's rathskeller. I don't have a girlfriend, and I don't go home often.

Spring comes in April 1955. The snow disappears. Boyce calls for workouts. "Tyler's not coming back. Says he's retired from baseball," he tells us.

"How about Paul Heath?"

"Heath's done, too. An' so's Al Bergeron. We're a little thin for players right now. But we'll be all right."

We start the season with an exhibition game at Strong. "Strong's not in the league this year," Boyce says. "I don't think they stack up well here. They'll probably go back into the North Franklin League."

"Who's coming in?" I ask.

"Bingham," he answers. "And North Jay is comin' back. They'll play in the Northern Division with us. We'll have six teams. Should be fun."

After the warm-up with Strong, Boyce declares us ready. On Memorial Day we travel to Bingham for the league opener. On the way upriver, Boyce talks about the Bingham Bears, the baseball power of the upper Kennebec River valley. They have, he tells us, produced some of the best baseball players in Maine, including at least one major leaguer. Listening to him, it occurs to me that the Bingham baseball field may be no place for the Townies, but I keep quiet. Boyce doesn't listen to pessimists.

The Bingham ball field is located on a flatland by the river. The Bears are taking batting practice. A Bingham hitter drives an arcing fly ball over an outfielder racing for it near the fence, and another hulking batter waits for a turn. He hits another, and I wonder how long the game will take. "Get loose," Boyce says. "We're next."

Boyce puts the best he has on the field: Gil Leslie on the pitcher's mound; Bob Parlin, Bernard Davis, Hall, and me at the infield positions; Art Mitchell, West Farmington's Bob Bell, and Bucky Buchanan in the outfield. Roger Parlin will catch . But Al Bergeron is gone; and Paul Heath and Cal Tyler, too.

The game seems long. Leslie goes the distance, but we suffer a predictable and convincing loss, 8–2. "They beat us because they're a better team," Boyce reminds us on the drive home. "We're respectable. We'll be all right."

North Jay and lefty curveballer Don Oakes come to Hippach Field. We haven't seen Oakes and his loopy curveball since the 1953 pennant race, when he pitched for the Monmouth Ms—nor have we hankered to. We first faced him in 1952—twice. It was our first year in the Lakes Region League. Oakes, one of the league's premier pitchers, bested Cal Tyler early in the season at North Jay; Tyler evened the score at Temple, and we finished a game ahead of the North Jays in the standings. But at Hippach, Oakes baffles us. Leslie keeps the game close, but without runs, we are forced to start the season with consecutive losses.

Rain washes out the North Anson game, and before we can play a makeup, Gil Leslie leaves for his summer job in Connecticut and Art Mitchell moves to Gorham, where he earns his college tuition in a Westbrook paper mill. Boyce is in another pickle. We trail the field two games—the rainout is our best performance to date—and the lineup has blanks to fill again. We go to Kingfield with a 0–2 record and a hopeful attitude. The Legionnaires are winless as well.

Boyce starts Lyle Hall on the mound. He represents the entire pitching staff. "No one's in the bullpen today," Boyce tells us before the game. But our hitters have a good day—Bob Parlin, Edgar Davis, and I each get three hits—and Hall is able to keep the game close. In the top of the eighth, we score a half-dozen runs when Kingfield starter Marty Sillanpaa runs out of gas. Before Howie Dunham can quell the uprising, we build a comfortable lead. Boyce sends Hall back to the mound in the bottom of the eighth confident of our first victory of the season. He also sends rookie Gary Bergeron, who played for the high school as a freshman this past spring, to left field. "You'll make a fine shortstop for us someday," he tells Bergeron, "but you need to get some playing time first."

Gary Bergeron was five years old when the Townies played their first game at the new Temple ball field on Independence Day, 1946. Al Bergeron, his older brother, played shortstop that day, and Gary's dream was born: he would be a shortstop, too—for the Townies.

Growing up, Bergeron hung out near the dugout and watched and listened to Boyce. He came up with a battered hand-me-down baseball glove, and Boyce sent him into foul ball territory to retrieve errants that had ricocheted off parked cars or flown into roadside bushes.

Eventually, like many of us, he stood on the infield during batting practice—shortstop was his hangout—with his ragged glove and snagged ground balls hit his way, all the time listening to Boyce, "Keep the glove low, Gary. Keep it low. The glove comes up quicker than it goes down."

By age ten, he had grown big enough to swing a bat, and occasionally Boyce let him swing at Tyler's batting practice pitches. "Keep the bat still, Gary, and when you step into the pitch, turn your belly button at Tyler. 'Belly button it,' they say. It'll give you room to swing the bat."

Bergeron stuck with Boyce as if he had no place else to go. He had so many brothers and sisters at home, he probably figured they wouldn't miss him anyway. Boyce would take him on the bakery wagon for a day and they'd talk baseball; perhaps stop by a school yard for a few minutes and watch a game. Boyce counseled him: "Don't reach for the runner when he's stealing second, or he'll slip by you. Reach for a spot between the runner and the bag. He'll slide right into the ball." Later he took Gary to a sporting goods store fifty miles away in Auburn, and they picked out new uniforms for the Townies. "Whaddaya like, Gary? Red stripes?"

Bergeron went to high school in Farmington and, in 1955, made the baseball team as a freshman. Boyce fitted him to one of the Townies' new, red-striped uniforms and found a seat for him on the bench—until the eighth inning in Kingfield, when the Townies pull away to what Boyce thinks is a safe lead, 15–7.

But Lyle Hall is pitching. The Legionnaires erupt for seven runs off Hall's erratic right arm in what *The Franklin Journal* will call a "wild eighth inning." But Boyce, absent any pitching backup, is forced to stick with Hall, and he fidgets on the bench and watches the Kingies close in on the luckless Townies. Rookie Bergeron, the high school freshman, also fidgets in unfamiliar left field, fearful the ball will be hit his way, wishing—praying—that it go somewhere else.

With two runners on base, two outs, and the Townies leading by a single run, Bergeron's fear appears. Howie Dunham lofts a towering fly ball into left field. Bergeron scurries backward after it. But the drive twists away from him. Just as it soars past, he lunges to his right, and the ball snags in his outstretched glove. Bergeron comes off the field grinning. Boyce clasps his hand. "Nice catch, Gary. You made me look like a genius putting you out there." Hall weathers the ninth without more damage and we claim our first victory of the season.

The win over Kingfield makes the Townies legitimate. North Jay—Don Oakes on the mound—outscored the Bingham Bears earlier in the day, and turned the division into a horse race. *The Franklin Journal* will report on Tuesday that the race "could find any one of the six teams picking up the marbles." *Kingfield, after their loss to the Townies, will have to be figured a long shot,* I think. Unlike the Townies, they haven't showed they can win a game. And the pitching Kingfield will face at Bingham, North Jay, and likely Livermore Falls will make it tough for them to pick up any marbles at all. But without Leslie, or some other reliable pitcher to go with Hall, it will be tough for Boyce and the Townies to pick up any marbles, too.

During the years Boyce managed the Townies, he found only two effective pitchers in Temple: Tarmo Sade and Calvin Tyler. The rest of his pitching staff—Heath, Larry Davis, Leslie, Lyle Hall, and others—came to the Townies from out of town. Though they pitched well, they could not be counted on to spend more than a season with us. In the Lakes Region League, a team needed an ace, a stopper that could consistently keep the games close, and a reliever to back him up. The good teams had a stopper: Randolph's Bill Verhille, Monmouth's Dick Grondin, North Jay's Don Oakes, Tri-corner's Earl Tibbetts. The Townies haven't enjoyed a stopper since Tyler and Heath left the team after our first year in the league, yet we face such pitching game after game.

On Independence Day, Kingfield, still looking for its first win, is scheduled to face North Jay. On the same day, the Townies will host North Anson. Boyce believes we can still pick up some marbles if he can put a stronger arm on the mound. He calls Cal Tyler. "The third-place North Anson Aces are only a game ahead of us," I envision him saying. "You can do it." Tyler shows up early Sunday afternoon at the Temple ball field with his dusty leather glove and spikes and wearing a Townies' uniform that fits a dite tight. Boyce greets him and sets him to work loosening for the game.

In 1952, the Townies's first year in the Lakes Region League, Tyler was the league's preeminent pitcher, a star. He struck out 100 batters that year in seventy-one innings, a league record. He threw three score-less innings in the league's all-star game under the lights at Hippach Field against the North Franklin League all-stars and former New York Yankee pitcher Lefty Gomez. And he finished the season with a 7–2 record for the second-place Townies. By all accounts, his mixture of pitches, a changing-speed fastball, fast-breaking curve, and wildness, was as daunting as anyone's in the league. Tyler was a star—and then the army drafted him.

Back from the army, Tyler had no interest in furthering his base-ball career and looked to settle down. He went to work for the paper company in Jay, married, bought a house in Wilton, and started a fam-ily. But when Boyce called him to pitch against the North Ansons, he agreed to come and test the current condition of his once-dominant right arm.

He looks heavier than when he last pitched in 1952. Army food, contrary to popular notion, was likely an improvement over his diet in Temple. Some folks think the extra weight will add zip to his fastball. Boyce hopes it will. But I wonder how he can go without pitching for most of three years and then just walk to the mound and overpower the Aces, a scrappy team that we lose to regularly. It turns out he can't.

Tyler takes the mound to a ripple of applause from fans. "You get 'em, Cal," and "It's just like the old days, Cal," they shout. But North Anson shows no respect for the returning star. By the end of the fourth inning, the Aces have ten hits and almost as many runs. Tyler is wild.

When he takes a tad off the fastball to get it over the plate, they smack it to all corners of the field. In the fifth inning, Boyce summons Lyle Hall.

When it's over, North Anson claims the win, 12–7. They keep pace with the Bingham Bears, who have shellacked Kingfield with twenty-five hits and twenty-two runs in a record fifty-four at-bats, both teams one game behind the Livermore Falls Indians and North Jay. We fall to 2–5, virtually out of the competition. My three-hit game goes for naught. Tyler goes home to Wilton, puts his glove and spikes in the back of the closet, and reports for work at the mill on Monday. "Who wouldda thought?" Boyce mutters.

Hall pitches against cellar-dweller Kingfield the following week in Temple, a game that we win without any theatrics. But a week later in Livermore Falls when Boyce writes the name of the starting pitcher in the score book, he writes Clyde Pingree.

Pingree, a right-hander, last pitched in 1954 for Strong in a double-header at Temple. He threw the customary variety of fastballs and curveballs, but his asset was the strength of his arm. He starred at shortstop for four years at Strong High School and made the 1954 Lakes Region League all-star team as a shortstop, but during Strong's hapless 1954 season, manager Ike Spencer often called Pingree and his strong right arm to the mound to quell an uprising. Spencer viewed Pingree's arm as a valuable backup to Strong's weak starting pitching. He could relieve the starter in the middle innings after the opposing team had built an insurmountable lead and throw the ball hard enough to finish the game before darkness set in.

But Boyce, persuaded by Pingree's youth, sees him as a starter and takes him to Livermore Falls to face the league-leading Indians. It's a step up for Pingree, and he admits to some nervousness. But he goes to the mound with the determination of a rookie and the deportment of a veteran. The game is close. Pingree throws well for five innings. But the Indians nick him for eight runs in the sixth, including a round-tripper by ex-Farmington Flyer Mike Puiia, and settle any doubt over the outcome. Lyle Hall finishes. The Townies threaten to come back but fail to take full advantage of their eighteen hits—three by me—and we go down, 12–10.

We travel to North Anson the following Sunday. "Pingree won't be going." Boyce tells us. Hall pitches—and loses again, this time to Ralph Manzor, the Aces workhorse who carries them to third place, one game away from all the marbles, ending the Townies' long, somewhat dispiriting season against superior teams.

Though Boyce's judgment in the use of pitchers might have been questioned—should he have put so much faith in Pingree, for example, or Tyler—his enthusiasm and optimism did not falter. "Of course we had a losing season," he says after the North Anson game. "We were playing big leaguers. That doesn't make us a bad team. We're a good team."

We finish the season with three wins and seven losses, ahead of only Kingfield, who lost eight. Gary Bergeron's catch in Kingfield kept us out of the cellar. My three hits at North Anson put my batting average at .360 for the season, but I can find little to celebrate. Gil Leslie has left for Connecticut, I don't have a girlfriend, and the money I earn working for the highway department goes directly into Aunt Marion's bank account.

Chapter Seventeen
MACK'S ALL STARS

I n the spring of 1956, after the final tuition bill has been paid at the university, Aunt Marion buys a new car, a spanking-new four-door Chevrolet Bel Air, the top of the line, a car with loopy chrome stripes and racy tail fins. To me it seems a bit out of character for her, but she doesn't see it that way. "Of course I'm going to have a Chevrolet," she remarks. "I've *always* driven a Chevrolet."

She lets me use her new Chevy on weekends. I wash it for her on Saturday to show my appreciation—polish the shiny chrome to draw attention to its newness—and drive it to my customary Saturday-night haunts: the State Theater in Farmington, the Riverside Hotel's lounge in Livermore Falls, or the top of Titcomb Hill in Farmington, where my friend Stew and I listen to Mel Allen broadcast Yankees' games on WINS New York and sip, as Allen suggests during the commercial breaks, from a bottle of Ballantine Ale. Though Aunt Marion does not caution me to drive her new Chevrolet slowly or safely or sanely, I am aware of the consequences of being indiscreet and respect her unspoken wishes. I treat the Chevy carefully.

Aunt Marion was proud of her new car. When she drove, she sat upright in the driver's seat. She motored slowly and waved to bystanders and lingerers outside the general store. She took neighbors shopping in Farmington and offered rides to surprised pedestrians. But as much as she obviously adored and showed off her upscale Chevy, it had one trait that aggravated her: it was two long to fit in her barn. She was forced to leave the tail fins sticking out the door into the driveway. Though most of the Bel Air was undercover, knowing that the car was not compatible with her storage space and that neighbors would likely gossip with each other about her buying such an outsized car in the first place, gnawed on her. She knew, too, that snow would come eventually and blow up against the barn as it had every year for a hundred years, requiring the door to be closed. Unless an arrangement was made before fall, the Bel Air would be forced to suffer winter's trauma outside.

She does what she often does when things don't fit together right. She calls Dick Blodgett, former Townies' second baseman and the carpenter of choice in Temple: kitchen cabinets, parlor furniture, sunlit verandas. He comes to the house with a variety of saws, a pinch bar, and an outsize ball peen hammer and goes to work knocking a sizable hole in the back wall of Aunt Marion's 1840s barn. I am stunned. What's he doing?" I ask her.

"Putting a little extension on the back of the barn," she answers.

"So the car will fit?" I ask, as if I don't know what she is up to.

"Yes," she goes on. "You know, winter and all."

I look at what Blodgett is doing. A capable job, no question, but I don't like the notion of corrupting her aged barn, building a homely node in the back wall with modern lumber, galvanized nails, and a piece of cement for a foundation, all just to hide the Chevy's tail fins. "Why don't you just buy a smaller car?" I ask her.

"A small car!" she retorts. "You know I'm not going to buy a small car. Who would think I'd buy a small car? I've always had a big car, and I'm going to have one now."

I am unable to avoid—as I should have—pursuing the matter further. After all, I think, she sent me to engineering school to learn how to logically solve a host of diverse problems, and this one barely dents my acquired sense for the right answer. "But the big car you owned before this one," I argue, "fit in the barn. Why not buy another one the same size?"

She is not impressed by my reasoning. "That car was the biggest Chevrolet I could buy, and this one is the same," she blurts. "I'm not buying a small car—why, who would think?"

I drop my objection to lengthening the barn.

"Good gosh! What's left for us?" I hear Boyce remark from behind the newspaper in his parlor chair. He has just read that the hapless Kingfield Legionnaires have dropped out of the Lakes Region League's Northern Division and will be replaced by Skowhegan, a town the size of Farmington twenty-five miles east. Boyce realizes for the first time that he shouldn't be in the Lakes Region League, that the competition here has improved well beyond the Townies' ability to compete. We lack dependable pitching, and our hitters will face such stalwarts as former Yankee farmhand Toppy Washburn, Bunky Davis, future Maine Baseball Hall of Famers Drig Fournier and Don Oakes, and whoever the potent Skowhegans put on the mound. Unlike Aunt Marion, Boyce has no barn he can lengthen. I think if the news had come sooner, Boyce'd have withdrawn the Townies from the league as well. Now we face the 1956 season virtually alone. It's too late to withdraw. Boyce has committed us to play, and he will live with the decision. "Whatever happens will be all right," he says.

He settles on Lyle Hall as starting pitcher and, desperate for help on the mound, recruits Farmington's Collis Ames and Bobby Roux to back up Hall in the bullpen. He also has his eye on Gary Bergeron's arm. The position players, Boyce thinks, will be the same as last year: Roger Parlin will catch; Bob Parlin, Bernard Davis, and Edgar Davis will be in the infield with me; Art Mitchell, Bob Bell, and batting champion Bucky Buchanan will be in the outfield.

I tell Boyce I might not play. He is surprised, as I expected him to be. I enjoyed my best year in 1955 and became a valued Townies player. Boyce started me every game—at second, third, shortstop—and I fielded flawlessly, hit .360, and drove home a few key runs with a well-placed extra-base hit or two. He has no reason not to expect me back.

"Why not?" he asks.

"I may not be around," I stammer. I struggle to tell him something about beginning my life, that I am growing up, that I have acquired a job—two jobs—in civil engineering and don't know where I'll be working, and that I look forward to doing as well in civil engineering as I have with the Townies. "I'll know soon," I say.

In June, graduation over, word comes from the highway department to report for work. "See Dave Smith up there," Vinton Savage, the new head of highway engineering, writes me from Augusta. "He'll be looking after some construction for us and will keep you busy with him." *How ironic*, I think. *My mentor, the same man who took me out of Magoni's soda shop and inspired me to study engineering.*

I find Smith in Mexico, Maine, as Savage promised, in an eight-by-ten-foot shack filled with plans, file boxes, reference books, and myriad tools and supplies. A sheet of plywood nailed across one end serves as a desk. He rolls out a set of plans and shows me the work. "The job stretches four miles east to Dixfield. And when we get this one going we'll start up another one in Farmington Falls." He introduces me to my crew and hands me the roll of plans. "You're the boss," he tells me. "You'll be with me all summer, no doubt." *Boyce will be pleased*, I think.

Boyce endures his most frustrating season ever. His pitching options severely limited, he starts Lyle Hall in the season-opener at North Anson. It is a dreary day, and I am reminded of the season-ending game two years ago when Hall came in to relieve my college pal Gil

Leslie, I made a crucial error in that game, and we were beaten. Now the Aces nibble at Hall for nine runs before Boyce brings in Bobby Roux, a young lefty who has pitched well for the high school team in Farmington. Roux finishes the game with the Townies on the losing end of an 11–3 score. The Bingham Bears, whom experts refer to as the league's elite, are next.

Boyce is confronted by a quandary best described, he says later, by one of his players who comes to him and asks, "Who in hell is going to pitch next week?" Boyce can't answer the question. He wants to challenge Bingham, make them earn their reputation, but he feels that neither Hall nor Bobby Roux, nor the untried Collis Ames is capable of keeping the Bears in check. He needs a pitcher who has been tested, one who has shown he can pitch at this level. Desperate, he calls Kingfield and talks to Bob Tufts, an all-star pitcher and shortstop for the Kingies the year before. Tufts agrees to travel to Bingham with the Townies.

It's two games into the season, the Bears are undefeated, and in the early stages of what looks to be a tight race with the North Anson Aces for the league pennant. The Townies are winless, and perhaps faint-hearted. But they play well in the face of the mighty Bears; Tufts duels Toppy Washburn inning for inning in a close contest. But the Bears come up with key hits late in the game, and the Townies drop, predictably, to 0–2. The following Sunday at Temple, Tufts takes the mound again. It's a battle between cellar-dwellers and the Townies loses to the Livermore Falls Indians, 9–3. After three games, the Townies are alone in last place. Tufts leaves for North Anson, where he will play shortstop for the Aces and be selected for the Northern Division all-star team.

The Townies continue to lose. They lose to North Jay and Don Oakes' curveball. They lose to Skowhegan and then again to the North Anson Aces. The losing streak reaches six games. Mercifully, the next

Boyce arrives at Hippach Field with a box of baseballs and the score book, c. 1956.

game, Bingham at Temple, is rained out in the second inning. Boyce reschedules the game for Friday night—at Hippach Field in Farmington.

Boyce credits the Sunday rain to Divine intervention. The delay gives him time to look for a pitcher. He calls Clyde Pingree. "I'm playing shortstop for Strong," Pingree tells him, "in the North Franklin League."

"I know it," Boyce answers, but when he finishes talking, Pingree agrees to come to Hippach Field and throw his fastball at the undefeated Bingham Bears.

A large crowd comes to Hippach Field on Friday to enjoy a summer evening. They sit in the bleachers along each foul line and in the grandstand behind home plate. The Bears arrive from Bingham with both pitching aces, Toppy Washburn and Bunky Davis. But Hank Washburn, Bingham's canny manager, needs aces Washburn and Davis rested for a doubleheader on Sunday against North Jay. With the league championship at stake, he isn't taking any chances and he names untested rookie Les Nicolas starting pitcher. "Les will be able to handle Temple all right," I envision Hank Washburn saying.

The determined Townies, buoyed by seeing Pingree on the mound, play well. Nicolas is a pleasant change from the customary pitching in the Northern Division, and the Townies build up a 6–2 lead on the Bears. The crowd turns their attention to the game. In the sixth inning, Hank Washburn owns up to his flawed strategy and summons Toppy Washburn from the bullpen. But it is too late. Pingree meets the challenge straight on and pitches a complete game. We knock off the league leaders. Final score: Townies 6, Bears 2. Hank Washburn and his rested pitching staff retreat to Bingham and the doubleheader with North Jay.

The Townies deservedly gloat a bit. They have escaped being skunked for the season by the fortunate blink of a second-inning rain shower, and they reside in last place, though with distinction. Two days later, the Bingham Bears outscore North Jay twice—Toppy Washburn pitches a no-hitter and Bunky Davis a two-hitter—and climb back into a first-place tie with North Anson. But the loss to the Townies is telling. When league play ends, the Aces have won all the marbles. The Bears finish one game behind and the Townies stay in the cellar with honor. Following the season, the team are invited to show off our skills at "Mac McLaughlin Night" at Hippach Field.

Frank "Mac" McLaughlin was born in 1882 in Starks, Maine, a somewhat homely farming settlement located in a Somerset County no-man's land four miles north of Mercer on the west bank of Lemon Stream. As a boy, he played baseball in the pastures and meadows, but when he graduated from Starks High School, he determined to be a businessman. He left Starks for a two-year business college, likely in nearby Waterville, and learned the rudiments of keeping journals and ledgers and analyzing profit and loss statements. Following the classroom experience, he returned home and looked for a way to apply his business know-how. But McLaughlin failed to profit in Starks and focused his idle time on his first love: baseball.

Baseball popularity grew quickly in the early 1900s. The major leagues organized into two leagues and culminated their seasons with a World Series that captured people's fancies all across the nation. Local teams formed, expanded their schedules, and new teams organized to meet the demand for baseball. In 1905, McLaughlin put together a youth team in Starks, the Somerset Juniors, and they played a schedule of games with similar teams from nearby Farmington, New Sharon, Mercer, and Norridgewock. Baseball continued to gain popularity, and the demand for skilled players increased. A team in Farmington recruited McLaughlin. He moved there and played his favorite game with such Farmington stalwarts as Roland Dingley and George McGary. Business was bustling in Farmington as well, and McLaughlin acquired a gasoline station, where he applied his business-school learning between baseball games.

Gasoline sales flourished at the intersection of Hill Street and New Sharon Road. The automobile—mainly Ford Model Ts and Hupmobile Runabouts—had come into use in Farmington, and McLaughlin was kept busy filling tanks with gas and tires with air. The competitive McLaughlin hired a pump tender, added a general store to his station, and put horseshoe pits in the side yard to attract people. Kids came and tossed horseshoes; older men sat on the benches McLaughlin put outside, talked, played cards, and waited their turn with the shoes. And after a morning of tossing horseshoes, folks picked up a small bag of penny candy or a quart of Bailey's milk at the general store and drove the Runabout, newly filled with McLaughlin's gasoline, home for lunch.

About 1920, perhaps a mite earlier, McLaughlin, looking for something more to attract customers, formed his own baseball team, Mack's All Stars. He recruited players from Farmington and nearby Farmington Falls, West Farmington, Temple, and perhaps New Vineyard. Local iceman Refino Collette, pump tender Apple Oliver, postal clerk Ken Brooks, undertaker Vint Davis, Clayton Berry, Stewart (Stoogie) Whittier, and part-time promoter Jack Callahan, later to be organizer of what would be known as Callahan's Hard Cider Boys, all played for McLaughlin. And Lawrence Boyce, who had learned baseball in the Pine Tree League with the Norway-South Paris nine as a youth and in 1920 or so had moved with his parents to West Farmington, joined Mack's All Stars as well.

Mack's All Stars barnstormed throughout Franklin and Somerset Counties, entertained large crowds, and won the preponderance of their games and the hearts of their followers. They lost some, too, but baseball was fun. The All Stars' popularity grew, and they attracted large crowds. Outlying towns put together local teams and sought Mac's presence on Sunday afternoons.

McLaughlin treated his players well. He bought them snappy uniforms—his gasoline station likely advertised on the back—and filled them with after-game nourishment. They loved him and gave him their best performances. He rewarded their winning with more recognition. McLaughlin's life came together in Farmington. He could make it all work here: a baseball team, a business, and horseshoe pits.

When World War II broke out, local baseball took a break. Mack's All Stars took off their baseball suits and put on service uniforms. "I'll wait for you," McLaughlin told them. But after the war, small towns everywhere began to put together town teams—Farmington had four—and there was no more room for Mack's All Stars. His players dispersed to hometown teams, and the remnant all-stars, too few to form a team of their own, recruited a few new and younger players and campaigned under the tutelage of Jack Callahan as Callahan's Hard Cider Boys. Mack's All Stars were consigned to history.

But McLaughlin's loyal followers did not forget. Ten years later, in August 1956, his baseball team shut down by World War II, his gasoline station, general store, and horseshoe pits victims of post-war road construction, Farmington turned out for "Mac McLaughlin Night" at sold-out Hippach Field. The man, the all-stars who played so zealously for him, and appreciative fans and followers all came together once more in gratitude for the many years McLaughlin devoted to Farmington baseball. The feature entertainment was a baseball game between the former Mack's All Stars—the old timers—and the Temple Townies.

A marching band led the parade, former Mack's All Stars followed the band, then the Temple Townies, youth teams in uniform, fans and followers. They marched down Farmington's Main Street to Intervale Road and Hippach Field. They took their places in preparation for the game. Youth in a baseball uniform were admitted free in tribute to Mac's love for the kids, and coaches from Farmington, Fairbanks, Strong, and Phillips brought their young teams. Mac was dressed in a coat and tie—"He looks like Philadelphia manager Connie Mack," someone said—and paced in the dugout telling stories, "Do you re-member the time we went to Bingham?" he asked a player. "I was scared to the heavens—but we gave 'em a game, I'll say."

"How'd you come to go there? Bingham was the best around."

"We gave 'em a helluva game—they only beat us, 1–0. Best they could do," Mac chuckled.

"You were that good, were you?"

"Won thirteen straight one year," he said. "An' then I bought 'em new uniforms. They strutted around in them uniforms with their heads in the clouds, and we never won another game all year. Those uniforms were a big mistake, I'll say."

"And there's the time," he went on, "that I had to bail my catcher out of jail on Sunday mornin' so's we could play. I only had one catcher then, and he'd gone and got hisself likkered up and locked up for bein' too rowdy someplace. I had to bail him out." McLaughlin laughed. "It's the only thing I coulda done, I'll say."

Boyce put on an old Mack's All Stars uniform and took the field against his own team. With no manager to guide him, Lyle Hall, the Townies' pitching mainstay, took the mound. Though the night was undoubtedly a gala tribute to "Mac" and the memory of his All Stars, the outcome of the game is unknown. I suspect the silence is because no one kept score, the outcome unimportant. The night belonged to McLaughlin.

Chapter Eighteen
LAWRENCE BOYCE (II)

I n June 1956, in Mexico, Maine, with graduation behind me, I am titled Assistant Engineer. My surveying crew comprises three other people: a civil engineering student at the university, a part-time highway department technician, and a mechanical engineering student at the university who has been in and out of various schools and jobs looking for himself. Mechanical engineering student brings the newspaper to work and fills in any idle seconds with a stab at the daily crossword. I sense civil engineering student and technician will establish the pace of our work. Mechanical engineering student will moderate it.

Highway 2 through Mexico is a mess. Narrow and cracked, full of potholes, it no longer serves well the loaded logging trucks that labor to the paper mill in Rumford, or the tourists who motor alongside the Androscoggin River on their way to Bar Harbor or South Bristol. Road machinery has arrived and is tearing it apart. Our job is to put in reference points—wooden stakes and six-penny nails—to guide the bulldozers as they put the road back together. We set stakes outside the work area and note elevation and distance to roadway features—centerline points, culvert ends, inlet basins—on the stakes with blue lumber crayon. It is busy work, and each person has a role: civil engineering student operates the instrument; techie and mechanical engineering student operate the measuring tape, leveling rod, and a sledge to drive the stakes. I'm the note keeper, mathematician, work planner, and problem solver. Though we are not well acquainted, we quickly adapt to each other's peculiarities and work well together. The job goes smoothly—with one exception. Mechanical engineering student, solver of crossword puzzles and measurer of work time left in the day, moves to new digs—perhaps part of Dr. Pierce's shifting population—and is without transportation. He asks me to pick him up on the way to work.

The first morning, I honk at six a.m. Ten minutes later, he appears at the door, then goes back for his lunch box. The second morning is the same, and the third. "I expect you to be ready," I tell him. "You're costing us." He doesn't change. Two days later, I honk, wait, then go inside, where I find him still in bed. "Last time," I tell him. "I'll wait five minutes. Then I'm gone."

The next day he is prompt. The following day, I wait five minutes and then leave. He arrives on the job at ten o'clock with a pal he has cajoled into driving him to Mexico. Without a word of greeting, he takes the sledge from technician and starts driving stakes. The incident is behind him. He has lost three hours of pay and will be on time the remainder of the summer. I go back to engineering.

At the end of July, we finish the work in Mexico on Dave Smith's timetable and move to the job at Farmington Falls. "The work here will go a little easier," Smith tells us. In open farmland, inspired by civil engineering student, we exceed the production rate we established in Mexico. Despite rainy weather and soggy tramping in the millet fields, we are done at the end of August. Smith is pleased, and when it comes time for me to leave for Orono, he appeals to me to return to the highway department. "We want you back," he tells me. "You've learned our business—and we can rely on you." I mumble something about him being helpful, how grateful I am, and, yes, I will be back when my faculty job ends. "But I've got the army to deal with, too," I caution him, thinking of the disruptive draft, a national two-year conscription of men between eighteen and twenty-five years old

I drive to Orono and meet with Professor Wes Evans, Chair of the Department of Civil Engineering at the university. He has appointed Gil Leslie and me to interim faculty positions for the school year. I suspect his search for legitimate candidates was impeded by a lack of desirable resumes, the same predicament Boyce often finds himself in at the beginning of a baseball season. So he's turned to Leslie and me to fill blanks in his twelve-person faculty, a risky move for him—and for me as well. I vow not to let him down.

At the meeting, he assigns me an office on the third floor of what he still calls the New Engineering Building, a classic brick structure built after World War II complete with downstairs labs and top-floor drafting rooms, a place I am intimately familiar with. We examine my course work: six one-hour lectures each week in highway design for juniors and seniors, two three-hour labs each week in engineering surveying, and two one-hour lectures in highway and railroad design fundamentals for students in the School of Forestry. "I think you'll find this sufficient to keep you busy," Evans tells me, "though the real work will come from preparing for the lectures in highway design." I set about preparing for my first class.

By September 19, 1956, I am prepared, but I am also frightened. Students stop chattering when I enter the classroom and look at me, curious, I suppose, to know whether I am actually the person who sat in one of these seats last year. The class comprises a mixture of traditional college students—young, attentive, carrying notebooks and texts—and former soldiers, older and more moderate in demeanor. There is at least one woman in the class.

I do not pretend that I belong here. I know that Evans is desperate. I deposit my teaching paraphernalia on an oak table at the front and smile. I introduce myself, describe the syllabus and its elements, and sketch the ranking system on the chalkboard. I poll the students—whether any of them have prior work experience in highway design or construction—and ask them to observe the engineering features of roadways as they ride over them. I assign reading for the next class. Then, as students stir and put away notepads, I interrupt their anticipation: "I recall some of my first classes," I say. "I suppose you came expecting that I would use only ten or fifteen minutes to describe the course and then you could leave—but I have more."

They settle into their seats. I spend the remaining time on the history of highway evolution worldwide. I start with the biblical prophet Isaiah and then the Romans. I laud the French engineer Tresaguet, who built the first roads in France for Napoleon; Scotsmen John MacAdam and Thomas Telford, whose military roads are still in use; and finally the coming of highways—delayed a century by railroad expansion—to America: the Philadelphia-Lancaster Turnpike, the Old National Pike to St. Louis, and the National Road, the first to cross the country. Finally, our network of interstate highways, America's version of earlier road systems built by the Romans, the French, and the British. The students sit quietly attentive throughout. "Come to class often," I encourage them. "My goal is to teach you to think." At the end, I feel that something big has come. I am no longer frightened.

I confront my obligation to military service. Thus far, I have avoided the draft by being eligible for an educational deferment. But now the draft is inevitable. I have no one to counsel with. Pa is no help; Uncle Lawrence has not served in the military; Aunt Marion will be acquiescent about it. "Take what comes," she'll say. "Chin up."

I look into what else might be available, a way I can make something useful out of my two years. Neither the Air Force nor the Coast

Guard interests me. The Navy and Marine Corps are no different—except for a branch of the Navy I discover called the Civil Engineering Corps. I don't know much about the Civil Engineering Corps, only that Seabees constructed airfields on Pacific islands during World War II, but I store the information away and carry on teaching.

I don't wait long. In March, Uncle Austin—who serves on the county draft board—sends word that my notice is in an envelope and will be mailed in a few days. I drive to Boston and join the Navy.

"The Seabees are full-up," a lieutenant tells me at the Milk Street recruiting station.

"What about the surface navy? Officer Candidate School at Newport?" I ask.

I take a physical for the surface navy. Afterward, the lieutenant asks me into his office. "You're the only one of seven candidates today who is not color blind," he says. "Instead of officer training at Newport, we'd like you to go to Pensacola, the Aviation Officer Candidate program."

"I've never flown."

He pauses. "I can fix that. Where you from?"

A few days later, I report to the Navy's air station in Brunswick, Maine Two aviators strap me into a twin-engine, navy aircraft. "Where'd you like to go?" the pilot asks me at about three thousand feet.

"Temple," I holler.

"Where the hell is Temple?" he shouts and pulls out a map. He flies over Temple, up the windy stream valley, and I look down on the village, the snowy intervale, the stringy shadows of maples and beeches on snow-covered ridges. A vehicle moves through the village in what seems like slow motion. Folks I likely know step in and out of the general store. I feel like a spy.

"Wanna get a closer look?" the pilot asks at the upper end of the intervale. He tips the plane onto its wing and into a dive. He flattens it out a few hundred feet over the general store, then climbs, turns, and tips again. He flies an encore from the opposite direction, circles the village at low altitude, and then climbs out toward Brunswick. My introduction to naval aviation is over.

On the first Saturday in April I meet Pa at his brother's in Farmington, a refuge for him, and we go to Temple to observe the sap run. He totes a fishing rod. It's trout-season. "I've joined the Navy," I tell him. "I was about to be drafted, so I drove to Boston and enlisted. I'm leaving in a month for Pensacola. I'll train to be an aviator, fly navy aircraft."

"Fly!" he exclaims. "You shouldda been here last week. Some crazy sonovagun swooping and diving all over town. Round and round. Military airplane. I thought he was gonna fly the damned thing right into Staples Hill. You shoulda seen it. Crazy sonovagun. I hope you never get mixed up with anything like that."

I grin at him. "I'll be careful, Pa."

May comes and I leave Professor Evans in my classroom with my students. I leave Pa fishing on Temple Stream. I leave Boyce putting together an independent schedule for the Townies and building a new baseball field on the Intervale Road for the Temple Tigers, a youth team that will begin its first season next month. I take the train to Boston and fly Eastern Airlines—my second time in an airplane—to Pensacola, Florida.

By May 28 I am three weeks into a pressurized, tight-scheduled flight-training program that includes enough military matter to qualify me for an officer's commission—ensign—at the end of the summer. My class comprises sixteen cadets. We are gathered in a drab classroom studying the operation of a radial engine mounted on a stand there. A seaman comes into the classroom and interrupts the class. "Hodgkins?" he asks. "Telephone call—emergency. Come with me."

I could barely hear Aunt Marion's voice. "It's Lawrence," she sobs

"He's gone. Happened today . . . seizure . . . working on a roof . . . I wanted you to know . . . don't come. You're too busy."

I am stunned. I have lost a friend and a model He set a standard for living. He showed those around him, particularly me, that a life of integrity, hard work, and trustworthiness works. He showed me right- eousness and never knew how much it meant to me. He chased dreams and didn't complain that he never caught one. I go to the air station chapel, pray for his soul and recall his goodness: never a cross word to me during my critical passages—boyhood baseball, my first job, driving a car. He was forever fair.

Funeral services are held for Boyce in Farmington. Former Townies Larry Barker, Al Bergeron, Vilio Hellgren, and Howard Mitchell carry him to his resting place in Riverside Cemetery, just up the hill behind Hippach Field. Later, in ceremonies prior to the open- ing game of the Temple Tigers' first season, the new ball field is dedi- cated to Boyce. The Reverend Donald Elliott praises him as a builder of sportsmanship and character. Selectman and former Townies center fielder Vilio Hellgren dedicates the field "to Lawrence Boyce's mem- ory." Former outfielder Larry Barker unveils a sign in center field des- ignating the new field "Boyce Park."

For twenty-seven years, kids in Temple didn't need movie theaters, soda shops, or basketball hoops. They had Boyce and baseball. And thanks to him, whose inspiration brought them the Tigers, they will have baseball for many years—perhaps forever—just a few steps from Dana Barker's hayfield where Boyce, wearing a Mack's All Stars uni- form, played his first game in Temple.

EPILOGUE

I t is May 2006. Forty-nine years have passed. I live in Yarmouth with Beth, my wife of forty-one years. Our three grown children and seven grandchildren are sprinkled here and there across New England. A bright day, the sun's heat is tempered by a fair breeze off Casco Bay. The telephone rings. "This is Ron Smith, coach of the Temple Tigers," says a husky voice.

Temple is much the same now as it was in the 1950s, when the Tigers started playing at Boyce Park. Yes, the general store is closed, and the Grange hall and Baptist church are gone. The one-room schoolhouse has been turned into a house. Town roads are paved, and automobiles take folks to jobs as far away as Waterville, Augusta, and Lewiston. The loss of the one-room schoolhouses to a school district has made Temple attractive to outsiders, however, and the town's population has doubled. But the logging trucks still roll through a Temple that remains largely the same: tin roofs, independent living, a post office in the corner of the former general store, a baseball team, and hardworking folks who care about their town. Dr. Pierce's gloomy predictions of no initiative, lost institutional life, doomed government, and the end of Temple's history have been ignored.

Beth and I own the old Burt Mitchell place on the Intervale Road and grow Christmas trees there. And we make maple syrup across town when spring comes. We go to Temple often, but folks in Temple seldom call us here in Yarmouth. I listen to Ron Smith.

"We've tidied up the ballpark some," he tells me. "A new infield, new outfield fence, new scoreboard. We're gonna rededicate the field at the opening game. Like to have you come up—be part of it."

It's been forty-nine years since that first Tigers game against the Farmington Braves. Hundreds of Temple youth have learned the lessons Boyce taught the Townies: sportsmanship, fair play, trying your best. The Tigers have won three championships in that time and put their losing seasons behind them in anticipation of winning the following year. Though the fiftieth anniversary of Boyce's inspiration is a year away, somehow it seems right that the rededication take place now.

Nearly two hundred people come to Boyce Park on a June evening: former coaches, players, parents of players, and townsfolk. I see a familiar face here and there, and memories come rolling back. Vilio Hellgren's son, lefty Weikko Hellgren, who threw a 2–1 victory for the Tigers against the powerful Farmington Pirates to force a playoff for the league championship in 1961; Larry Barker Jr., who played second base for the Tigers as a six-year-old and for six years after that; Bill Hodgkins, home-run hitter on the Tigers' first championship team in 1962 and coach of the second thirty years later; Doug Brackett, who also pitched for the high school and the Farmington Flyers. Gary Bergeron, former Townies' shortstop, is here also, and his brothers Michael and Terry, shortstops in turn for the Tigers. I tell Gary I'm writing a book. "Do you know any former Townies still around?" I ask.

He mentions Bill Mosher and Cal Tyler. "Ernie Danforth?" I query.

"Lives in Gardiner."

"Lyle Hall?"

Gary shakes his head. "Don't believe so."

Someone mentions Boyce and that forty-nine years ago his inspiration created the Tigers. At the mention of Boyce's name, I recall his moderation, his vision, his strength, his resolve. It's been seventy-five years since Boyce arrived here on the intervale in his Mack's All Stars uniform, sixty since I came under his influence. He was mostly invisible then, and virtually no one here now knew him, or remembers. But his influence remains. His passion for the game, his commitment to Temple, and his inspiration made this moment necessary. Bergeron remembers him.

"Like a father to me," he says. "A good man."

I tell him I've nominated Boyce for the Maine Baseball Hall of Fame.

"Do you think . . .? Gawd, I hope so. That'd be wonderful."

"Maybe. Sometime. The next election is November. We'll see what happens."

Before the Tigers take the field for a game against the New Sharon Yankees, Ron Smith greets the crowd. He introduces coaches and players and speaks of the Tigers' history. In a demonstration of former skills, Weikko Hellgren tries to replicate the curveball that subdued the Pirates so long ago and bounces it to his catcher. "Arm's not what it was once," he confesses. Bill Hodgkins pops up a high fastball from Doug Brackett. After a few minutes the crowd quiets, and Larry Barker Jr. unveils the new scoreboard.

More than a year later, on a brilliantly hot summer Sunday in July 2007, I am sitting in an air-conditioned banquet room in Portland. Five hundred of us are here for lunch, and to honor eleven new inductees into the Maine Baseball Hall of Fame. Since the first inductees in 1969, four hundred fifty have been so honored, including Harris Plaisted, South China Clippers; Galen Sayward, Farmington Jewels; Bud Ochmanski, Farmingdale Chiefs; Drig Fournier, Toppy Washburn, and lefty Don Oakes, all former opponents of the Townies. And now Lawrence Boyce, the Townies' player-manager for twenty-seven years, the inspiration behind the Temple Tigers, the man whose baseball team arguably saved Temple from predicted oblivion, will take his rightful place with Maine's baseball best.

The call came on Christmas Day. "A present for you," the voice said. I'd been hoping for months, never sure it would happen, and I'm elated. Boyce has caught a dream.

Time stops for the commemoration. The sun is still. Night does not come. Folks are introspective. We pledge allegiance to our flag, and five hundred voices sing "God Bless America." We celebrate America's game with remembrance. At the dais, the inductees, one by one, tell their story. Men can't stop talking about what it was like when baseball was king. They laugh. They choke up. They sob. One tells how, in his early years, he set a record for sacrifice bunts in a season. Another tries to relive his memories and is so overcome he can't speak.

I speak for Boyce. I introduce the other four Townies present—Ernie Danforth, Gil Leslie, Roger Parlin, Gary Bergeron—and I recall that Lawrence Boyce cared about us. I tell a story and speak a moment of his goodness. Someone puts a plaque in my hand.

The celebration goes on for four hours. At the end, a woman who came three thousand miles to be at the ceremony is rewarded with a ten-pound box of chocolates for coming the farthest distance. Presumably she will eat the chocolates on the way home. The oldest lady in the crowd—ninety-eight years—is awarded a vase of wilted black-eyed Susans to dispose of. It is baseball. It is Americana: politicians and car salesmen, lobstermen and families and fried chicken, baseball players and baseball fans, five hundred strong.

Lawrence Boyce was a good man.

ACKNOWLEDGMENTS

A t the time of this writing, twelve former Townies survived. (There may be others who played a few innings that I have forgotten or couldn't find. To those, if any, I apologize.) Though we lived separate lives, we are held together by a common remembrance. I talked with each one then, some at length and some for only a moment or two, and listened to their stories. I am grateful to them—Collis Ames, Gary Bergeron, Ernie Danforth, Bernard Davis, Edgar Davis, Paul Heath, Gil Leslie, Art Mitchell, Bill Mosher, Bob Parlin, Roger Parlin, Cal Tyler—for their memories.

I am also grateful to many others for their help and inspiration: *The Franklin Journal* for its thorough reporting in the 1940s and 50s of Franklin County baseball happenings; the Mantor Library, at the University of Maine Farmington, for allowing extensive use of its microfiche files; the Central Maine Writers—Lisa Audet, Nicole Gervais, Hannah Hinckley, Ron Laing, Karen Merrill, Tom Pelletier, Jill Pierce, Lynn Ross, Maggie Roy—for listening and commenting and inspiring me; baseball-specialist Stewart Goodwin and baseball-tyro Lynn Ross for their reading and editing; and, of course, Beth, who read my drafts and insisted that my writing make sense. I thank also the Temple Historical Society, which generously permitted liberal inspection of Townies' memorabilia and the use of several period photographs, and Maine baseball authors Wes Johnson (*Good Old Town Team Baseball*) and Jim Baumer (*When Towns Had Teams*), whose writing provided background information. And, finally, thank-yous to Anna Field Harding Fernald (letters), Larry Barker Jr., Audrey (Mrs. Al) Bergeron, George Blodgett, Bill Hodgkins, Patty Hodgkins, and Joe Suga for their agreeable assistance as well.

JOHN E. HODGKINS lives in Yarmouth, Maine with his wife Beth. A retired civil engineer and adjunct civil engineering professor, his writing has been published in *Maine Times, Library Journal, Down East,* and *Discover Maine*. He is also the author of the memoir *A Soldier's Son: An American Boyhood During World War II*.

He and Beth maintain ties to his native Temple and spend a few months there each year producing maple syrup and raising Christmas trees for the local folks.